D1217665

Urban Forms
and Colonial Confrontations

The publisher gratefully acknowledges the contribution provided by the Art Book Endowment Fund of the Associates of the University of California Press, which is supported by a major gift from the Ahmanson Foundation.

Urban Forms
and Colonial
Confrontations

Algiers under French Rule

Zeynep Çelik

UNIVERSITY OF CALIFORNIA PRESS
Berkeley / Los Angeles / London

University of California Press
Berkeley and Los Angeles, California

University of California Press, Ltd.
London, England

Library of Congress Cataloging-in-Publication Data

Çelik, Zeynep.
    Urban forms and colonial confrontations : Algiers under French
rule / Zeynep Çelik.
       p.   cm.
    Includes bibliographical references and index.
    ISBN 0-520-20457-3 (cloth: alk. paper)
     1. Architecture and society — Algeria — Algiers. 2. Architecture,
French — Algeria — Algiers.   3. Architecture, Colonial — Algeria —
Algiers. 4. Architecture, Domestic — Algeria — Algiers. 5. Algiers
(Algeria) — Buildings, structures, etc. I. Title.
NA2543.S6C44 1997
720'.965'3 — dc21   96-37606

Printed in the United States of America
9 8 7 6 5 4 3 2 1

To Ali and Perry Winston

ン

Contents

Illustrations

Acknowledgments

I benefited from the intellectual generosity of many colleagues and friends during the research and writing phases of this book. I am particularly indebted to Janet Abu-Lughod, Oleg Grabar, Ira Lapidus, and Susana Torre, who supported the project in its early phases. I would also like to single out Philippe Aigrain, Katharine Branning, Eric Breitbart, Ibrahim and Sylvie Çelik, Diane Favro, Alice Friedman, Mireille Grubert, Barbara Knecht, Mary McLeod, Christian Otto, Attilio Petruccioli, Grahame Shane, Eve Sinaiko, Jeannette Wakin, and Ayşe Yönder for their help, advice, and friendship. I am grateful to Marc Garanger for his kind permission to publish three of his archival photographs, and to Roland Simounet for granting me an interview. I thank Urs Gauchat for his appreciation and for juggling my teaching schedule to allow me writing time. For the hospitality my family and I received in Algiers and for many challenging and informative conversations, my heartfelt thanks go to Muhammed Kouaci, Madame Kouaci, and Rachid Ouahes. Without the learned and passionate introduction of Rachid Ouahes to his city, I would not have been able to undertake this project. The memories of our many excursions, long discussions, and friendship are interwoven into my book.

The research was funded by senior fellowships from the Social Science Research Council and American Council of Learned Societies, as well as a summer research grant from the National Endowment for the Humanities. I thank these institutions for their financial support. In addition, I would like to express my appreciation to Columbia University Seminars for assistance in the preparation of the manuscript for publication. Material drawn from this work was presented at the Columbia University Seminars on the City and on Arabic Studies, as well as at Cornell University, Harvard University, University of California at Santa Cruz, University of Texas at Austin, University of Washington, University of Pennsylvania, University of California at Los Angeles, and the 1995 annual meeting of the Society of Architectural Historians in Seattle. The questions and suggestions I received on each of these occasions helped me broaden my vision and rethink many issues discussed in this book. The American Institute for Maghrib Studies conference, "The Living Medina: The Walled Arab City in Literature, Architecture, and History," held in Tangier in spring 1996, gave me the opportunity to present my research to a knowledgeable and interdisciplinary audience. While it was too late to incorporate some of the suggestions into my book, the support I enjoyed from many colleagues helped me reaffirm my belief in the project. I especially appreciated comments from Jamila Binous, Ali Djerbi, Susan Gilson Miller, Djilali Sari, and Susan Slyomovics.

John McKenna created the line drawings and the majority of the maps, demonstrating great professionalism and efficiency. Lynne Withey, my editor at the University of California Press, was patient, meticulous, and gracious. It has been my pleasure to work with her and with the University of California Press on this project, too. I am particularly indebted to the project editor, Dore Brown, and the copy editor, Ruth Veleta, for their very fine work.

This book owes something to the cultural climate of Turkey in the 1960s and to my parents, Nevin and Edip Çelik: I was first introduced to Third World politics and to a critical approach to colonial policies in my parents' bustling home in Istanbul. I am now beginning to understand the significance of those years in my formation and I am grateful for all I was exposed to. But, above all, I thank my husband, Perry Winston, and my son, Ali Winston, who lived with me through the seemingly endless process of research and writing, who traveled with me, who put up with my absences, and who shared my enthusiasm and frustrations. As always, Perry's intellectual contribution and critical feedback have been invaluable.

A Note on Arabic Terms

The standard Algerian transliteration of Arabic names and places has been used throughout the text.

Introduction

Algiers was conquered by the French in 1830. From 1830 until its independence in 1962, Algeria remained the most important, the most cherished, the most invested in, and the most problematic of all French territories *outre-mer*. Intricately entangled in every aspect of the French empire-building process, Algeria also endured an unmatched longevity as a French colony. It became the site of a multitude of colonial experiments, ranging over the course of 132 years from early militaristic and assimilationist tactics to softer associationist policies to a modern iron-fisted rule. Algiers, the major urban and administrative center of the colonizing activity, was the colonial city par excellence, the terrain of many battles—cultural, political, military, urban, architectural.[1]

This book is a detailed look at Algiers as the site of colonial policies, based on an understanding that architecture and urban forms are key players in definitions of culture and identity.[2] My focus on architectural and urban spheres allows for an investigation of the cultural dimension of empire building. For colonialism not only involved economics and politics but also was a cultural phenomenon. In Eric Hobsbawm's words, "The conquest of the globe by its 'developed' minority transformed images, ideas and aspirations, both by force and institutions, by example, and by social transformation."[3] For Edward Said, the cultural sphere is a main actor in the "processes of imperialism" which occur "by predisposition, by the authority of recognizable cultural formations, by continuing consolidation within education, literature, and the visual and musical arts." Culture is a crucial element in the power struc-

1

ture of the colonial condition, because "the enterprise of empire depends upon the *idea* of *having an empire.*" Culture enables the formation of this idea.[4]

Architecture and urbanism have an obvious advantage over other cultural formations in shedding light on social relations and power structures: they constitute an essential part of the human experience and their experiential qualities make them accessible to everybody. They express cultural values, but they are also firmly grounded in material and daily life. Their connection to the everyday world is so substantial that they can never transcend or be divorced from worldly associations—a phenomenon often observed in other cultural and artistic formations. The everyday life of the colonial order occurred in the public and private spaces of Algiers, the metaphorical and the practical, the confrontational and the compromising clashing as people (colonized and colonizer) went about their routine activities. Because architecture and urban forms frame all human activity, and because the particular evolution of Algiers under French rule was so dramatic, the physical city kept its residents constantly aware of political conditions and power relations.

My analysis of Algiers evolves around two general themes: urban form and urban process. I subscribe to Spiro Kostof's approach to studying cities—that is, to an architectural historian's urban history. Unlike social historians, architectural historians place their emphasis on the "physical frame of things" and the "spatial characteristics of the city." They focus on urban form in a historical perspective, looking for specific intents.[5]

In its broader manifestation, the form of a city is determined by its "image." Kevin Lynch defined "imageability" as "that quality in a physical object which gives it a high probability of evoking a strong image in any given observer." This "legibility," Lynch argued, plays a social role as well, because it embodies elements that lead to the emergence of collective memories and symbols.[6] Yet even the clearest and sharpest of urban images evokes different readings, recalling Henri Lefebvre's probing question: "To what extent may *a* space be read or decoded?"[7] Granted that the French colonial city is characterized by a powerful visual character that culminates in the contrasting images of the European and indigenous quarters (Fig. 1), consider the following passages.

Frantz Fanon, the passionate critic of French colonialism, drew the image of the generic colonial city:

Figure 1. Aerial view from 1935, showing the juncture of the casbah (on the right) and the French quarters (on the left). The intersection is marked by Boulevard Gambetta (now Ourida Meddad), the Grand Theater, and Place d'Aristide Briand (now Square Port Said).

The settlers' town is a strongly built town, all made of stone and steel. It is a brightly lit town; the streets are paved with asphalt, and the garbage cans swallow all the leavings, unseen, unknown, and hardly thought about. The settler's feet are never visible, except perhaps in the sea; but there you're never close enough to see them. His feet are protected by strong shoes although the streets of his town are clean and even, with no holes or stones. The settler's town is a well-fed town, an easygoing town; its belly is always full of good things. The settlers' town is a town of white people, of foreigners.

The town belonging to the colonized people, or at least the native town, the Negro village, the medina, the reservation, is a place of ill fame, peopled by men of evil repute. They are born there, it matters little where or how; they die there, it matters not where, nor how. It is a world without spaciousness; men live there on top of each other, and their huts are built one on top of the other. The native town is a hungry town, starved of bread, of meat, of shoes, of coal, of light. The native town is a crouching village, a town on its knees, a town wallowing in the mire. It is a town of niggers and dirty Arabs.[8]

Le Corbusier, the foremost modernist architect, focused on the same duality, with specific reference to Algiers:

Seen from the sea, European Algiers is nothing but crumbling walls and devastated nature, the whole a sullied blot. We have seen the agglomeration, the juxtaposition of dwelling units one on top of the other, one next to the other, randomly, enclosing the inhabitant in stone ramparts and roughcast, folding over him the walls, blocking the horizons, hiding all natural spectacles, and making people live, in Algiers of Africa, like anywhere on the continent; very poorly. Europeans did not exploit the fortune offered to them. . . .

The casbah of Algiers [in contrast] *made* the site: it gave the name of White Algiers to this glittering entity, that welcomes, at dawn, the boats that arrive at the harbor. Inscribed in the site, it is irrefutable. It is in consonance with nature, because from every house, from the terrace— and these terraces add on to each other like a magic and gigantic staircase descending to the sea—one sees the space, the sea.

Le Corbusier concluded, elsewhere, that "the 'civilized' live like rats in holes," whereas "the 'barbarians' live in solitude, in well-being."[9]

The same urban image, then, has the potential to signify different messages. Because a form—even a seemingly crystalline one—can be viewed from a myriad of perspectives, focusing on physical aspects alone does not allow for a meaningful analysis of the city. As Lefebvre insists, spaces are read according to the specific codes developed at specific historic periods and under specific conditions.[10] While the colonial city embodied for Fanon everything that was problematic in colonial occupation, the duality he despised because of its unegalitarianism and hegemony, which left the native inhabitants in miserable conditions, is reversed by Le Corbusier; in his interpretation, it is the European who lives in unacceptable spaces, while the natives enjoy a decent town that is spacious and embraces nature. The two visions can be attributed to historic conditions and to particular agendas. Fanon's piece was written at a time marked by liberation movements in colonies and in particular the Algerian War, whereas Le Corbusier made his observations in the 1930s in a seemingly subdued Algiers, where the colonizer could choose to overlook colonial conflicts. Fanon's goal was to display the horrors of colonialism in support of resistance struggles; Le Corbusier's critique, in contrast, centered on the promotion of his own projects for Algiers.

To look at such shifting readings becomes crucial in the urban historian's quest to begin to reveal the multitude of meanings associated with forms and spaces. The historian thus borrows a research tool from sociology: triangulation. In Janet Abu-Lughod's words, triangulation is based on the understanding that "there is no archimedean point *outside* the system from which to view historic reality."[11] This new dimension in the writing of urban history is intertwined with the study of the "urban process" that embodies the intricate interaction of social, economic, political, technical, cultural, and artistic forces that bring the form about and give dynamism to the city through time.[12] Lefebvre proposes that, to avoid the "trap of treating space as space 'in itself'" (not an uncommon trend among architectural historians and critics), the urban historian must look at the "production of space and the social relations inherent to it" and uncover social relationships. This involves not chronologically fixed urban forms, but the "long history of space" and "accounts for both representational spaces and representations of space, but above all for their interrelationships and their links to social practice."[13] Moreover, as Hobsbawm observed, cities reflect great social transformations better than any institution.[14] We gain a broader understanding of colonialism—a determining force in the history of the modern era that brought about one of the most important transformations in the world order—through the analysis of its cities.

The dual structure of the colonial city described by Fanon and Le Corbusier, the unlikely partners of this introduction, is a fragment of the broad discourse of colonialism which accommodates the exercise of colonial power by an "articulation of forms of difference." Separation plays an important part in defining otherness and allows for a critical distance needed for surveillance.[15] Racial, cultural, and historical otherness constituted the main paradigm that dominated all building activity in Algiers during the French occupation, and spatial separation in the most concrete sense reinforced the difference.

Behind the clear message conveyed by the image of dual cities at first sight, however, hide more complicated implications. As argued by Homi Bhabha and others, the colonial relationship is not symmetrically antagonistic, due to the ambivalence in the positioning of the colonized and the colonizer. Ambivalence is connected to "hybridity," in which the other's original is rewritten but also transformed through misreadings and incongruities, resulting in something different.[16] The architecture of colonialism reveals levels of ambivalence and hybridity while persistently maintaining the overriding theme of difference.

Architecture and urbanism in the colonial context should thus be viewed among the practices that make up the colonial discourse. My argument here is based on an expansion of Peter Hulme's definition of colonial discourse as "an ensemble of linguistically based practices unified by their common deployment of colonial relationships."[17] To Hulme's repertoire, which ranges from bureaucratic documents to romantic novels, I would like to add architecture, whose expression is also coded by linguistic conventions, albeit visual and spatial ones. As different practices in the discourse complemented each other and culminated in an interconnected knowledge of the colony, I expand my study of Algiers with references to other fields of knowledge following an interdisciplinary approach. My goal is to gain a better understanding of architectural and urban forms by situating them in their historical, political, and cultural contexts. I rely particularly on ethnography, because as a discipline historically entangled in the politics of colonialism (an association explained by Michel Leiris in a memorable article in 1950[18]) ethnography played a major role in defining the sociocultural characteristics of the "Algerian" society as well as its spatial parameters. These definitions, in turn, were instrumental in shaping colonial designs.[19]

This book examines two related topics: urbanism and housing design. I study the city-building activities carried out in Algiers under French rule and the large housing projects (*grands ensembles*) designed and constructed by the colonial administration for exclusive use by Algerians. The chronology is framed by the French occupation from 1830 to 1962. I extend briefly beyond these dates in both directions by references to the historic development of the precolonial city and to some issues of the postcolonial period.[20]

Algiers occupies an exceptional place in the history of French colonial urbanism. As a city with already several centuries of history and as a pioneer outpost of what would grow into a huge colonial empire, it posited unforeseen problems for French invaders, who were not equipped with the urbanistic tools to meet Algiers's challenges. Yet by the 1830s, the French were experienced modern city builders who had developed impressive large-scale renovation plans and whose incremental interventions since the early seventeenth century had changed the faces of several cities at home, particularly Paris. While this expertise came in handy, the presence of powerful local urban forms and a well-coded Muslim urban culture, in addition to the complex topography of the site, complicated the task of French technocrats in Algiers. The city became the trial-and-error case of French colonial urbanism, and the mistakes made there were used as lessons in other colonies. Compared with the carefully orchestrated urban design practices in cities colonized later by the French, the case of Algiers stands out in its irregular processes, as well as the resulting "chaos" so feverishly criticized by the French themselves throughout their tenure. Even though the colonial administration managed to use urban design for establishing and expressing power and control over the local population, the output was always fragmented and the policies never matched the all-encompassing and meticulously calculated interventions in other colonies, most notably Louis Hubert Gonzalve Lyautey's Morocco.

From the 1930s on, urban design in Algiers became associated with large housing projects. Paralleling the dual structure of the city that was well in place by then, the colonial policies kept the housing built for Algerians separate from the housing projects that sheltered Europeans. The separation was not only physical, but also highlighted by architectural difference in various attempts to synthesize the collective housing typologies with socioculturally loaded elements deemed appropriate to represent and accommodate Algerians. The "traditional" Algerian house, as already studied by ethnographers and architects, written about by travelers, and replicated in artistic productions, constituted a major resource in identifying the most "characteristic" pieces.

Chapter 1 describes the old city. After surveying the precolonial history of the casbah, as old Algiers is commonly called, and analyzing its spatial characteristics on the eve of the French occupation, I introduce its treatment in colonial discourse, which crystallized in the development of a "myth of the casbah." The bulk of the chapter then deals with interventions to the upper and the lower casbah (the Marine Quarter)—operations fluctuating among ruthless carving and piercing into the existing fabric, attempts to preserve its romantic authenticity, and benign neglect. Chapter 2 traces the urban development of Algiers and the insistent struggle of the colonial administration to turn it into a modern French city. I analyze a selection of executed projects as well as proposals that remained on paper, my view being that eventually both contributed to the shape of Algiers. Among the unexecuted projects are Le Corbusier's renowned schemes, widely studied by architectural historians as masterpieces of modernism, but systematically abstracted from their context. Situating them within the history of urban planning in Algiers casts new light on their exaggerated originality.

With my analysis of city building in Algiers, I hope to contribute to filling a major lacuna in urban histories of modernism, which center routinely on Europe and North America. Yet, linked to the colonial expansions, some of the most challenging experiments of city building in the era covered here happened in other parts of the world—a phenomenon that has begun to receive attention only recently.[21] It is also noteworthy that urban planning operations designed and carried out in French colonial cities, especially in Algiers, were closely linked to their counterparts in France. Many issues regarding city planning had interconnected histories in Algeria and France. Among them were historic preservation, problems of *îlots insalubres* (unsanitary districts), the poorly housed populations (*mal-logés*), building of large housing projects (*grands ensembles*) in immediate suburbs, policies regarding the shantytowns (*bidonvilles*)—topics of the following chapters. While the *métropole*/colonial paradigm held true for other French possessions, Algeria's special status made its relationship to France much more arduous than was the case for other colonies.

After drawing the broader framework in the first two chapters, I turn to housing, which received unprecedented priority as part of the reforms introduced in Algeria to celebrate the centennial of the occupation, in 1930. During this time the indispensability of colonies formed the core of political debates. Albert Sarrault, the former governor of Indochina and minister of colonies, stated: "Henceforth, the European edifice rests on colonial *pilotis*." Left on its own, Europe would not have the resources to feed itself and would collapse economically without primary materials and labor from the colonies and their "vast exterior markets."[22] The much-publicized centennial was exploited to disseminate the importance of colonies and to develop further the notion of *la plus grande France,* an "imperial French doctrine," and a "colonial consciousness." It was also utilized to consolidate Algeria's ties to France. Algeria was presented as an integral part of the "France of one million inhabitants" that extended over five continents.[23] A government official elaborated this notion: "Here [in Algeria] there is truly a new France . . . [its] people have but one desire, one ambition: to be intimately fused with the Mother Country."[24] The celebrations were multifaceted, varying from sumptuous military parades to an impressive range of publications on different aspects of the country, from cultural and artistic exhibitions to ambitious projects to renovate the cities of Algeria and provide decent housing.[25]

Before looking at the actual housing projects built by the French for the Algerians, I trace the definition of the parameters that served as sociocultural guidelines for architects. Chapter 3 discusses the idea of a "traditional Algerian house" constructed by the colonial discourse, specifically by ethnographers and architects, but also by artists and photographers. Because domestic space in colonial discourse on Algeria is interlaced with Algerian women, understanding and explaining women's social condition and their daily life patterns were considered essential. Although this "construction" process began in the late nineteenth century, it reached a critical moment in the 1930s.

Chapters 4 and 5 deal with the provision of housing for the indigenous people of Algiers and cover the period between 1930 and 1962, the former date corresponding to the first projects built by the French for the Algerians. Chapter 4 analyzes the general policies regarding housing, developed from the knowledge accumulated over the years of French rule in Algeria. Chapter 5 surveys a cross-section of *grands ensembles*, examining how the sociocultural structures and life patterns of the Algerian people (as described and codified in various fields of knowledge) were interpreted to fit into these massive structures. I deliberately do not elaborate at length on certain themes that constitute the essence of most studies on housing, such as quantitative issues, ownership patterns, management structures, and agencies. I focus instead on architectural and sociocultural aspects, in keeping with the underlying theme of the book that architecture is a cultural formation.

The Epilogue ties together the material presented in individual chapters and bridges the colonial and postcolonial eras. I suggest that many issues discussed in this book did not end with the French rule but persisted into independent Algeria—in a transformed framework. If the complexity of the present-day situation cautions against drawing quick parallels and conclusions, it also heightens the importance of understanding the entangled nature of the colonial and postcolonial situation in Algeria.

CHAPTER I

The Casbah and
the Marine Quarter

A whitish blur, cut into a trapezium, and dotted with silver
sparkles—each one of them a country house—began to be drawn
against the dark hills: this is Algiers, Al-Djezair, as the Arabs
call it. We approach; around the trapezium, two ocre-colored
ravines define the lower edges of the slopes, and shimmer with such
a lively light that they seem as though they are ends to two sun
torrents: these are the trenches. The walls, strangely crenellated,
ascend the height of the slope.

Algiers is built as an amphitheater on a steep slope, such that
its houses seem to have their feet on the heads of others. . . . When
the distance gets smaller, we perceive amid the glare the minaret
of a mosque, the dome of a sufi convent, the mass of a great
edifice, the casbah.

Théophile Gautier,
Voyage pittoresque en Algérie

The term *casbah* refers to the ancient core of Algiers, the triangular-shaped town carved into the hills facing the Mediterranean (Fig. 2).[1] The sea forms the base of the triangle; a citadel is at the triangle's summit. It is defined on the south by Square Port Said (formerly Place d'Aristide Briand, earlier Place de la République) and Boulevard Ourida Meddad (formerly Boulevard Gambetta), on the west by Boulevard de la Victoire and the Palace of the Dey, on the north by Boulevard Abderazak Hadad (formerly Boulevard de Verdun), and on the east by Boulevards Ernesto Che Guevara, Anatole France, and Mohamed Rachid (formerly all three comprising Boulevard de la République, ear-

Figure 2. Plan of the old city, c. 1900, showing the casbah (1) and the Marine Quarter (2). For a more detailed plan of the street network, see Fig. 14.

lier Boulevard de l'Impératrice), which define the waterfront. The town's border being fixed by fortifications, it developed vertically into a high-density settlement. Its striking urban aesthetics were defined by the interlocking masses of white, geometric houses with roof terraces opening onto the bay.[2] As will be traced in the following chapter, under French rule Algiers extended along the coastline, gradually filling in the valleys and climbing up the hills in the hinterland.

Historic Development

The settlement was founded by the Arab Zirid dynasty in the tenth century and named al-Jaza'ir ("the islands") in reference to the islands facing the waterfront. Its fate locked to the rest of North Africa, it was ruled by successive Arab dynasties as a minor port until the sixteenth century, when it was made the capital of Algeria by the Ottomans.

A major turning point in the history of medieval Algiers was the re-capture of Spain by Christians in the fifteenth century, which resulted in a wave of Muslim refugees to Algiers. The Muslims from Spain con-tributed further to the "Western" Islamic taste that already characterized the artistic and architectural culture, but perhaps more important to the livelihood of the city they established themselves as corsairs, or pirates, in response to the *reconquista,* the Spanish expulsion of Muslims to North Africa. To suppress the corsair activity, Spain imposed a levy on Algiers in 1510. With support from powerful Ottoman corsairs (first Aruj, then Khayr al-Din), however, the Spaniards were driven away and Algiers became an important port of the Ottoman Empire in 1529. Piracy remained the main income-generating activity for the city, providing for all sections of the population but also provoking frequent attacks from Europe.[3]

Not much is known about pre-Ottoman Algiers. The walls of the Arab settlement might have corresponded to the later Ottoman walls, but the density was considerably lower than that of the post-sixteenth-century period. The Ottoman walls ran continuously for 3,100 meters and enclosed the town from all sides, including the sea. They were dotted with towers and had five gates: Bab Azzoun to the south, Bab al-Jadid to the southwest, Bab al-Bahr on the sea front, Bab Jazira on entry of the harbor, and Bab el-Oued to the north. The streets leading from the gates met in front of the Ketchaoua Mosque. The citadel at the highest point on the fortifications was built in 1556.[4]

The road connecting Bab el-Oued to Bab Azzoun divided Algiers into two zones, in accordance with André Raymond's notion of "public" and "private" cities: the upper (private) city, called al-Gabal or "the mountain," and the lower (public) city, called al-Wata or "the plains."[5] The lower part developed as an administrative, military, and commercial quarter (Fig. 3). It was inhabited mostly by Turkish dignitaries and upper-class families whose luxurious houses synthesizing Eastern and Western influences dotted the neighborhood. The Dar al-Sultan, or the Janina Palace, built in the 1550s as the residence of the dey, was also located in this area, together with the major mosques and the military barracks.[6] The souks (markets) and warehouses were concentrated along the main streets, with the al-Souk al-Kabir (the road connecting Bab el-Oued and Bab Azzoun), only 3 meters wide, standing out as the largest artery of Algiers. Commercial structures also provided accommodations for foreigners and "bachelors" from other parts of the country. The commercial zone was shaped according to concentrations of different merchandise, and merchant associations were strong and well organized.[7]

The upper city was comprised of approximately fifty small neighborhoods. As was typical of the decentralized Ottoman urban system

Figure 3. View of the waterfront, c. 1830. In the foreground is the al-Jadid Mosque; to the right is the al-Kabir Mosque. The Bab al-Bahr (Sea Gate) is to the left of the al-Jadid Mosque.

throughout the empire, every neighborhood was under the administrative responsibility of religious chiefs and *qadis* (judges), hence each community was controlled and supervised by its own leaders. The population was mixed. Old families with Andalusian and Moorish roots engaged in commercial and artisanal activities; Kabyles formed the working class; Jews, who had three distinct neighborhoods in the upper casbah, were tradespeople. The presence of European consuls and businessmen, Saharans, and Christian slaves made the population of Algiers truly cosmopolitan.[8]

The street network—considered thoroughly inadequate and irrational by the French—demonstrated a clear and functional hierarchy, made up of three distinct types of thoroughfares.[9] It revealed a carefully articulated logic, a "system of filtered access."[10] The streets of the lower town, catering to commercial, military, and administrative functions, differed in their physical character and the concentration of their activities: they were lined with shops, cafés, and large structures, and crowded with people and merchandise all day long, but especially during morning hours. The arteries leading to the gates were particularly prominent. The transversal roads that climbed to the upper town formed the second category; as straight as the topography permitted, they cut through the urban tissue and provided efficient communication between the two sections of Algiers. The neighborhood streets made up the third and the largest category. Narrow, irregular, often with dead ends, they accommodated the introverted lifestyle that centered around the privacy of the home and the family; their configuration also enabled the use of gates to close off a neighborhood in the evenings to ensure its safety (Fig. 4). Respect for privacy dictated the design of facades as well: windows and doors were carefully located to prevent views into the houses across the street. Neighborhood streets had the lightest circulation; they functioned instead as playgrounds for children, especially boys. The citizens of Algiers took great pride in the cleanliness of their streets, where, they boasted, one could sit on the ground, even to eat.[11]

The urban structure of Algiers, dominated by its short, crooked neighborhood streets, is a hallmark of the "Islamic city"—a problematic construction by European historians, which has been recently subjected to serious revision. Janet Abu-Lughod, the most convincing critic of this concept, has argued, nevertheless, that Islam shaped social, political, and legal institutions, and through them, the cities. She pointed out that gender segregation was the most important issue, and by encouraging it, Islam structured the urban space and divided places and functions.[12] To put it schematically, in the "traditional Islamic city," public spaces, hence streets, belonged to men, and domestic spaces to women.

Gender-based separate "turfs" prevented physical contact and relegated the lives of the women to their homes. Privacy thus became a leading factor and resulted in the emergence of an interiorized domestic architecture. Regardless of the family's income level or the size of the building, the houses of the casbah were organized around a court surrounded by arcades (Figs. 5 and 6). This was the center, indeed the "principal room," the setting for the "theater of work and women's leisure, for children's games."[13] Some houses had water fountains here, with water coming from the aqueducts that tapped the sources in the hills around Algiers.[14] Entrance to the court was indirect and achieved through several labyrinthine lobbies. The largest room of the entry level could be used by the man of the house to entertain his friends without interfering with women's activities. The upper floors contained the

Figure 4. Street view in the upper casbah.

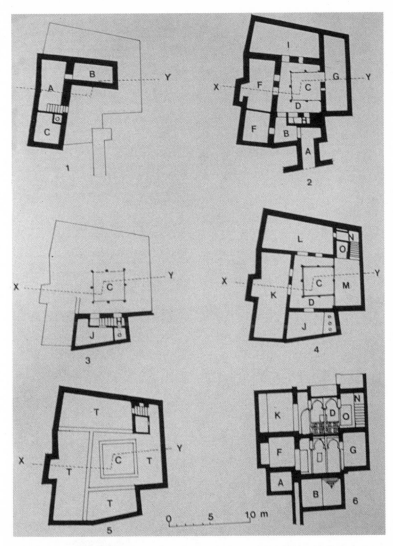

Figure 5. Plans and section of a modest house in the casbah. (1) Basement floor plan: A, room; B, cistern; C, laundry room; (2) first-floor plan: A, entrance hall; B, vestibule; C, patio; D, portico; F, G, I, rooms; (3) a half floor between the first and second floors, where the latrines are located; (4) second-floor plan: J, kitchen; K, L, M, rooms; (5) plan of the terrace level; (6) section through the courtyard (X–Y).

Figure 6. Courtyard view from an upper-class house (Dar Aziza) in the casbah.

main rooms, all opening onto the arcade. A stairway led to the roof terrace, which often had a cistern to collect rainwater.[15]

Like the court, the terrace was an essential part of the house where women spent many hours of the day, working and socializing with their neighbors. The dense configuration of the casbah made it possible to pass from one terrace to the other and visit other homes without having to use the streets. The rooftops of the casbah functioned as an alternative public realm that extended over the entire city. In contrast to the interiorized court and the relatively contrived rooms, the rooftops opened up to the city, to the sea, to the world (Fig. 7). With the appropriation of this space by the women of Algiers, the casbah became divided horizontally into two realms: on the top, occupying the expanse of the entire city, were the women; at the bottom, the streets belonged to the men.

Algiers boasted religious and public buildings throughout. Right before the French conquest, there were about a dozen major mosques and sixty smaller ones.[16] The primary mosques, namely the eleventh-century al-Kabir (Fig. 8), Ketchaoua from 1612 (transformed into a cathedral in 1838), Ali Bichnin from 1632, al-Jadid from 1660, and al-Sayyida, perhaps the most elegant of all the religious buildings in Algiers and reconstructed in 1794, were concentrated in the lower section.[17] Nevertheless, the entire city was dotted with *masjid*s (smaller prayer halls), endowing every neighborhood with its own prayer spaces. Minarets were placed strategically around the city so that the calls to prayer could be heard from every house. Religious schools were scattered throughout, as well as public fountains and *hammam*s (baths). The management of all religious and public buildings was in the hands of the religious leaders, regulated by the *waqf* system.[18]

Mosques and religious schools were frequented by the male population, but the baths were used by women on special days reserved for them. Their outings included visits to the tombs of venerated figures, some inside the city walls, some outside. It was not uncommon to see small groups of women passing through the streets of Algiers, creating an "exotic" scene much cherished by the French.

When the French occupied Algiers in 1830, they found a dense, fortified town, nestled against steep green hills facing the Mediterranean (Fig. 9). The city was crowded with monuments and public buildings, criss-crossed by an efficient street network, well maintained, and cosmopolitan. However, the urban image owed its uniqueness and

Figure 7. *(above)* Rooftops of the casbah; sketch by Charles Brouty, 1933.
Figure 8. *(below)* Exterior view of al-Kabir Mosque, c. 1930. Part of this
mosque was demolished to make room for the Rue de la Marine. During the
operation, one row of interior columns was turned into an exterior colonnade.

Figure 9. Nineteenth-century view of Algiers from the sea.

integrity to the residences, collectively an impressive mass of white, cubical structures that had evolved incrementally.

The Myth of the Casbah

The image of the casbah from the sea, described, drawn, painted, and photographed repeatedly by travelers, artists, and architects, became engraved in the collective imagination and, nurtured with the Orientalist cultural repertory on Islam, enhanced the creation of a "myth." For Roland Barthes, myth is a "system of communication," a "message." It is defined by the "way in which it utters this message," and not by the "object of its message." It is "chosen by history" and is "filled with a situation."[19] In this case, then, the myth was about the colonial discourse and not the casbah itself; it was colonialism (the historic "situation") that framed the casbah with certain concepts. In turn, these powerful and enduring concepts played an important role in shaping colonial policies regarding the casbah. The myth and the politics of colonialism continued to nurture each other throughout French rule.

The myth of the casbah developed around three concepts: gender, mystery, and difference. The first was linked to the broader project of the feminization of the Orient; yet in the colonial context, the gendering of Algerian society and culture became blatantly referential to power structure. As Winifred Woodhull has shown, French intellectuals, the military, and administrative officers made Algerian women the "key symbols of the colony's cultural identity." In a typical formulation, J. Lorraine, writing at the turn of the century, called the entire country "a wise and dangerous mistress," but one who "exudes a climate of caress and torpor," suggesting that control over her mind and body was essential.[20]

The casbah, too, became identified with a single and undifferentiated Algerian woman. Popular literature abounds with descriptions of Algiers as a woman, often an excessively sensuous one. In the travel accounts of Marius Bernard, for example, Algiers is a woman to fall in love with. Even its name carried a special appeal:

> Algiers! Such a musical word, like the murmur of waves against the white sand of the beach; a name as sweet as the rippling of the breeze in the palm trees of the oases! Algiers! So seductive and easy-going, a town to be loved for the deep purity of her sky, the radiant splendor of her turquoise sea, her mysterious smells, the warm breath in which she wraps her visitors like a long caress.[21]

Similarly, Lucienne Favre, a woman novelist writing in the 1930s, described the casbah as "the vamp of North Africa," bearing a "capricious feminine charm" and a great "sex appeal."[22]

Le Corbusier's gendered description of Algiers extends this tradition to architecture. Provoking associations between the curved lines of his projects and the "plasticity" of the bodies of Algerian women, Le Corbusier described at length his enchantment with these women and consistently represented the casbah as a veiled head in his reductive drawings (Fig. 10). He also likened the city to a female body: "Algiers drops out of sight," he noted, viewing the city from a boat leaving for France, "like a magnificent body, supple-hipped and full-breasted. . . . A body which could be revealed in all its magnificence, through the judicious influence of form and the bold use of mathematics to harmonize natural topography and human geometry."[23] The cover sketch of his *Poésie sur Alger* depicts a unicorn-headed, winged female body—supple-hipped and full-breasted—the city/poem caressed gently by a hand (the architect's) against the skyline of new Algiers, to be designed by Le Corbusier himself (Fig. 11).

Figure 10. Le Corbusier, sketch showing the casbah as a veiled head.

Le Corbusier elaborated on the sensuality of Algiers by describing the city's intimate relation to nature and recycling the formula that equates nature with woman. The casbah complemented its surrounding geography and absorbed all senses:

We are in Africa. This sun, this space created by azure and water, this foliage have formed the set for the actions of Salambo, Scipio and Hannibal, together with those of Kheir-ed-dinn the Barbaresque. The sea,

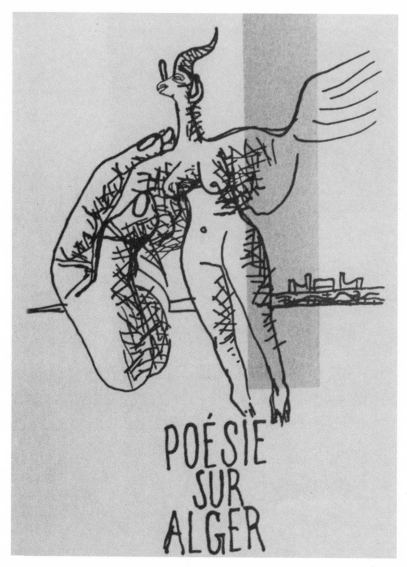

Figure 11. Cover of Le Corbusier's *Poésie sur Alger*.

the chain of the Atlas Mountains, the slopes of Kabylia unfold their blue displays. The earth is red. The vegetation consists of palm trees, eucalyptus trees, gum trees, cork oaks, olive trees and fig trees; the perfumes, jasmine and mimosa. From the first plane to the confines of the horizon, the symphony is imminent.[24]

The casbah was so intertwined with landscape and nature that it *made* the site: "The casbah of Algiers . . . has given the name Algiers-the-White to this glittering apparition that welcomes at dawn the boats arriving from the port. Inscribed in the site, it is irrefutable. It is in consonance with nature."[25]

Hand in hand with its gendered sensuality, the casbah evoked mystery. It represented the attractions of unknown dangers, as expressed by one writer: "The Kasbah! This magic word intrigued me when I was a child. It pursued me over the years, evoking so much mystery, such hazy and disturbing images. When it was spoken it had a special sound. . . . I imagined a den of danger and enchantment, straight from the *Arabian Nights*."[26] Furthermore, it marked the difference between cultures and even formed for some observers an inspiring contrast to the "vulgarity of the Occident," with its "trams, machinery, cylindrical costumes, stupidity of words": "And to know that simply two steps from all this is the possibility of perpetual beauty . . . which is only to push open a door, to take a few steps in order to enter right away into a magic land."[27]

Even when the observer did not romanticize about the casbah, he or she attributed elements of mystery and unfamiliarity to it. Eugène Fromentin, for example, noted the dramatic transition from culture to culture and its immediate effect, but claimed to have transcended mere appearances and to understand the hidden meaning about the civilization the casbah represented:

> Opposite [the European town] . . . open discreetly contemplative quarters of old Algiers. . . . Bizarre streets like mysterious stairways that would lead to silence climb [the hill]. The transition is so rapid, the change of place so complete that one recognizes the better, the more beautiful sides of Arab people, those sides that make a contrast with the sad example of our social state. . . .
>
> Their town, whose construction itself is the most significant symbol, their *white town* shelters them, more or less like the national *bournous* that they wear, in a uniform and crude envelope. . . . [A] single mass of masonry, compact and confused, built like a sepulchre . . . such is the strange city where a people who had never been as grand as we believed . . . lives, or rather extinguishes itself. I spoke the truth when I mentioned a sepulchre. The Arab believes he lives in his white town; he is buried there.[28]

Descriptions and commentaries on the casbah perpetuated the myth that restricted the city and remade it according to favorite colonial paradigms. In addition, the freezing of the old town in a mythical frame abstracted it from history. Colonial discourse attempted to reserve history making for the colonizer alone; the casbah was relegated to acting as a background that highlighted the colonizer's "innovative dynamism."[29] Years later, struggling with the problems of the casbah in independent Algeria, Dr. Amir, the president of COMEDOR (Comité permanente d'études, de développement, d'organisation et d'aménagement de l'agglomération d'Alger) felt the need to undo the myth to be able to face the urgent issues. He argued that the colonial discourse that had made the casbah an "exotic town . . . something different to look at" carried serious political implications. By focusing on the "picturesqueness of its streets and beauty of its patios" as the only impressions to be retained from a visit to the old town, the "colonial mechanism" in reality dismissed the essence of the old town and its sociocultural realities.[30]

Replanning al-Jaza'ir

FIRST INTERVENTIONS

The casbah posed a great challenge to French planners for a variety of reasons: high population densities, concentration and form of the built fabric, topography, and sociocultural texture, as well as their own romantic/Orientalist appreciation of its aesthetic values, accompanied by a growing consciousness of historic preservation. In part due to these reasons, but also to the need to provide new quarters to lodge Europeans, interventions in the casbah remained incremental throughout the French occupation and no grand plans were ventured. While the upper part of the town was left practically untouched, the lower part underwent certain transformations that accentuated the preexisting division during the colonial period. The greatest changes to the lower city, known later as the Marine Quarter or the Quarter of the Ancient Prefecture, took place during the initial phase of colonization, between 1830 and 1846.

A solution that essentially characterized almost all later projects was proposed by Théophile Gautier in 1845: the high casbah should be preserved "in all its original barbary," while the Europeans should stick to the lower part, close to the harbor, because of their penchant for "large streets . . . cartage . . . and commercial movement."[31] This was exactly what had happened in the early years of the occupation, when the main concerns were militaristic (not yet commercial) and before it became clear that expansion beyond the Ottoman fortifications was a necessity. The documents from the first decade of the French regime reveal an overwhelming obsession with potential offensives from Europe and only a secondary consideration for possible conflicts and confrontations with local people. Military engineering dominated all urban design operations during this period.

The pressing issues of the 1830s consisted of lodging military troops and cutting through the necessary arteries to enable rapid maneuvers. Appropriation of houses, shops, workshops, and even religious buildings was commonplace during the first years of the occupation and often involved modifications in the buildings to accommodate the needs of the army.[32] The abrupt brutality of the first interventions caused an immediate controversy, making the city and its architecture prime actors as contested terrains in the colonial confrontation. Oral literature from the time of the conquest is rich with examples that voice the collective sentiments of local residents. One such song lamented the invasion and appropriation of the city and highlighted the violation of its most revered cultural icons:

O regrets for Algiers, for its houses
And for its so well-kept apartments!
O regrets for the town of cleanliness
Whose marble and porphyry dazzled the eyes!
The Christians inhabit them, their state has changed!
They have degraded everything, spoiled all, the impure ones!
They have broken down the walls of the *janissaries'* barracks,
They have taken away the marble, the balustrades and the benches;
And the iron grills which adorned the windows
Have been torn away to add insult to our misfortunes.
O regrets for Algiers and for its stores,
Their traces no longer exist!
Such iniquities committed by the accursed ones!
Al-Qaisariya has been named Plaza
And to think that holy books were sold and bound there.
They have rummaged through the tombs of our fathers,
And they have scattered their bones
To allow their wagons to go over them.
O believers, the world has seen with its own eyes.
Their horses tied in our mosques,
And they and their Jews rejoiced because of it
While we wept in our sadness.[33]

Expropriation and demolition were rampant, but on a fragmented and relatively small scale. True French urbanism in Algiers originated with the carving of a Place du Gouvernement and the widening of three main streets off this square that led to the main gates: Rue Bab Azzoun going south, Rue Bab el-Oued going north, and Rue de la Marine east to the harbor.

The idea of a Place du Gouvernement developed immediately after the conquest. Noting right away that the existing town lacked a large, conveniently located space for assembling the troops, the chief army engineers decided to open an "immense" area in front of the Palace of the Dey (Figs. 12 and 13).[34] The initial clearing—which involved the demolition of the minaret of the al-Sayyida Mosque,[35] as well as "many shops in bad shape and several houses," in the words of Lieutenant Colonel Lemercier—was based on practical goals: to shelter the troops, to enable the movement of carriages, and to establish markets. Lemercier added, however, that with later enlargements according to a plan, this square would turn the quarter into "the most beautiful and the most commercial" in town. Successive projects attempted to regularize the square: a pentagonal piazza, planted with trees, dotted with fountains, and surrounded by two-story residential buildings with arcades on the ground level was proposed in 1830.[36] A rectangular proposal by a government architect named Luvini called for the demolition of the al-Jadid and al-Sayyida mosques in 1831, but was opposed by Lemercier out of sympathy for the local population in order "not to hurt the religious sentiments of the Moors" (Fig. 14).[37] Al-Jadid survived the demolition fever, but al-Sayyida was torn down to allow for a building with a regular facade on the square.[38]

Capitalizing on the damage caused by a fire to parts of the Janina Palace in 1844, numerous projects attempted to readjust the plaza's overall shape in the following decades. Over a long period of time it acquired a loosely rectangular shape with arcades on three sides, the irregularity of the east side a result of Lemercier's desire not to tear down the al-Jadid Mosque (Fig. 15).[39]

The enlargement of Bab Azzoun, Bab el-Oued, and Marine streets did not involve such drastic demolitions. Adhering to preexisting patterns, they followed an irregular route but were widened to 8 meters to allow for two carriages to pass (Fig. 16).[40] In 1833 two other streets, Rue de Chartres and Rue des Consuls, were classified with the first three as the main arteries of Algiers, although only Rue de Chartres could be enlarged and that in 1837. Between Bab Azzoun and Rue de Chartres a

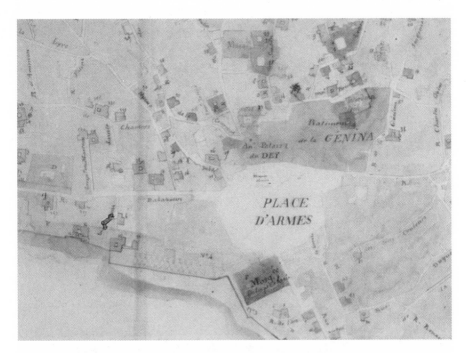

Figure 12. *(above)* Plan of central Algiers, showing the Place d'Armes (Place du Gouvernement), 1832. Figure 13. *(below)* View of the Place du Gouvernement, c. 1835. The building to the left in the foreground is the al-Jadid Mosque.

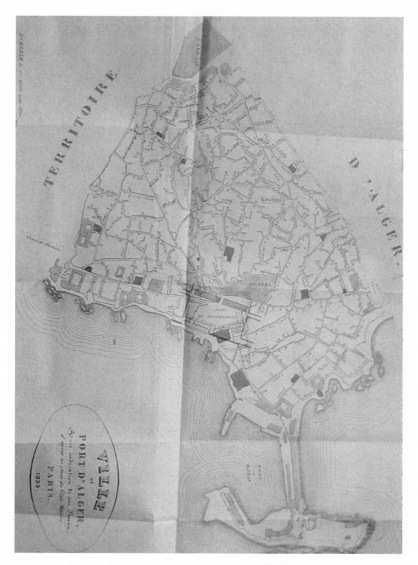

Figure 14. Proposal for regularization of the Place du Gouvernement, 1831.

square, Place de Chartres, was carved by demolishing a small mosque and a series of commercial structures (Fig. 17). To compensate for the loss of the latter, the urban administration constructed here a covered market with 250 shops for the exclusive use of indigenous populations. Boulevard de la Victoire, defining the highest boundary of the town,

Figure 15. Aerial view of the Place du Gouvernement, 1934. The al-Jadid Mosque is to the right.

also dates from this period.[41] To facilitate military movements and vehicular circulation in the upper casbah, a plan in 1834 proposed a new gate on the south walls and an artery connecting this gate to the citadel. In addition to serving the army, the new "grande route" would bring life to the residents of the upper town by providing an alternative to the existing "exceptionally narrow" streets, totally inaccessible to vehicles.[42] The project, which also regularized the central square, was not executed.

REGULARIZATION, REDUCTION, AND ISOLATION

Comprehensive urban design projects that targeted the reorganization of the entire settlement were few and far between. Engineer Poirel's 1837 proposal to regularize and widen the street network, bringing the secondary streets to 3 and 5 meters wide, received a great deal of criticism due to its excessive catering to private interests.[43] Later designs focused on the extension of the city and only marginally ad-

Figure 16. Rue Bab Azzoun, c. 1900.

dressed the old town. One example is Charles Delaroche's 1848 project, which doubled the size of Algiers by new fortifications and a modern settlement with wide arteries and squares in the European quarter (Fig. 18). Delaroche's unrealized interventions to the casbah consisted of broadening three major streets that cut across the old town and carving a few squares at important intersections.

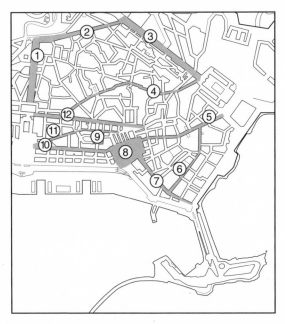

Figure 17. Plan of the casbah. (1) Boulevard Gambetta, (2) Boulevard de la Victoire, (3) Boulevard Vallée, (4) Rues Randon and
Marengo, (5) Rue Bab el-Oued, (6) Rue d'Orléans, (7) Rue de
la Marine, (8) Place du Gouvernement, (9) Place de Chartres,
(10) Rue Bab Azzoun, (11) Rue de Chartres, (12) Rue de la
Lyre.

The realization of a main artery on the waterfront, Rue Militaire, first
presented in a sketch by Poirel in 1837 and intended to serve the harbor
as well as act as a promenade, was delayed until 1860. When construction began, the artery was named Boulevard de l'Impératrice, celebrating the visit of Empress Eugénie and Napoleon III to Algiers the same
year. It was completed in 1866 according to Charles-Fréderick Chassériau's plans (Fig. 19). A particularly difficult feat of engineering due to
the drastic difference in level between the boulevard and the embank-
ment, the structure was supported by a series of high arches recalling a
bridge or an aqueduct. The ramps connecting the Boulevard de l'Impératrice to the harbor level took another eight years to build.[44] The
project gave Algiers its memorable waterfront: the continuous high arcade of the lower level, animated by the changing scale of the arches
supporting the ramps and in juxtaposition to the more delicate arcades
of the Boulevard de l'Impératrice on the upper level—all in white.

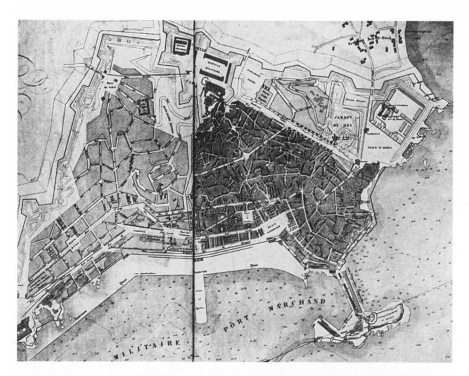

Figure 18. *(above)* Plan by Charles Delaroche, 1848.   Figure 19. *(below)* Aerial view of the arcades and the Boulevard de l'Impératrice, 1933.

While providing a spectacular edge to Algiers, this project also engraved the power relations of the colonial order onto the urban image: the casbah was locked behind the solid rows of French structures.

The obsessive focus on defense generated persistent demands for the enlargement of the fortified areas—a debate that had started in 1840.[45] By 1849, the old fortifications were replaced by new ones, enclosing an area three times larger than the one occupied by the old town. The lower part of the casbah had acquired a more regular street network with two main arteries, Rue de la Marine and Rue d'Orléans, which connected Rue de la Marine to Rue Bab el-Oued (see Fig. 17). The European settlers—French, but also Italian and Spanish—lived here, while the upper casbah became an exclusively indigenous town. The distinction between the two parts was reflected in their new names: the upper casbah became the "casbah" proper and the lower town became the Marine Quarter.[46]

The conjuncture of the casbah and the Marine Quarter was subjected repeatedly to regularization proposals. In 1917, for example, a project devised for the area defined by Chartres, Vialar, and Bab Azzoun streets and Place du Gouvernement, advocated the enlargement of Rue Bab Azzoun by appropriating 6-meter strips from its west side, thereby changing the width from 8 to 14 meters. In addition, Rue de Chartres and Rue de Vialar would be widened to 10 meters, and transversal streets, 8 meters wide, would connect the main arteries running parallel to the waterfront.[47]

Of various plans devised for the Marine Quarter, the one proposed by Eugène de Redon in 1884 has been revived several times, most significantly in revised versions between 1901 and 1914, and in 1922 (Fig. 20). Redon's project was initiated by the municipality's growing concern about public hygiene in the Marine Quarter, in the area between Rue Bab el-Oued and Boulevard de la République on the waterfront (the original Boulevard de l'Impératrice). The municipal authorities agreed to "raze whatever existed" here.[48] Although Redon's project addressed the entire city, its main impact was restricted to the proposals for the Marine Quarter, because it established clear strategies to resolve the chaotic structure of this area. The essence of the proposal involved the displacement of half of the population residing in the quarter, specifically the urban poor, who would be relodged in new housing projects to be built on the hills of the Bab el-Oued Quarter to the northwest of the old town. This depopulation would enable the replacement of narrow streets with large arteries lined with luxurious buildings to attract the wealthy bourgeoisie. A 25-meter-wide main avenue, Avenue de la

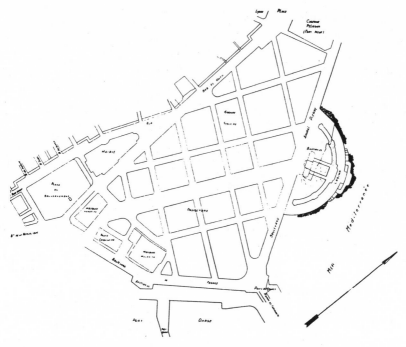

Figure 20. Eugène de Redon's plan for the Marine Quarter, 1925.

Préfecture, would extend the Boulevard de la République. At the begin-ning point of the avenue, close to the Place du Gouvernement, place-ment of the stockmarket and the Tribunal of Commerce expressed the ambition to turn the Marine Quarter into an impressive business center. The reorganization of the area would result in the reorientation of the al-Jadid Mosque and demolition of the al-Kabir Mosque, with plans to rebuild it on the northern flanks of the casbah.[49]

The 1922 version of the Redon plan emphasized once more the quar-ter's congestion and the necessity for erasing the entire area to accom-modate circulation and called for the displacement of twelve to fifteen thousand people. The new buildings would cater above all to the needs of commerce.[50] In this version, however, the two mosques were pre-served and a prominent casino was placed where the main avenue met the waterfront in the north.

Interventions to the casbah proper were relatively few. The north-south Rue de la Lyre (present-day Rue Ahmed Bouzrina), parallel to the Rue Bab Azzoun, stood out with its straight layout and continuous col-onnades amid the irregular street fabric surrounding it. Projected in

1845 but completed in 1855, it connected the center with the newly planned suburb Bab Azzoun and eased the heavy circulation on the axis of Rue Bab Azzoun and Rue Bab el-Oued.[51] Its architectural qualities made it especially significant to the French as a reminder of the Rue de Rivoli, a cherished urban fragment from Paris now implanted in Algiers. Rue Randon (now Ali la Pointe), its extension Rue Marengo (now Arbaji), and Rue Bruce were also cut through at this time.[52] Other major alterations carried out in the 1840s included two straight boulevards, Boulevard Vallée (present-day Boulevard Abderazak Hadad) on the north and Boulevard Gambetta (present-day Boulevard Ourida Meddad) on the south, both built on the glacis of the Ottoman fortifications.[53] Remaining at the edges of the old town, the major interventions during the early phases of the colonial rule may seem to have had little effect on the core of this introverted settlement. Nevertheless, the boulevards encircled the casbah and signified the surrender of the original residents of Algiers to the French—literally and metaphorically.

French architects early on acknowledged the immense difficulty of cutting through the casbah. A report submitted to the governor general of Algeria in 1858 pointed to the futility of fighting "against nature," against the capricious, "tormented," and "accidental" topography of the casbah. Arguing that the needs of the French were different from those of the indigenous people, the report proposed the construction of a new town, which would cater to European tastes, next to the old one.[54] Napoleon III's "arabizing" policies enhanced the conservation of the casbah further. The new policy of "tolerance" that dominated the 1860s criticized former demolitions and European constructions in the old town, which had pushed the local population to upper slopes and resulted in highly congested living conditions. The report that followed the emperor's research maintained that

> the town must conserve its actual physiognomy, that is to say, the high town must stay as it is, because it is appropriate to the customs and habits of the indigenous; cutting through grand arteries may result in causing them great suffering, and all these improvements may impose hardships to the indigenous population, which does not have the same lifestyle as the Europeans. The emperor thinks that the lower town should be reserved for the latter and it is in that part that all works of improvement and beautification should be made.[55]

In the late 1870s Eugène Fromentin summarized the early colonial policies Napoleon III aimed to change and commented on the rationale and extent of the French appropriation of Algiers:

France took from the old town everything that was convenient for her, everything that touched the waterfront or dominated the gates, everything that was more or less level and that could be easily cleared, and readily accessible. She took the Djenina, that she razed, and the ancient palace of the pachas, that she converted into the house of her governors. . . . She created a little Rue de Rivoli with Bab Azzoun and Bab el-Oued streets, and peopled it with counterfeiting Parisians. She made a choice between mosques, leaving some to the Qu'ran, giving others to the Evangelists.[56]

After these initial interventions, the casbah was left on its own. If demolition was no longer the issue, neither was maintenance. Algerian urban sociologist Djaffar Lesbet argues that the implicit menace of destruction to the casbah posed by neglect played a constructive and catalyzing role on the residents and forced them to pool their resources to stop the "natural" demolition of their neighborhoods. The basis for an alternative urban administration was established, operating on two levels: the maintenance of public open spaces by designated officers from the casbah and the maintenance of individual houses by the collaborative and organized labor of renters and owners. The residents of the casbah thus spoke back to colonizers by turning to themselves, consolidating their unity, and establishing their own system. With this move, Lesbet maintains, the casbah was transformed into a "counter space" (*espace contre*) that represented the oppositional voice of Algerians to colonial power.[57] The diametric stances of the casbah and the French Algiers, crystallized further by the former's "counter space" character, destroyed any possibility of overall harmony in a situation distinct to French colonial urbanism. In the words of Fanon, "The zone where the natives live is not complementary to the zone inhabited by the settlers. The two zones are opposed, but not in the service of a higher unity. Obedient to the rules of pure Aristotelian logic, they both follow the principle of reciprocal exclusivity. No conciliation is possible."[58]

THE IDEOLOGY OF PRESERVATION

The polarization in the urban form and social structure of Algiers was well in place after a century of French occupation. This did not mean, however, abandoning the casbah and its inhabitants to their own destiny. The attempts to renovate Algiers in celebration of one hundred years of French rule and in preparation for its leadership role in French Africa brought the old city—both the casbah and the

Marine Quarter—into focus. By this time, the first colonial interventions into the old city were subject to widespread criticism among the French in Algeria. The critics focused on two points: demolition of the old fabric and the poor aesthetic quality of the European structures. According to one critic, before the arrival of the French,

> The capricious urbanism of Algiers had the great merit of unity; Arab architecture only had buildings that accommodated their goals and that presented an ensemble of habitations all built according to a uniform plan. From the first stroke, we abolished this harmony.
>
> The most beautiful indigenous quarters thus were hollowed out; hundreds of houses were torn down; either the military administration or the entrepreneurs, after demolishing and ravaging, replaced the oriental dwellings with villain structures in the European style for renters.[59]

The foremost scholar of Algiers, René Lespès, also emphasized the "uniformity of the Moorish houses of Algiers," which harmonized with the lifestyles and customs of the residents. Grieving over the destruction of the ancient town, he pointed to the need to understand the particular character of these houses, as well as the intentions and the necessities that dictated their plans against the "stupidity and inelegance . . . of the desire to Europeanize them."[60]

The new directions adopted during the two decades from the 1930s to the 1950s agreed on the preservation of the precolonial heritage of the casbah. In essence, the policies pursued Napoleon III's notion of *royaume arabe* (arab realm) and, building on decades of French colonial experience, brought a clearly articulated ideological justification to all the design decisions.

Hubert Lyautey, governor general of Morocco from 1912 to 1925, is acknowledged for his development of distinct French colonial urban policies and an ideology of preservation in the colonies. The essence of his urbanism aimed to accommodate a new order, based on diversity, where people of different social and cultural circumstances could coexist.[61]

Lyautey's two main principles, which recall Napoleon III's policies for Algiers—namely, preservation of medinas out of respect for the local culture and building of new, modern cities for European populations—formed the backbone of all later urban planning decisions in Algiers. For Lyautey, the preservation of the Arab town had several meanings, some emotional, some practical. Above all, he savored the aesthetic qualities of the Arab town, its "charm and poetry," which he attributed to the sophistication of the Arab culture.[62] To understand the difference between this culture and the European one was essential to building a colonial policy that would endure: "The secret . . . is the extended hand, and not the condescending hand, but the loyal handshake between man and man—in order to understand each other. . . . This [Arab] race is not inferior, it is different. Let us learn how to understand their difference just like they will understand it from their side."[63]

This major difference between the two cultures required the separation of the indigenous from the European populations in the city, according to Lyautey:

> Large cities, boulevards, tall facades for stores and homes, installations of water and electricity are necessary, [all of] which upset the indigenous city completely, making the customary way of life impossible. You know how jealous the Muslim is of the integrity of his private life; you are familiar with the narrow streets, the facades without opening behind which hides the whole of life, the terraces upon which the life of the family spreads out and which must therefore remain sheltered from indiscreet looks.[64]

Consequently, Lyautey made the conservation of the Moroccan medinas one of his priorities in urban planning. He announced proudly, "Yes, in Morocco, and it is to our honor, we conserve. I would go a step further, we rescue. We wish to conserve in Morocco Beauty—and it is not a negligible thing."[65] Behind these compassionate words, however, lay an economic goal: the medinas were essential for the development of tourism, especially for the romantic traveler and the artist.[66]

The International Congress on Urbanism in the Colonies, held during the 1931 Colonial Exposition in Paris, recorded the powerful influence of Lyautey's ideas and practice on the new rules of planning in French colonies. Among the goals of the congress, as listed by Henri Prost, were "tourism and conservation of old cities" and "protection of landscapes and historic monuments." The "wish list" of the participants included the creation of separate settlements for indigenous and European populations, respecting the beliefs, habits, and traditions of various races. Whenever possible, a greenbelt, sometimes referred to as a *cordon sanitaire*, would divide the European town from the indigenous one.[67]

In Algiers, these principles were already written into ordinances by the late 1920s, and the "indigenous quarters" were placed under a special regime destined to conserve their character—despite the fact that "they were in opposition to principles of hygiene and urbanism."[68] The architects in Algiers knew that conservation was not sufficient to preserve the picturesque character of the casbah; given the buildings' fragility, rehabilitation was an important issue. One architect, Jean Bévia, proposed regulations to prohibit changes, to fix the height limits, and to impose "the Arab style." Nevertheless, he advocated demolishing buildings in bad condition and using their lots to "ventilate" these congested neighborhoods. Furthermore, a special municipal commission of hygiene had to be established to educate the residents—a most difficult task, Bévia maintained, given that the local people ignored all rules of health and hygiene.[69] A recurring theme in the discussions on the casbah, the "lack" of hygiene (together with the "lack" of order, material civilization, and so on) is a key mechanism in what Ella Shohat and Robert Stam call "the transformational grammar of colonial style racism," which reiterates the hierarchical structure of the colonial society.[70]

A special regulation, dated 13 June 1931, intended to conserve the "character and aesthetics" of the casbah by "imposing on the inhabitants the obligation to restore their houses and to build new ones only in ways that serve to that effect, following the proportions and characteristics of the indigenous architecture of Algiers." A newly created commission of consultants would supervise the casbah. Accordingly, Henri Prost, René Danger, and Maurice Rotival drafted a master plan for Algiers in 1931 that aimed to preserve the casbah.[71]

The abstract notion of the preservation of casbah was further articulated during the following years. Now the upper city itself was divided into two. The efforts of the Commission of Historic Monuments contributed greatly to the regulations concerning the "picturesque physiognomy" of the new "upper" casbah, defined by Rue Randon and Rue Marengo and Boulevard de la Victoire. This quarter would be neither demolished nor rebuilt as pastiche in the manner of "exhibition pavilions," a term used derogatorily. The rules were clearly specified: all new houses would conform to Algerian and Moorish styles; cornices, windows, wood lattices, canopies, doors, polished tiles, and painted or sculpted woodwork would be either preserved or reconstructed according to the original; a few new interpretations could be allowed if the output conformed to the general style; demolished European houses would be replaced by ones in the indigenous style; no building would be higher than three floors, including the ground floor; and all plans had to be submitted to the Technical Services section of the municipality for approval.[72]

While intervention to the upper part of the casbah was minimal and its residential function was maintained, the lower part, between Rue

Marengo and Rue Bab el-Oued, would be turned into a "museum quarter." Here, careful restoration of the few authentic buildings of aesthetic value and the preservation of the "tortuous and vaulted" Rue Emile Maupas and Rue de l'Intendance, considered by Lespès as "the most remarkable in old Algiers," would be undertaken. The archdiocese, the Palais d'Hiver, the headquarters of Indigenous Military Affairs, the old Moorish baths, the Bibliothèque Nationale, and the palace that now sheltered some offices of the secretary general would form an easily accessible ensemble as a museum complex.[73] In addition, schools for the indigenous would encourage the development of local art forms. As an integral part of the greater mission to preserve Algeria's historic heritage, an impressive number of new schools and workshops had already been established by the colonial authorities to develop local crafts—embroidery, leatherwork, copperwork, metalwork, carpentry, pottery, masonry, and decorative arts—with the goal of increasing their commercial value.[74]

Le Corbusier's projects for Algiers (spanning from 1931 to 1942) pursued the prescribed policy of preservation, used the same terminology, and gave the familiar rationale in explaining what to do with the casbah. Le Corbusier's casbah was also "beautiful," "charming," and "adorable," and it "never, no, never must be destroyed." Its historic significance as the "place of European and Muslim life during centuries of picturesque struggles" was held to be of great interest to the entire world. Therefore, its historical and aesthetic values, the vestiges of Arab urbanism and architecture, should be protected to enhance the "gigantic" touristic potential of Algiers. The overpopulation of the casbah, however, posed a difficult problem because it sheltered four to six times more residents than it could contain. If Algiers was to become the capital of French Africa, the misery of its Muslim population had to be addressed, the casbah "purified" and reorganized, its population reduced.[75]

Le Corbusier thus proposed to preserve the upper casbah in its integrity while restricting the densities and intervening in the patterns of use, in accordance with the planning decisions made before him. A number of buildings were to continue to function as residences, but others were to be converted into arts and crafts centers to initiate an indigenous "renaissance." The slums of the lower casbah, in contrast, would be expurgated; only the mansions would be preserved, yet converted into specialized museums for the indigenous arts. Parks and gardens would replace the areas cleared from the slums, but the existing street network

Figure 21. Le Corbusier, project for Algiers, photomontage, 1933. The business center, shown in the foreground, is connected to the residential areas on the hills by means of an elevated structure that forms a bridge over the casbah.

would be maintained to link the high casbah to the Marine Quarter and to the harbor.[76]

Le Corbusier interpreted Lyautey's idea of a greenbelt separating the European city from the casbah. In his 1932 plan, for example, a giant linear structure that connected the hillside residences for Europeans to the *cité d'affaires* in the Marine Quarter formed a bridge over the casbah, transforming the sanitary greenbelt into an air band and reversing the horizontality of the former into a vertical element (Fig. 21). Repeating the concept in his later plans, Le Corbusier himself emphasized the essential separation of the two settlements: "This artery will be separated entirely from the indigenous town, by means of a level difference."[77] Le Corbusier's project would thus establish constant visual supervision over the local population and clearly mark the hierarchical social order onto the urban image, with the dominating above and the dominated below.

POST—WORLD WAR II REALITIES

The casbah entered a crisis in the late 1930s. Political and economic conflicts and instability stalled all plans for the casbah in the

later part of the decade. World War II shifted the focus of political concerns away from the local populations, pushing the casbah further into
the background. The result was an intensification of the problems noted
repeatedly in the early 1930s, namely the pace of demographic growth
and physical decrepitude.

According to the 1931 census, the population of the upper casbah was
about 54,000 people, with nearly 3,000 inhabitants per hectare, as compared to 1,430 in 1881 and 2,028 in 1921. The growth was largely due to
immigration from Kabylia. The majority of the casbah's population
consisted of indigenous people, Arab or Kabyle, although there was a
considerable Jewish contingent; the few Europeans were often married
to locals. As indicated by the very high densities, housing conditions
were dreadful, with often an entire family crammed into a single room.
The majority of the houses did not have electricity or running water,
but sometimes a well in the shared courtyard. Remnants of the former
lifestyle could be found in a small number of houses that belonged to
the Turkish bourgeoisie on Rue de la Grenade (now Kheireddine Zen-
ouda), Rue Kléber (now Rue des Frères Bachara), and Rue Sidi Moham-
med Cherif.[78]

By 1949, the population had increased to 64,000 in the 38-hectare
area defined by Boulevard Gambetta, Boulevard de la Victoire, Boulevard de Verdun, and Bab el-Oued and Bab Azzoun streets, raising the
density in certain locations to 3,500 inhabitants per hectare. Of the 2,250
buildings of the upper casbah, 7 were mosques, 5 synagogues, and 1 a
Protestant church; only 15 residences were "classified," that is, in good
condition. E. Pasquali, an engineer in charge of the Central Division of
Technical Services in the municipality, reported that the rest of the residential fabric, "several centuries old," would be subject to a municipal
program. The first step in this program consisted of a survey of all buildings, to be followed by necessary interventions to assure the safety of
the inhabitants, and, eventually, by demolition. While the municipal officer regretted the disappearance of these "last witnesses of the barbaresque period," he argued that in the interest of the residents and the
quarter itself, there was no other alternative. The demolition of thirty-
three houses in 1948 marked the beginning of a new era for the upper
casbah: it was now essential to draft a redevelopment plan for the old
town.[79]

Two years later, such a plan had not been drafted and Pasquali still
advocated the demolition of most of the casbah, pursuing the dominant
attitude toward historic cities everywhere at the time. He now proposed
that before demolitions, however, a new *cité* should be built for the resi-

dents who would be displaced. He attributed the unhygienic conditions to overpopulation and the age of the buildings, pointing to physical as well as social diseases that would result from the crowding of eight or ten persons into a single room and two hundred into a single house. Under attacks from the conservationist camp, Pasquali eventually had to "admit, in spite of everything, that tourists did not come to Algiers to contemplate (our) Isly and Michelet streets," and that it was the casbah that made Algiers a tourist attraction due to the originality of the siting of its houses and to its "sympathetic disorder." His solution was to convert the upper casbah in its entirety into a museum and to remove its actual residents.[80]

The loss of old Algiers was an eventuality agreed on by many European observers. The only unchanged section was the heights, the quarter bordered by Rue de la Casbah on the north, Boulevard de la Victoire on the west, Rue Rampart-Médée and Rue du Centaure in the south, and Rue Randon and Rue Marengo in the east. With the goal of limiting historic preservation to this relatively small area, planners argued that here the original street network and the Moorish houses should remain intact. European constructions were negligible and the population exclusively Muslim. Given that the rest of the casbah had been intersected by several arteries and that old age was in the process of destroying whatever was left of the original buildings, the area once occupied by the old town was diminishing rapidly. Already in the first period of colonization the great triangle of old Algiers had lost its base, with the two great mosques left freestanding and isolated from their community of worshipers.[81]

The overcrowding of the casbah began to push the limits of the old settlement with pockets of shantytowns at its borders in the early 1950s. The first *bidonvilles* appeared to the west and the northwest of the casbah; the construction was made of any available material, including reed, zinc sheets, and large metal containers (*bidons*). Here immigrants from the countryside lived in congested conditions, often more than ten people inhabiting a single shack. Carrying the aspect of a "real village of *gourbis*," or huts, such settlements maintained a rural lifestyle and contrasted not only with the European parts of Algiers, but also with the urban form and life of the casbah itself. Nevertheless, the casbah had undergone some transformations as the waves of immigration changed its population cross-section to predominantly Kabyle residents, "a truly rural proletariat" that maintained its customs and traditions and resisted the urban culture.[82]

The urban administration proudly announced its success in introducing some elements of "modernization" to the casbah. By the first years of the 1950s, public fountains, at intervals of 200 or 300 meters, dotted the quarter; because the majority of the houses did not have running water, water carriers provided service for a fixed price. Garbage was collected every morning by small carts pulled by donkeys (regular carriages could not pass through the narrow streets), and the streets were washed by sea water. Electricity had also entered the casbah: not only the major streets, but also many houses were lit electrically.[83]

The debates between those who favored the preservation of the casbah (for historic and touristic reasons) and those who favored radical surgery (for hygienic—later political and militaristic—reasons) continued until the liberation. Even after the Battle of Algiers turned the historic city into a war zone, a romance with the beauty of its site and architecture lingered among many sectors of European society. In 1959, for example, the chief engineer of the Urbanism Section of the Municipal Council of Algiers gave an extensive tour of the casbah to a delegation of European mayors, who, according to newspaper accounts, were seduced by the "cascades of white terraces, diving into the harbor in a dreamlike golden light."[84]

On 3 October 1957, Gen. Charles de Gaulle revealed his extensive development plan for Algeria. The Plan de Constantine, named after the city where de Gaulle's famous speech was delivered, was based, according to its promoters, on "human promotion." Its premise, as outlined by de Gaulle, emphasized the role of France as the bearer of civilization, now a modern civilization: "Algeria in its entirety must have its share of what modern civilization can deliver to men of well-being and dignity." Together with education, decent housing was deemed essential to improve the standard of life of the Algerian people, but also to ensure their "social evolution" and "to modify their life habits and familial needs."[85]

Interpreted by its defenders as "the hope for the renaissance of the casbah," the Plan de Constantine addressed its problems on two levels: socioeconomic promotion and humanization of the daily life of the inhabitants. According to Jean Fabian, the municipal inspector for the casbah, the sociocultural project involved establishing new clinics and schools, and encouraging commercial enterprise. As congestion was the main issue, ventilating the casbah by means of demolition would allow for good traffic circulation and improve the transportation problems, as well as endowing the quarter with a "decent and modern" face, one that would be perceived as "a very great French work." According to the

Plan de Constantine, the residents would be relodged in new housing projects specifically designed for them. Of the three possible solutions—to raze the casbah entirely, to keep it as it was, or to redevelop it—the last was deemed the most productive. The houses in poor condition would be taken down, while others whose salvage was possible would be restored according to an effective technical plan. This option would not only bring down the population densities, but also establish an equilibrium between open space and built form.[86]

Despite regulations and the innumerable debates on how to improve the conditions in the casbah, the administration did not take any action. With the intensification of local resistance against French rule, the casbah became a "high risk" war zone. Ultimately, it was abandoned by the urban administration altogether. As noted by Lesbet, Algiers and the casbah were played against each other during the war, expanding on their oppositional roles established earlier.[87]

IMPACT OF THE DECOLONIZATION WAR

The image of the casbah changed fundamentally in 1954, when the region became the site of urban guerrilla warfare. For the Algerians, it became the locus of "the legend and the slum," that is, the legend of the Revolution and the slum of daily life. The National Liberation Front's Committee of Coordination and Execution had reorganized the administration of the casbah by dividing it into zones and establishing a system of *planques* (hideouts) and caches of resistance.[88] The complex configuration of the casbah, with interlocking terraces and passageways and tortuous dead-end streets, made penetration by French authorities difficult and facilitated defense.

As the site of war, certain locations in the casbah became associated with unforgettable moments for Algerians. The houses where resistance fighters were caught, tortured, and sometimes murdered became engraved into public memory. For example, the Rue Sidi bin Ali was the hiding place and explosives laboratory of Yacef Sadi, who escaped miraculously during the invasion on 6 February 1956; the same night, on Rue de la Grenade, Djamila Bouhired's father and brother were tortured in her presence for hours; two months later, Djamila herself was shot and arrested in the same location. On Rue Caton, Yacef Sadi and Zohra Drif were caught on 24 September 1958; on 3 October 1958 a group of houses was blown up by parachutists, resulting in the death of Ali la Pointe and Hassiba ben Bouali, in addition to thirty others.[89]

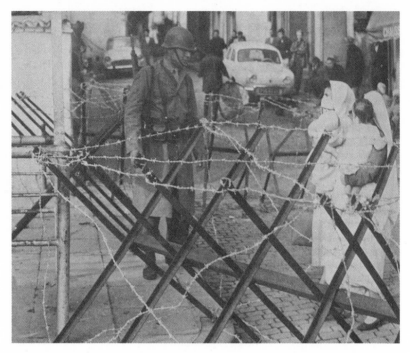

Figure 22. Barricades in the casbah.

From 1956 on, it was common practice for the French security forces to invade the casbah and cut it off from communication with the rest of Algiers (Fig. 22). Even a random selection of news items conveys the change in the daily life of the casbah, now frequently interrupted by unexpected police raids. On 28 March 1956, in an attempt to "decontaminate" the casbah of troublemakers and "to protect the lives and properties of many families . . . whose only desire is to work and live in peace," the police forces blocked unexpectedly the Rue Marengo and Rue Randon, together with adjoining smaller streets, to question more than two thousand people; five hundred were taken to the police headquarters for identity checks. The same evening, a similar operation was carried out in the upper casbah, and still more people were put into custody. Another "giant control operation" imprisoned sixty-five hundred residents in the casbah on 26 May 1956 for twenty-four hours, during which more than four thousand people were interrogated and all contact with the exterior was halted. The casbah was surrounded at midnight, and machine guns and grenade launchers were placed at key locations, such as Boulevard de la Victoire and Rue de la Lyre. Colonial

newspaper accounts commented tongue in cheek on the lack of picturesqueness in the casbah during those twenty-four hours, when the residents were locked inside their houses and allowed to open their doors
only to the police. On 8 January 1957, armed forces two thousand strong
undertook a search operation in the upper casbah. A secondary objec-
tive of this massive action, which had started at 3 : 00 A.M., was to recruit
unemployed people as construction workers. On 23 September 1956,
twenty-four smaller streets around Rue Bab el-Oued, Rue Bab Azzoun,
and Rue de la Lyre were barred from circulation "for an indeterminate
amount of time."[90]

The French considered the defeat of Ali la Pointe the end of the
Battle of Algiers, with the paramilitary forces as the victors. From that
point military order reigned in the casbah and marked the region with
its own symbols of war and occupation. Military and police officers had
increased in great numbers, all strategic crossroads were wired, entries
and exits from the casbah were controlled, and public spaces were decorated with propaganda posters (which were in turn covered with graffiti
expressing themes of resistance and independence).[91] In December
1960, a tract signed by several resistance organizations and published in
El Moudjahid, the official journal of the National Liberation Front
(FLN), called the casbah the "new ghetto of Warsaw," in reference to
the two hundred thousand people besieged here.[92] Yet though the casbah was locked off from the rest of Algiers and under military occupation, it still functioned as a theater for resistance, with parades echoing
others elsewhere in the city until the end of French rule.[93]

The Story of the Marine Quarter

The divergence of the Marine Quarter and the casbah be-
came definitive in the 1930s. In response to the debates to create a truly
appropriate capital for French Africa, René Danger, Henri Prost, and
Maurice Rotival drafted the first master plan for Algiers, which was approved in 1931. In accordance with the new enthusiasm for "urbanism"
among French technocrats and administrators, the three architects were
applauded as "true '*urbanistes*' of highest quality, and of an indisputable
fame."[94] This statement implicitly expressed doubt about Le Corbusier's credibility as an urbanist at the time when he had started working
on his alternative designs for Algiers.

Within the framework provided by the master plan, Tony Socard, an

Figure 23. Aerial view of the Marine Quarter, with the casbah behind, 1935.

architect working with Prost, developed a project for the Marine Quarter that was based largely on Redon's earlier scheme.[95] In the early 1930s, this quarter was densely inhabited by a low-income cosmopolitan population, mainly consisting of Neapolitan Italians, Spaniards, Jews, and "indigenous immigrants" (Fig. 23). Its street network was inaccessible to motor vehicles and its buildings extremely fragile—as witnessed by a building collapse on Rue des Consuls in 1929 in which over fifty people were killed. It was generally agreed that there was little here worthy of preservation. René Lespès defined the Marine Quarter at the time as "a small town, bastard, neither Moorish, nor entirely European." Joseph Sintes reaffirmed Lespès' statement by arguing that "this old quarter responded neither to aesthetics, nor to material or moral hygiene," the last reference to the scale of prostitution.[96] The few protests from the Comité du Vieil Alger to preserve several small and scattered "historic corners" were rebuffed (even by members of the committee itself) as "false Orientalism . . . now outmoded."[97] It was common sentiment that there was nothing worth saving from the residential and commercial framework and that valuable fragments—columns, tiles, woodwork, etc.—could easily be salvaged for incorporation into new buildings.[98]

The Marine Quarter was of crucial importance to Algiers, however, because it provided the connection to the harbor. It had also maintained a commercial character, with the Rue Bab el-Oued as the center of this activity, being the first stop for people descending from the casbah. Yet Bab el-Oued was lined with small shops that were deemed no longer efficient.[99] The presence of the two "untouchable" monuments, al-Kabir and al-Jadid mosques, caused several daily visits by Muslims in large numbers, inevitably making the quarter a meeting place—a notion that Le Corbusier would expand into a "meeting place" between the two cultures.

Socard's plan aimed to destroy the quarter entirely with the exception of the two historic mosques; their asymmetrical relationship, which betrayed the essence of Beaux-Arts urban design, would be "corrected" with landscaping (Fig. 24). A "magnificent boulevard," 450 meters long and 30 meters wide, would pass between the two mosques and act as the "great collector" of traffic circulating between Bab el-Oued and the streets to the west and northwest, on the one hand, and the waterfront and the ramps of the harbor, on the other. The Rue Bab el-Oued would be enlarged to 22 meters; the west part of the quarter would be divided into four sections by means of 16-meter and 10-meter streets, each part occupied by a building with a large garden court. The patchwork of houses between the Place du Gouvernement and Rue Mahon were to be demolished to give way to a park that would include the landscaped plaza in front of the al-Jadid Mosque and end in a curve to the west; the curve would be reflected on the east side of the grand avenue, creating a transversal axis. The east part of the quarter was differentiated as the locus of institutions, such as the chamber of commerce, stockmarket, Palace of Justice, library, and possibly the National School of Fine Arts. The project was seen as favorable in terms of circulation and a well-balanced distribution of built and open spaces; the resulting displacement of about fifteen thousand people would be resolved by settling them into the new housing projects.[100]

The project came under the attack of critics defending a more radical approach sympathetic to Le Corbusier's ideas. Emphasizing the importance of "scientific control by urbanists who know their job" and agreeing on the necessity to change the scale of the quarter, Jean-Pierre Fauve expressed his dissatisfaction with the Prost-Socard plan. According to Fauve, this plan was not "large enough." The widening of Bab el-Oued as proposed by Prost and Socard was in the spirit of the plans applied in Algiers in the 1850s and thus on a pre-automobile scale. The 35-meter width envisioned for the grand avenue was not daring enough, either.

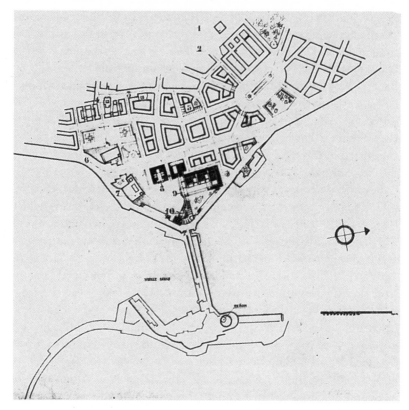

Figure 24. Tony Socard, plan for the Marine Quarter, 1935. Al-Jadid and al-Kabir mosques are labeled 6 and 7, respectively. The buildings marked in black form the institutional complex.

The best solution would be a *ville radieuse,* a radiant city that would let the sun in by decreasing the built surface and increasing the open space.[101]

Fauve also criticized Prost's overall master plan for shifting the city center away from old Algiers toward Agha in the south. Arguing that centers historically develop according to many good reasons, he challenged the Prost plan for not being functional and for turning its back on the history of Algiers. There was also a political issue at stake: as the capital, Algiers had a most important mission as a "Franco-Muslim" city. The Place du Gouvernement, the contact point of the two communities, had to remain the center of the city.[102]

Le Corbusier's designs preserved the central functions of the Marine

Quarter. In the 1932 plan, for example, a skyscraper sheltered the main activities of the *cité d'affaires*.[103] The "air belt" that separated the casbah from new Algiers began at this point with the proposal for a bridge-like structure that connected the skyscraper to the residential buildings for the Europeans on the hills above the casbah. Le Corbusier's successive proposals elaborated on the idea of the Marine Quarter as the "business center" and "civic center" of Algiers. Cleared and rebuilt with large blocks that left plenty of open space for parks and gardens, the quarter would provide the link between the European and Arab cities. Certain Arab institutions, such as offices, shops, and meeting halls, would be placed here. Le Corbusier maintained that the location was most convenient for overlapping functions because of its proximity to the port, its centrality in terms of future growth, and its significance as a historical axis for Arabs. The two mosques to be preserved, but cleared of the impeding fabric, would be returned to their original condition, sitting on a rock base. The presence of the new "indigenous institutions" in a "vast ensemble of new [and] grand Muslim architecture, as monumental as it would be picturesque," would complement the historic buildings.[104] In short, Le Corbusier's cleansing in the Marine Quarter would be urbanistic, architectural, and social, at once providing for controlled activities for Arabs and racial contact in an ordered environment.

After a long political battle, laced with intrigue, concessions, and compromises between the urban administration and Le Corbusier and his defenders, his project was rejected definitively in 1942 and the Prost plan was revived.[105] The war years stalled its implementation, however, and only in 1945 was the grand axis, Avenue du 8 Novembre (now Avenue du 1 Novembre), opened to circulation. The demolitions rekindled the sentiments of the citizens who feared the loss of their historic heritage. In a public letter, well-respected Algerian theologian and intellectual Omar Racim likened the destruction of Algiers to that of Hiroshima and argued that with the opening of the Avenue du 8 Novembre the mosques were "chipped" and found themselves as "old people deformed by age who in vain tried to hide their shame caused by their infirmities." He bitterly wondered when the city officials would "bury Algiers alive" by demolishing whatever was left of the old city in order to sell its pieces to tourists as relics.[106]

To enable the construction of the new artery, 340 buildings, covering an area of 45,800 square meters, were demolished, and 11,000 residents and 380 shopkeepers were evacuated (Fig. 25). Meanwhile 1,456 units of

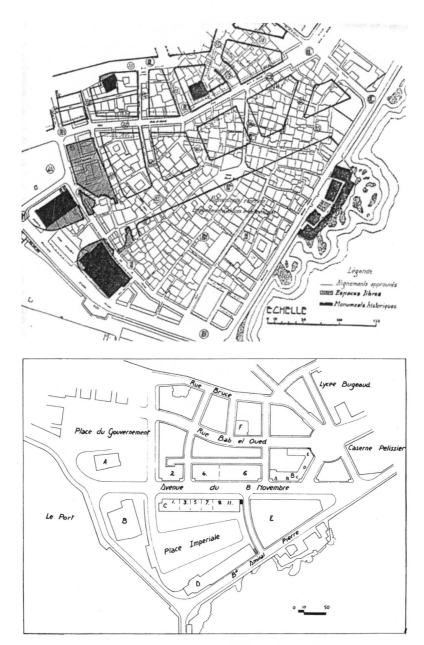

Figure 25. *(above)* Plan showing the extent of demolitions proposed by Socard's project for the Marine Quarter. Figure 26. *(below)* Plan for the Marine Quarter, 1950.

housing (amounting to 3,628 rooms) were constructed elsewhere, the city expropriated about 500 more buildings, and the construction of the first residential complex in the Marine Quarter was begun. P. Loviconi, the adjunct secretary general of the communal administration, summarized the status of the project in 1949, indicating clearly the extent of the demolition and construction work to be done.[107]

In 1950, a slight alteration to the project introduced a trapezoidal public place, the Place Impériale, open to the waterfront on the south but surrounded by buildings sheltering residential units and offices on the other three sides (Fig. 26). The Palace of Justice would define its narrow north side, and a skyscraper would be placed to the east, reviving Le Corbusier's 1932 scheme.[108] This project stalled again.

Mayor Jacques Chevallier refueled the efforts to renovate the Marine Quarter in a final, but doomed, attempt. By this time, the housing conditions had become even more urgent and the existing stock alarmingly decrepit. The 550 buildings over an area of 89,000 square meters, sheltering 18,000 to 20,000 residents, with densities approaching 1,500 people per hectare, were estimated unsalvageable in the Marine Quarter. The city official reiterated that there was no other solution than razing the area and rebuilding it.[109]

The project was commissioned to Gérald Hanning, who brought back the design principles of Le Corbusier's *cité d'affaires* without linking it to the heights. Hanning proposed to reduce the number of motor vehicles in the quarter by designating a peripheral route to transit traffic. Treated as a tabula rasa, the area was reorganized with tall blocks placed perpendicular to the casbah, with the highest structure at the tip of the triangle extending to the sea (Fig. 27). Hanning's rationalization of this decision focused on providing intriguing city views from the water and sea views from the hills. Four to five thousand people would be resettled in the new housing (the remaining population was to be transferred to the new projects in the Bab el-Oued Quarter), and the densities would not exceed four hundred persons per hectare.[110]

Hanning's project did not lead to any of the turmoil Le Corbusier had experienced two decades earlier. It was approved with great pride on the premise that "the orthogonal conception of the buildings will give the quarter an agreeable ambiance while providing for large open spaces between the buildings."[111]

Hanning proposed a "historic" enclave amid the entirely new buildings, a quiet spot between the two mosques below the Place du Gouvernement. Isolating the historic monuments from the modern quarter

Figure 27. Gérald Hanning, project for the Marine Quarter, photo-montage, 1959.

would put an end to their "suffering" and give them back their religious and artistic value, according to the architect. The Place du Gouvernement was to be enclosed on the north side by a horizontal block four stories high. Considering the area between Avenue du 8 Novembre and the foot of the casbah a transition zone, Hanning laid out here a network of short, rather narrow streets lined with modern, courtyard houses. In another attempt to relate to the casbah, the architect allowed for small shops on the ground level of the tall buildings that would correspond to the scale of souks and hence make the transition between the old city and the new quarters smoother.[112]

The project was received enthusiastically, despite its acknowledged departure from the urban structure of old Algiers, and this approval was solidified in a municipal publication. Hanning's project was promoted as another harmonious layer to the historic complexity of Algiers, characterized not by a stylistic and formal uniformity, but on the contrary, by a "happy juxtaposition of forms, of volumes put in place during centuries." Reconstituting preexisting structures had never been a concern before, and modern planners would be wise to pursue this philosophy.[113]

Like other ambitious projects envisioned for the Marine Quarter, Hanning's proposal was not implemented, except for demolitions on both sides of the Avenue du 8 Novembre and the rehousing of the inhabitants. While many residents were relocated in the new housing settlements on the hills of Bab el-Oued, the lack of available units forced others to move to the already crowded casbah, raising the densities to unbearable limits.[114] At the conclusion of the war, after eighty years of grand visions for the Marine Quarter, the Algerian administration inherited a wasteland of sorts—largely demolished, but not reorganized.

CHAPTER 2

An Outline of Urban Structure

Whether we take into consideration social, political, economic, or artistic points of view, we must recognize the essential role that cities play in the modern world and the influence they may have on the destiny of the people who have begun to evolve, on their environment, their organization, their health, their aesthetics.

Order and security are at play; social peace, prosperity of the nation, its artistic formation, [and] the attraction it may exert on foreigners can be compromised or assured by violation of or respect for principles of urbanism.

M. E. De Vivier de Streel,
Introduction to J. Royer, *L'Urbanisme
aux colonies et dans les pays tropicaux*

The dilemmas the French confronted in their interventions to the old town of al-Jaza'ir were paralleled and, furthermore, complicated by the considerable growth of the city following the occupation. French administrators placed great importance on urban planning as an instrument of colonization that would help establish their power and facilitate their control of the dominated society. The need for systematic urban design was acknowledged and voiced immediately following the conquest, but its translation into practice did not proceed smoothly. Several factors hindered the implementation of grand plans—among them the ambiguity of the role assigned to Algiers in the early decades of French rule; the topography of the site, complicated by steep hills separated by valleys behind a flat band along the water; and, stem-

58

ming from site conditions, the linear "organic" growth of the city toward the south, following the coastline. Political struggles within the
urban administration and economic problems played obstructing roles
as well. While these issues dominated the entire duration of French rule,
the planning of Algiers displays three distinct periods. The first period
covers the century between 1830 and 1930 and shows fragmented reac-
tions to ad hoc growth. The second period extends from 1930 to the
end of World War II and is distinguished by sweeping attempts to bring
order to the entire city through master plans. The third period, characterized by its concentration on the regional scale, leads to the end of
French rule.

From the first decades of French occupation, the organic expansion
of the lower city was linear; it followed the coastline and eventually resulted in a continuously built fabric in the flat zone at the water's edge,
meanwhile pushing the center of the city away from old Algiers. The
hills were dotted with dispersed settlements separated from the rest by
topographic conditions. Establishing a connection between the upper
and lower sections of the town constituted the main issue, and plans
were devised to construct a wide road that swept along the heights and
many cross-streets that climbed up the slopes to provide fast access to
upper neighborhoods. Starting in 1930, master plans attacked the same
problems, which continued to escalate with the growth of Algiers. The
master plans, like the regional plans that came later, prioritized zoning
and a road network that would unify the city. With the intensification
of the housing shortage in the 1950s, however, planning began to focus
on the design of large housing projects, the *grands ensembles*.[1]

Taming the Organic Growth

When the French invaded Algiers, they settled in the old
city. Uncertain about their future in Algeria, they kept urban intervention to a minimum during the first years of occupation. As seen in the
previous chapter, the main operations—the opening of the Place du
Gouvernement and the widening of the main arteries, Rue Bab el-Oued
and Rue Bab Azzoun—depended solely on militaristic and practical
necessities.

Even in the 1840s, when the French became convinced that they
would stay in Algeria for good, no clear role was envisioned for Algiers.

On the one hand, plans for its future did not extend beyond military functions, as articulated by the governor general of Algeria in 1844: "Algiers must rather be a place of war, which forms the citadel of Algeria, than a town of commerce."[2] Accordingly, an early planning decision called to replace the Ottoman fortifications with new fortifications "à la Vauban."[3] Built between 1841 and 1848, the new fortifications tripled the *intra-muros,* while enhancing the emphasis put on defense. On the other hand, a second camp approached city building with a broader vision. Arguing that French domination in Algiers would be permanent, a group of technocrats advocated converting Algiers from a battlefield (*champ de bataille*) to a workplace (*champ de travail*), where a large European population would either mix with local Arabs or live next to them in peace and friendship. To enable economic development, construction of harbor facilities and commercial buildings had to be given priority.[4]

Meanwhile, the growing population of the city had already pushed the city limits toward the south, creating a major settlement in Mustafa. As early as 1839, official reports pointed to the high densities in the old town, especially to the overcrowding of the Marine Quarter and the lower casbah, where most of the fifteen thousand Europeans lived. By this time, the population of Algiers was around forty-eight thousand.[5]

Attempts at a plan that would control the urban growth and introduce a "rational" street system go back to the early 1840s, but the first project to be approved by the ministry of war dates from 1846. The project replaced the Ottoman fortifications by large boulevards that encircled the casbah. The Boulevard Vallée to the north of the casbah and the Rue Rovigo to the south, which climbed the hills with its dramatic curves, provided communication with the interior of the country (Fig. 28). Rue du Rampart (later Boulevard de l'Impératrice, Boulevard de la République, and now Boulevard Che Guevara), completed in the 1860s, defined the border between the edge of the city and its harbor.[6]

Taking into consideration the organic extension of the city southward, a second project from 1846 (Plan Guiauchain) moved the center from the Place du Gouvernement to the site of the demolished Bab Azzoun gate. The Bab Azzoun Quarter, sheltering both residential and commercial functions, had a "double physiognomy": corresponding to its topography, the lower section displayed a rectilinear arrangement of streets, with the Rue d'Isly crossing it transversely and opening up to the Place d'Isly (later named Place Bugeaud) at its center, while the upper section was cut through by curving arteries. The short streets

Figure 28.   Plan of Algiers, c. 1900. (1) Rue d'Isly, (2) Rue Rovigo,
(3) Boulevard Vallée, (4) Rue du Rampart, (5) Place de la République.

linking the Rue d'Isly to the heights were, if straight, painfully stepped.
One among them, Rue Joinville, with its 150 steps, was considered by
Lespès to be "a curiosity . . . a challenge thrown at nature and also a
picturesque misinterpretation of urbanism."[7]

While the area around Bab Azzoun developed as a European quarter,
not much happened in Bab el-Oued, except for the establishment of a
few minor industries and a couple of mills. A planned working-class
neighborhood, the Cité Bugeaud, was designed for this quarter in the
late 1840s on the initiative of a German architect, M. Lichtenstein;
it offered refuge to victims of the Janina fire, which had devastated
the area surrounding the Janina Palace as well as the palace itself
(Fig. 29).[8]

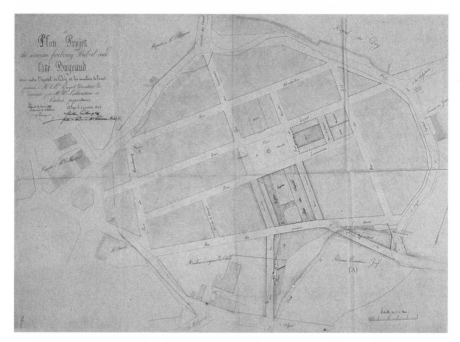

Figure 29. Plan of Cité Bugeaud, Bab el-Oued Quarter, c. 1845.

Several projects in the 1850s called for the extension of Algiers outside its fortifications toward the south. Chassériau's "Napoléonville" from 1858 proposed to sever the European settlement completely from the Muslim town and to settle sixty thousand Europeans in two-story houses filling an orthogonal grid in Mustafa (Fig. 30). The houses were grouped around green spaces, and densities did not exceed 282 people per hectare. Given the realities of Algiers, Chassériau's project was considered idealistic and "too beautiful to become real." Two similar projects, the Vigourous-Caillat plan and the MacCarthy-Génévay plan, reiterated the same ideas the same year. None of these proposals stirred an interest among municipal authorities, whose main concern focused on the private interests of landowners in *intro-muros*. In addition, Mustafa obtained its autonomy as an urban unit in 1871 and pursued its own ad hoc development.[9]

On the road that led from Bab Azzoun to Mustafa, another quarter, that of Agha, had developed organically since the 1840s along Rue de Constantine, which led to the town of Constantine. Agha attracted some commercial enterprises, as well as a considerable number of caba-

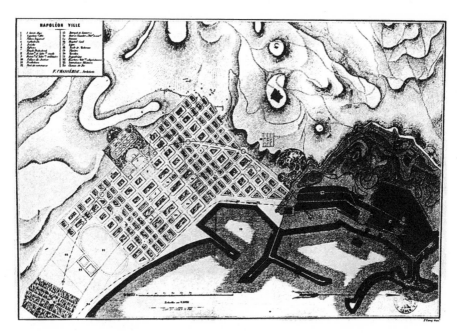

Figure 30.   Charles-Fréderick Chassériau, plan for Napoléonville, 1858.

rets that capitalized on the proximity of the army camp and the Champ
de Manoeuvres, the parade ground. According to Fromentin in 1852, the
Agha Quarter was "an interminable line of restaurants and cafés [*bu-
vettes*]," forming a striking contrast to the sombre Muslim town.[10]

Perhaps the most significant urbanistic event of the 1860s was the
completion of the Boulevard de l'Impératrice, which extended from
one end of the city to the other within the French fortifications, unifying the waterfront (see Fig. 19). This boulevard enhanced the planning
of adjacent areas, among them the Square Bresson (later Place de la République, then Square Aristide Briand; now Square Said), which definitively welded the old town to the new one. Defined on one side by the
Grand Theater, one of the first French monuments in town, Square
Bresson opened to the waterfront on the other. It was lushly planted
and decorated with statues; the music stand in the center was topped by
a dome from a demolished sixteenth-century building. The Boulevard
du Centaure (later Boulevard Gambetta, now Ourida Meddad), leading
from Square Bresson to the hills behind and following the line of the
former Ottoman fortifications, was an "immense stairway" with about
two hundred steps and periodic platforms (Figs. 31 and 32). On the up-

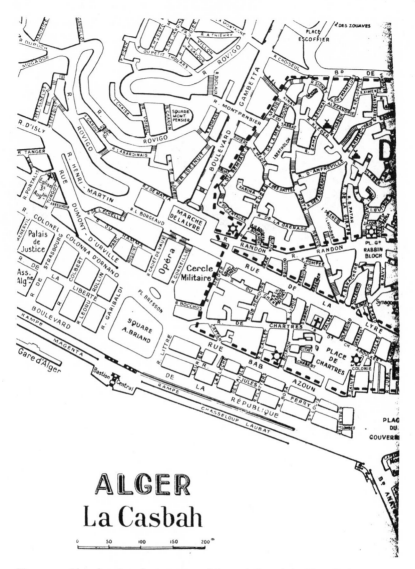

Figure 31. Plan showing the juncture of the casbah and the French city.

per parts of the Boulevard du Centaure the first casino in Algiers was built in the 1880s in an effort to accommodate the British tourists and to turn the city into an *hivernage* (winter resort).[11]

The Rue de la Liberté, parallel to the Boulevard de l'Impératrice, was also laid out during the 1860s, simultaneously with a network of or-

Figure 32. View of Square Bresson, with the Grand Theater in the foreground, c. 1900.

thogonal streets, creating a new neighborhood (Fig. 33). Due to the 10-meter width of its streets and the uniformity of the buildings lining them, this longitudinal quarter was considered the "best designed," the "best ventilated," and the "best built." The two government buildings back to back to each other in the center, the Central Post Office facing the Boulevard de l'Impératrice and the Palace of Justice the Rue de la Liberté, added further prestige to this strip.[12]

Mustafa's autonomy lasted until its reannexation in 1904. During the 1870s it grew considerably, in part due to employment resulting from the construction of the Civil Hospital. Random development of the neighborhood was difficult to correct, however, and the attempt of a master plan to regularize the quarter failed, because it did not take into consideration topographic characteristics. The Rue de Télemy (now Salah Bouakouir) remained a unique intervention. Originally conceived as a 10-meter-wide corniche that would span the heights of the city and offer spectacular views of the bay, its width was reduced to 7 meters for reasons of economy.[13]

The lifting of the forty years of military regime in favor of civilian rule in 1871 had important consequences for the city of Algiers. The military terrains and easements occupied a huge area encircling the city; within the fortifications, this amounted to 160 hectares, as opposed to the 86 hectares left for public use. The city walls had also become obsolete, acting only as artificial barriers between Algiers proper and its

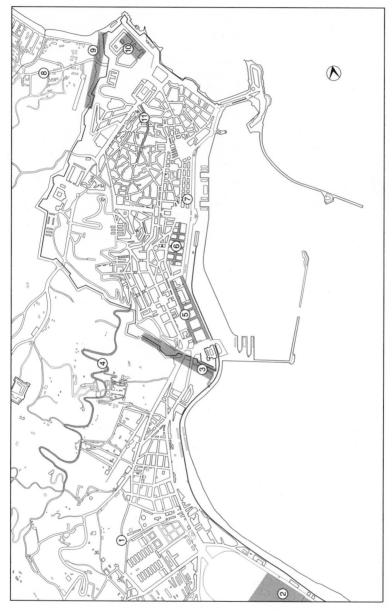

Figure 33. Plan of Algiers, c. 1900. (1) Mustafa, (2) Jardin d'Essai, (3) Boulevard Laferrière, (4) Rue de Télemy, (5) Rue de Constantine, (6) Rue de la Liberté, (7) Boulevard de l'Impératrice, (8) Bab el-Oued, (9) Boulevard Guillemin, (10) Square Nelson, (11) Rue Randon.

suburbs. After negotiations that lasted over a decade, the demolition of the ramparts began in 1894. The turbulent negotiations themselves constituted one of the two main urbanistic activities from the 1880s to the beginning of the demolitions (with the exception of one new street—the extension of the Rue Randon).[14]

The other major event in the planning of the history of Algiers at the time was the *Projet de transformation, d'extension et d'embellissement de la ville d'Alger,* prepared by Eugène de Redon in 1884. Taking into consideration the inevitable growth of the city southward, Redon proposed to connect Algiers and Mustafa by placing a maritime quarter in the Bab Azzoun area. Sheltering new sea and land transportation installations, a train station, and a large commercial area, and facing a new basin, this quarter would replace the Bab Azzoun fort. Redon extended the Boulevard de la République for 900 meters toward Agha and foresaw the development of the zone gained by the demolition of the fortifications, around a main boulevard that connected the waterfront to the heights—later realized as the Boulevard Laferrière.[15]

To compensate for the real estate lost by the military in the redesign of the Marine Quarter, Redon introduced a military quarter in the north, near Bab el-Oued. This quarter was organized by means of three arteries parallel to a 630-meter-long and 25-meter-wide boulevard on the waterfront, the Avenue Bab el-Oued; other streets perpendicular to those would ensure excellent ventilation. Furthermore, Redon proposed to renovate the Bab el-Oued Quarter entirely in an effort to balance development in the north of the city with the expansion of the southern suburbs. The corniche boulevard would be continued, and six principal roads parallel to it would be intersected by perpendicular streets, forming, once again, a well-connected and spacious network.[16]

As Lespès argued, even though actual city building was minimal between 1880 and 1896, an important development had taken place: the city administrators had formed a clear opinion on how to deal with the problems of Algiers. They understood that the future of the city was based on its merging with suburbs in the north and south; the Mustafa and Bab el-Oued quarters had to be incorporated into Algiers proper. In addition, Algiers was now considered the capital of French Africa and potentially a great city of commerce, not a mere military and naval outpost. In 1896, its population was over 120,000 people; of these, about 92,000 lived in Algiers proper and 35,000 in Mustafa.[17]

The heyday of building activity in Algiers occurred between 1896 and 1914. On the land bought from the army by the city administration, the municipality built sixty-six roads. The impressive developments to the south underscored the inevitable shift of the center: the Rue d'Isly, until then dotted with makeshift shops and insignificant buildings, became lined with large and "beautiful" structures; another well-built neighborhood emerged in the Isly Quarter and around the newly extended Bugeaud ramp; the terrains between Rue de Constantine and Boulevard Carnot also were developed. To the north, the Esplanade Quarter was built around a central square, the Square Nelson (now Square d'Istanbul); the heights of Bab el-Oued, below the el-Kattar cemetery, acquired twenty streets lined with impressive buildings. In addition, two new boulevards replaced the former fortifications: Boulevard Laferrière (now Mohamed Khemisti) to the south and Boulevard Guillemin (now Abderahmane Taleb) to the north, both alternating ramps with leveled platforms to soften the topography. The lushly planted central strips of these avenues acted as longitudinal mini-parks, compensating to some degree for the lack of open space in the city. Another important urbanistic gesture was the decision to create a large public park in the Jardin d'Essai in 1912.[18]

This intensive building activity could not always be controlled and regulated. While certain urban fragments benefited from careful plans, others were not so lucky. For example, the lower and upper sections of Mustafa, as well as Belcourt and Hamma, grew fast but without any plan (Fig. 34).[19] Inevitably, the more prestigious quarters became the focus of attention and benefited from urban design in the "grand manner," albeit in a piecemeal fashion. The location of a number of new monuments, such as the new Prefecture on the Boulevard de la République and the Central Post Office on Boulevard Laferrière—both built in 1906 in neo-Islamic styles—emphasized further the primacy of certain quarters (Fig. 35).

The ad hoc growth pattern set by Mustafa, Belcourt, and Hamma became the norm until 1930. Not only did the built fabric of the city begin to climb up farther onto the hills, appropriating any available land, but also the former pattern of "Moorish-style" villas in gardens on the heights gave way to much denser settlement patterns; the original owners of such villas now preferred to live in the fashionable apartments downtown. Densities in the older quarters of the city rose, too, due to the increasing building heights and new construction on every leftover open space. Yet it was the linear expanse that most overwhelmed people concerned with the future of Algiers. In 1930, Algiers extended for 8 kilometers along the shore from St.-Eugène to Hussein-Dey, in

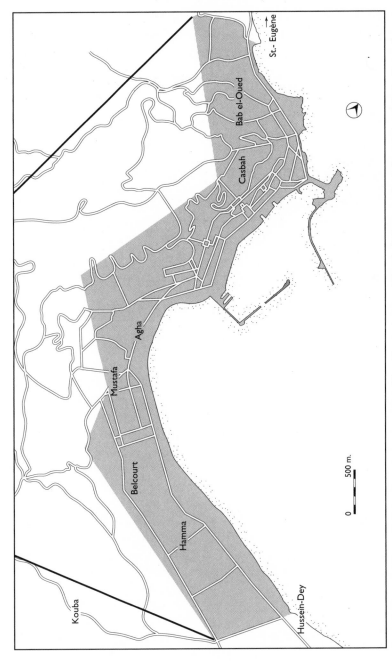

Figure 34. Schematic plan showing the area occupied by Algiers in 1930. The dark lines on the left and the right indicate the area covered in the 1948 regional plan.

Figure 35. View of the Prefecture on Boulevard de la République. The arcades of the harbor are in the foreground.

what was repeatedly characterized at the time as "chaotic growth." In between the built areas lay land that belonged either to the military or to the public (such as hospitals).[20]

Unlike other French colonial cities, Algiers was not strictly segregated into European and indigenous quarters. The exception was the casbah with its almost entirely Algerian population; other areas showed varying degrees of population mixture. In 1926, 212,000 people lived in Algiers (including Mustafa). The *intra-muros* had 112,000 residents: about 45,000 were Algerians, mostly concentrated in the casbah, and 67,000 were Europeans residing in the quarters to the south of the casbah and in the less affluent Marine Quarter. Mustafa's population consisted of 64,000 Europeans and 10,000 Muslims. Bab el-Oued had only 800 Muslims, out of a total of 26,000 residents.[21]

The Age of Master Plans

The first French law on "urbanism" dates from 14 March 1919. Considered "the charter of modern urbanism," this law called for a master plan for every town having more than ten thousand people in order to regulate growth and enable "beautification" (*embellissement*). The plan would thus determine the street network once and for all, specifying the layout and width of all the streets (including the design of new ones and modification of old ones) and the location and character of all open spaces—public parks, gardens, and squares—as well as of monuments and public service buildings.[22] Undoubtedly, the technological, social, and aesthetic lessons learned from city planning practices previously undertaken in French colonies played a primary role in devising official policies for urban development in both metropolitan France and *outre-mer*. Similar regulations for orderly urban development were in place in other parts of Europe at the time, and while the French were influenced by these trends, they relied more heavily on their own ideas about urban planning. To reiterate a familiar argument, the colonies were true laboratories of modern planning.

Yet although Algiers was the foremost among France's colonial cities, it had never been a real laboratory. Its development had followed a haphazard pattern; decisions were made on the spot, in accordance with the ambiguous and unsettled policies of the early colonial period. In fact, the mistakes made in Algiers were in part responsible for the more orderly planning in other colonies. In turn, the urbanistic lessons learned from the later colonies and empowered by the growing confidence in modernism were reformulated in the 1930s to be applied to France's oldest colonial city. The curious story of Algiers's "rational" planning after 1930 is indicative of the waves of changes in colonial policies, as well as the city's unusual status vis-à-vis France.

Algiers's master plan, a pioneering scheme that put the 1919 law into practice, was approved in 1931 and revised twice, in 1933 and 1934. Initiated by the newly created Service Municipale de l'Urbanisme, it was drafted by Henri Prost, René Danger, and Maurice Rotival. Prost was considered an especially fortunate choice to correct the former errors and offer "new and sound" rules because of his extensive experience in Morocco and the "happy and rational" results he had obtained there. Nevertheless, given the "disordered and incoherent character" of Algiers, expectations were conservative. Lespès, for example, could foresee only "partial improvements" succeeding in the old built fabric; he displayed more optimism for new quarters planned for vacant zones.[23]

Following the new trend in urban planning, the Prost plan (as the master plan came to be known) called for strict zoning, qualified as "methodical discrimination" but based on current needs and tendencies (Fig. 36). The city was divided into four zones, A, B, C, and D. The commercial area, zone A, covered the lower part of Bab el-Oued, the

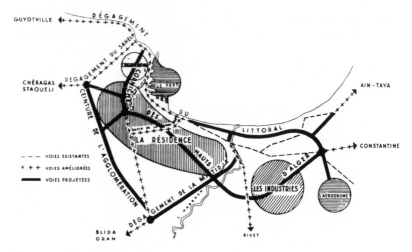

Figure 36. The Prost plan, 1930–37. Zone A follows the coastline; zone B covers the area marked as "la résidence"; zone C is on the heights of "la résidence"; zone D comprises the areas marked as "agglomération" and "industries."

Esplanade Quarter, the old town, Agha, and the middle and inner parts of Mustafa all the way to the Jardin d'Essai; it would be filled with apartment buildings, offices, shops, cafés, restaurants, small workshops, and garages; the roads would be a minimum of 12 meters wide. Zone B was residential and consisted of small, single-family houses (whose maximum height could not exceed 15.2 meters) covering a large and longitudinal area from Bab el-Oued to Mustafa; the streets would again be a minimum of 12 meters wide. Zone C, located on the heights of Mustafa, had "country cottages" in gardens, in an effort to preserve the natural beauty of the particular site. The industrial region, zone D, was on the southern border of Bab el-Oued, as well as to the south, past the Jardin d'Essai. But the real industrial suburb of Algiers was Hussein-Dey. The main roads of the industrial zone were envisioned as 18 meters wide, whereas the secondary ones could be 12 meters. In accordance with the tendencies already in place, industrial working classes were to be housed close to their workplaces, whereas the upper regions of the "amphitheater," which enjoyed a better climate and were in demand by upper classes, would be reserved for villas in gardens and parks.[24]

Within these general outlines, the plan had specific provisions. For example, the Marine Quarter would be demolished completely and rebuilt; new quarters were to be designed in the area gained by the appro-

priation of the Champs de Manoeuvres, in Mustafa, and on the waterfront near Bab el-Oued; in the densely built quarters, many existing
streets would be enlarged and new ones cut through; and the greenbelt defining the heights of Algiers would be preserved, because it was
essential for the health, charm, and beauty of the city. The construction of four new roads would improve the communication system of
Algiers radically. The corniche along the waterfront would continue the
Boulevard de l'Impératrice toward Hussein-Dey and extend for another
13 kilometers; a "ring road" on the zone cleared from the fortifications
would add picturesque and aesthetic values to the city; the middle region (the residential section) would be crossed with the help of tunnels
which also linked the waterfront to the heights; and, finally, another belt
road would envelop the entire agglomeration.[25] One of the first seg-
ments of the Prost plan to be completed was the ring road. The Boulevard Laferrière (on the site of the demolished French fortifications),
considered to be a great urbanistic achievement, was extended to a vast
esplanade of about 3,000 square meters—the "real forum of new Algiers."[26] No longer a traffic artery, it was turned into a lushly planted
park with spectacular views. Prost and his colleagues proposed a tunnel
under Boulevard Laferrière that would start at the docks (at the Maritime Terminal) and connect to the ring road at the heights (Fig. 37). An
exit at Rue d'Isly would enable access to a central location in "downtown" Algiers, close to the Central Post Office, and another exit would
lead to the new development of Tagarins farther up the hill.

Rotival justified this ambitious plan by defining the new role that
Algiers would play as the capital of an African empire, as a business,
commercial, and industrial center, and as a residential town. He likened
the task ahead to the rebuilding of Paris under Napoleon III. Confront-
ing the criticism directed at the plan he and his colleagues had drafted,
he argued that if Baron Haussmann had not been supported by Napoleon III against his own critics, Paris would now be a "poorly designed
village without a future."[27]

The main challenge to the Prost plan came from Le Corbusier, in the
form of several (unimplemented) projects for the city between 1932 and
1942.[28] Le Corbusier was not officially commissioned to develop a master plan; his involvement with Algiers had started through an invitation
from the Friends of Algiers in 1931 (to deliver a series of lectures on
urbanism within the context of the centennial celebrations) and was
pursued on his own initiative. While his designs are commonly seen as a
critique of French urbanism, in essence they did not diverge radically

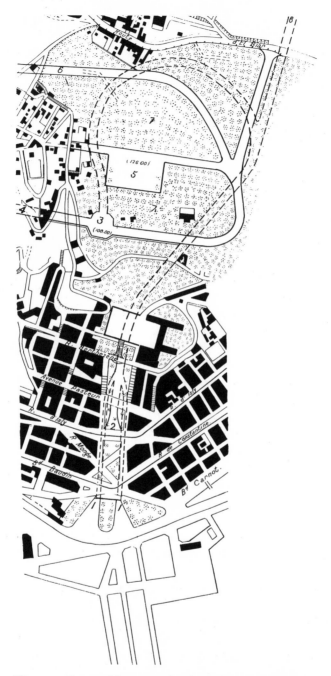

Figure 37. Proposal for a tunnel under Boulevard Laferrière by Prost, Danger, and Rotival, 1937. (1) Entrance to the tunnel from the maritime station, (2) access to Rue d'Isly, (3) exit from the tunnel at Tagarins, (4) rectified rail connection to Télemy, (5) terrace, (6) corniche of Fort l'Empereur, (7) Tagarins park, (8) exit from the tunnel at Frais Vallon.

from the proposals of Prost and his colleagues; the differences were formal, not conceptual, and exaggerated mainly by Le Corbusier's own vast and vigorous propaganda. Le Corbusier began his critique of contemporary urbanism by arguing that French interventions during the last five decades had caused the destruction of Algiers. He wrote: "The last fifty years of European colonization abolished without any regrets the natural richness and petrified the new city into a desert with its crowded houses leaning onto noisy streets." Like the cities of Europe and America, Algiers had sickened, for it had been shorn of its poetry.[29]

Curiously enough, Le Corbusier respected the original achievements of the French colonial oeuvre and credited the first decades of French rule with good urbanism. He had already clarified his standpoint in *La Ville radieuse*, where, including a plan that indicated the first interventions (the Place du Gouvernement and the Bab Azzoun and Bab el-Oued streets), he expressed his admiration for early colonial urbanism: "The military rulers of the conquest knew how to make beautiful city plans. They knew how to urbanize."[30]

While Le Corbusier's diplomatic plot to obtain the commission by associating the current administration with the glorified conquerors is quite transparent in this statement made on the centennial of the occupation, his repetition of the same theme in various contexts reflects his firm support of French colonial policies. For example, celebrating the *mission civilisatrice* in Morocco, he praised the instruction, loyalty, and justice brought by the French, as well as the network of roads and cities they had built—all "signs of civilization." These achievements, he argued, had created an atmosphere of admiration, enthusiasm, and respect among the Arabs: "The Arab discovered his educator, his instructor. He did not bat an eyelid of doubt. With two hands outstretched, leaving all his hopeless deceit behind, he loved, admired, understood the new times and respected France with all his conviction. Architecture and urbanism can be the great educator."[31]

In accordance with the colonial mission, Le Corbusier's Algiers—the "French capital of Africa," the "head of French Africa," and the "phoenix of France . . . reborn out of the ashes of the mother country"— would reinforce French rule not only in Algeria, but throughout the entire continent.[32] The architect expressed this view passionately in his writings, but also in several drawings where an axis originating in the north continues into Africa, connecting France, from Le Havre via Paris to Marseilles and across the Mediterranean, to Algiers and farther in (Fig. 38). Sketches of skyscrapers indicate the cities along the

Figure 38.
Le Corbusier, sketch
showing the unifica-
tion of the French
colonial empire by
urbanism.

axis, proposing to unify the greater France through a new architecture
and urbanism. With such drawings, Le Corbusier was reiterating the
notion of a geographical axis between France and Algiers, a repeated
theme in colonial discourse. For example, Cotéreau, a prominent engineer who worked for the urban administration of Algiers, argued in 1933
that the city must be renovated by means of a "sane architecture, following Aryan traditions," because of "its position on the axis of France."[33]
Le Corbusier's sketches depict, furthermore, the idea of *la plus grande
France*, which represents not only an imperial French doctrine, but also
a colonial consciousness developed in 1930. Minister of Colonies Paul
Reynaud summarized this new mindset at the time: "Everyone among
us must feel he is a citizen of the greatest France [*la plus grande France*]
that expands to five parts of the world."[34]

Le Corbusier's 1932 Obus A plan (the word *obus* being a reference to
the trajectory of an exploding shell) ignored the existing city by and
large and superimposed a new system. A curvilinear viaduct along the

Figure 39. Le Corbusier's Obus A plan, 1932.

waterfront connected Hussein-Dey to St. Eugène, emphasizing the linear development of the city and reinterpreting the corniche in the Prost
plan (Fig. 39).[35] Le Corbusier's desire to respond to the geography of
the site and to muster views of the Mediterranean was the driving factors
behind his proposal; the viaduct (which would house working classes)
can be regarded as a second, and raised, corniche running parallel to the
first one, the Boulevard de l'Impératrice. The Marine Quarter, entirely
demolished and transformed into a *cité d'affaires,* reflects a conceptual
similarity to zone A of the Prost plan. Yet the scale is radically different,
as Le Corbusier's scheme is dominated by high-rises. The housing
blocks of Fort-l'Empereur on the hills, intended for the middle and upper classes, can be seen as the equivalent to the zoning of the heights of
Mustafa for upper-class residences by Prost and his colleagues. The last
major element of the plan, the elevated highway that connected the
housing on the hills of Fort-l'Empereur with the business center in the
Marine Quarter, addressed the much-debated problem of linking the
coast to the heights—a problem that Prost and his colleagues had attempted to resolve by means of underground transportation.

Obus A was formally the most spectacular of Le Corbusier's Algiers
plans. In successive plans, he modified the original scheme in accordance to the responses he received. In Obus B of 1933, for example, he
eliminated the viaduct and gathered all the functions of the business
center in a single skyscraper. Obus C of 1934 was restricted to the Marine Quarter only and again proposed a single skyscraper. This building

became the principal focus of the proposals and took different forms: in 1938 it acquired a Y-shaped plan (Obus D), and in 1939 it was transformed into a building whose facades were defined by Le Corbusier's hallmark *brise soleils* (Obus E).

The 1942 project was the last and the most conventional of Le Corbusier's schemes for Algiers. Although it came closest to Obus A in its scope as a master plan, it diverged dramatically from the proposal of 1932 in terms of its formal qualities. A coastal road replaced the viaduct, approaching closer to Prost's corniche, and zoning dominated the plan, delineating separate functions that were not connected to each other. The business center was moved from the Marine Quarter to the eastern end of Boulevard Laferrière, away from the casbah and clearly serving the European community. Similarly, the civic center was transported to Agha, again shifting the center toward the European town. Recreation facilities were placed along the coastline of Bab el-Oued and in the vicinity of the Jardin d'Essai; industry was concentrated in Hussein-Dey, and the port maintained its commercial and transportational functions. Residential zones, distinguished with their Y-shaped high-rises, dominated the hills, affording good views and providing for public gardens and parks. The Marine Quarter was now reserved for "Muslim cultural institutions," with the argument that this transformation would enable the cleaning of the lower part of the casbah and bring a new vitality to the casbah-Marine ensemble.[36] The separation between the European and indigenous communities would thus be secured even more firmly than in the previous schemes.

Le Corbusier's progression from Obus A to the *plan directeur* reflected the architect's persistent efforts to secure the commission by conforming to established norms. As argued by Mary McLeod, the architect's involvement with the landscape became limited to details and moved away from broad gestures that had endowed Obus A with its lyrical plasticity.[37] Not surprisingly, it is the more "realistic" aspects of Le Corbusier's later plans that made an impact on the future architecture of Algiers. While the Algiers plans have become keystones in the architectural discourse on modernism, their impact on the city of Algiers itself remained minimal. The most memorable urbanistic aspects on paper—the daring proposals of Obus A—were the least influential, whereas the *plan directeur* surfaced in small fragments now and then in subsequent efforts to regulate the city. Le Corbusier's influence on Algiers remained on the architectural level and manifested especially in the 1950s.[38]

Expanding the Boundaries:
Regional Plans and *Grands Ensembles*

The international economic crisis of the 1930s hit Algeria seriously, although a few years later than it had disrupted France. Affected by an economic crisis that included a plunge in exports, high inflation, unemployment, and lack of funds for building investment, the master plan drafted by Prost and his colleagues could not be implemented. World War II made matters only graver and forced the colony into a closed economy.[39] Not until 1948 was the attempt to address the city's problems and to achieve a comprehensive solution revived. In the meantime, the housing situation in Algiers had deteriorated to the degree that the 1948 *plan d'urbanisme* (which literally duplicated the Prost plan and survived with minor alterations until 1976) prioritized housing over other issues in a move that would dominate all subsequent planning activities in Algiers until the end of French rule. In effect, the origins of the *bidonvilles* that became the nightmare of planners from the 1950s onward began in the early 1930s: as noted by sociologist René Maunier, gas barrels (*bidons*) were used "even to build walls" in 1932.[40]

Inflation and unemployment had hit all lower-income groups, but indigenous populations suffered the most. Attempts by colonial authorities to provide housing for all lower-income groups, and especially for Algerians, stemmed from a fear of uprisings. Private enterprise, however, favored lucrative luxury housing for the wealthiest sector of the European community and refrained from investing in the peripheries for more modest populations. It had become clear to all parties involved that large-scale housing operations should be relegated to the public sector.[41]

In spite of the lip service paid to the intellectual, administrative, military, judiciary, and religious centrality of Algiers and its role as the capital, the principal premise of the 1948 plan, implemented only in parts, revolved around developing residential zones on the heights. Housing would be built on the ridges and plateaus, while the actual center was reserved for tertiary activities and the valleys conserved as parks, with roads connecting the various quarters in the valley beds. In the already built-up quarters further growth would be blocked; the new residential zones would be defined by clear boundaries and divided into two categories. The "peripheral residential sectors," reserved for modest-income groups and kept to a maximum density of 124 persons per hectare, would be located near industrial zones or preexisting similar residential neighborhoods (such as Ouchaya). For the "sectors with special status," however, densities were envisioned to vary between 97 and 294 persons per hectare; here residential buildings could range from one to twelve stories in a "subtle" arrangement that would conform to the site; such quarters would occupy the more favorable ridges and platforms (like Les Annassers in Kouba) that afforded good views.[42]

Development of "industrial" and "rural" zones was the other component of the plan. Industrial zones were divided into three: the "mixed" areas in Hussein-Dey along the coast to the south, which also sheltered certain nonindustrial activities; the "first- and second-class" industrial areas situated well outside the city, along the railways leading to Oran and Constantine in opposite directions from Algiers; and the "third-class" industrial zone in the Kouba quarter on the southern hills. Following the zoning principles by now accepted universally, the concentration of industry intensified with distance from the city proper. "Satellite cities" for workers were to be situated in the proximity of factories, but separated from them by means of green areas. Finally, "rural zones" were projected for the borders of the settlement—to the west, in Sahel, fields for fruits and vegetables, and to the east, in Mitija, land for grapes and cereals—in a first-time gesture to organize the site around the city as part of a regional plan.[43]

The proposed road network consisted of two coastal exits, one from the east and the other from the west, reiterating once more the importance of the waterfront connection. Two arteries, going east and west, would connect the coastal road to the rural hinterland. A corniche running parallel to the waterfront divided the settlement in two and formed the spine of the residential settlement, ultimately connecting to the industrial zone and to the airport farther to the east. This first regional plan for Algiers thus defined a huge triangular area, with the waterfront as its base, Châteauneuf as its summit, and the valleys of Oued M'Kacel (Frais Vallon) and Oued Kniss (Femme Sauvage, now Mohamed Belkacemi) defining the sides (see Fig. 34).[44] A triangular pattern echoing the original settlement persisted, but on a dramatically enlarged scale. The urban image had changed radically, too. In contrast to the compact form of old Algiers, surrounded by vegetation on three sides, against a background of steep hills, the Algiers of the mid-twentieth century was a sprawling city. It circled the entire amphitheater of the bay and extended into the hills, its built fabric broken up by random green zones. Within this immense agglomeration, the casbah stood out in its urban-

istic configuration. Clearly in opposition to French Algiers, it still dominated the urban image with its uniqueness.

By the early 1950s, restricted use of the city's open zones was
no longer considered a viable solution to the housing problem. The
heights of the city and other areas not built on due to their difficult
topography were now seen as inevitable sites for development, if fur-
nished with a road network that, "inscribing itself into the site," would
conform to the specificities of the land. Sweeping plans could no longer
respond to the new scale and complexity of Algiers; a decentralized
strategy was proposed which divided the city into quarters and relegated
them to individual planners who would report to a central office of urbanism that coordinated the different projects.[45] Expanding the scope,
planners and administrators agreed that a regional approach had become necessary and developed the Plan Régionale d'Urbanisme. This
plan took two essential measures: regional management and zoning.
The principles that underlined the first measure included decreasing
congestion in Algiers, conserving the greenbelt around the city by limiting land occupation, placing new housing projects on slopes, and developing a road network between new quarters and employment centers. The second measure proposed six new zones, three dedicated to
housing, others to industry, green areas, and finally to rural development (at the edges of the city).[46]

Between 1948 and 1954, Muslim immigration to Algiers significantly
increased the population, deteriorating housing conditions and resulting in the multiplication of *bidonvilles*.[47] The growth of squatter settlements intensified ethnic segregation, with "European Algiers" becom-
ing more and more isolated from "Muslim Algiers." Europeans were
concentrated in the center, along the waterfront from Bab el-Oued
to Champ de Manoeuvres, extending as far as the coastal suburbs of
Hussein-Dey and St.-Eugène, and in neighborhoods on the slopes that-
dominated the amphitheater of Mustafa. The "Muslim" zones consisted of the casbah in the north, its extension Climat de France, the
"petite casbah" near Hamma in the south, sandwiched between two
larger squatter settlements, Mahieddine and Clos Salembier, and Kouba,
Hussein-Dey, and Maison-Carrée farther away. The divided nature of
Algiers was particularly evident in the daily life and commercial activities. The "Moorish cafés" and small shops of the casbah contrasted with
the "milk bars" and haute couture boutiques of the Rue d'Isly (formerly
Rue de Chartres). Although Algerian workers crowded the European
quarters, there were no Europeans visible in the Muslim quarters.[48]

In response to and in accordance with the spirit of the 1948 plan, the seven years from 1954 to 1961 were marked by intensive campaigns to build large-scale housing projects, a period characterized by Jean-Jacques Deluz as *l'ère française des grands ensembles.*[49] Jacques Chevallier, the mayor of Algiers elected to office in 1953, "attacked the problem [of shantytowns]," which in 1953 sheltered 125,000 Muslims in the region of Algiers, up from 4,800 in 1938. In Algiers proper, the mayor stated, 120 *bidonvilles* had "invaded like a plague any available land," condemning 80,000 Algerians to live in "unheard of conditions," while the casbah beat "one of the world records of human density" with its 70,000 residents.[50] The first *grands ensembles* in Algiers, Diar el-Mahçoul and Diar es-Saada, built on terrain cleared from squatter houses, date from Chevallier's tenure.

Jacques Chevallier also established the AEDAA (Association pour l'Etude et le Développement de l'Agglomération Algéroise, known from 1955 on as "l'Agence de Plan") in 1954. Divided into three sections—technical studies, ethnographic and economic studies, and general services—this organization brought together a team of architects, urbanists, cartographers, and sociologists under the direction of Gérald Hanning, an urbanist.[51] The mayor's goal was to "represent all organisms interested in the harmonious development of the city."[52] The official philosophy of the agency was publicized as "an empirical and evolutive urbanism, concerned with operations, rather than plans." According to this approach, a good plan matured slowly and responded to the life of a city or a region; nevertheless, urbanism went beyond the realm of plans, which were not ends in themselves, but served only to limit the margin of error.[53]

Hanning's ideas on urbanism differed from those of classical urbanists, who favored rigid functional zones, and from the "macro-architecture" of Le Corbusier. Hanning argued that, within a general framework (the plan), the city should have the capacity to provide continuity even if conditions changed. To accommodate flexibility, he proposed a conceptual plan he named the *trame d'Alger,* the "frame" of Algiers (Fig. 40). Debating that the stereotypical acceptance of the crescent shape of the Bay of Algiers related only to the coastal zone and that it was a mistake to base master plans on this form (as had been done in the past), he maintained that the edge of Sahel ridge that gave way to a sudden faultline should be taken as the starting point to reorganize the city. The site thus presented a T-shape configuration with the stem of the T toward Maison-Carrée about 10 kilometers long and its shorter

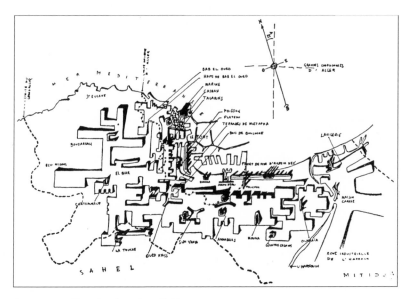

Figure 40. Hanning's *trame d'Alger*, 1958.

line extending 5 kilometers. This conceptual organization divided the
site in two, in a pattern reminiscent of previous developments: the lower
zone and the upper zone.[54]

Hanning proposed an orthogonal frame, based on his interpretation
of the site and with a transversal axis at an angle turned 28°30' northeast.
This shift, he argued, allowed for the best conditions in the orientation
of buildings, as well as conforming to the topography. Even though
Hanning was opposed to the zoning principles of "classic" planners, his
own solution separated functions to a certain degree, affiliating his
scheme with the earlier ones. For example, his lower zone, the coastal
one, was reserved mainly for economic activities; here, housing and administrative and public services were limited. The slopes of the valleys,
from where access to the waterfront was easy, were to be developed for
mass housing, the *grands ensembles*. The heights of Algiers were maintained as residential, but converted from "dormitory" to "satellite" settlements and endowed with administrative, professional, commercial,
and even some industrial functions. Main industries were pushed farther
away. The new road network, the *trame*, did not conform to the existing
one, deemed insufficient by Hanning, but reorganized the city on the
east-west axis; it thus diverted the former focus on the waterfront to the

Figure 41. Project for the waterfront, 1951.

heights by establishing a strong connection between the coastline and the inner quarters.[55]

Considered an absurdity, Hanning's proposal remained on paper. Mayor Chevallier's tenure was marked by other achievements, foremost among them large-scale housing projects. Furthermore, two initial sections of the *grands boulevards supérieurs* that would eventually form a new ring connecting the hills of the city were constructed under Chevallier.[56] Projects to regulate the waterfront and the detailed plan to reorganize the Mahieddine Quarter along a large promenade were, however, ignored by the next wave of urban administrators, technocrats of the Plan de Constantine (Fig. 41).

Even though the Plan de Constantine aimed to encompass the entire country in a well-balanced manner, cities and especially the capital reaped the greatest benefits and grew disproportionately during the last years of colonial rule. A great deal of housing was built during this last French campaign to keep Algeria, but the desperate rush was not systematically and sensitively managed. The master plans based on arbitrary concepts were strong on zoning and functional segregation—in direct opposition to the master plan developed by Hanning a few years earlier. They were devised by engineers, practical-minded graduates of the *grandes écoles* (mainly the Polytechnique and Ponts et Chaussées), who were newly arrived from France and who considered the architects and urbanists previously involved in the planning of Algiers hopelessly romantic. The goals were numerically clear and should be achieved efficiently: two hundred thousand housing units had to be built, four hundred thousand employment opportunities created, two million children schooled, and so on.[57]

The novelty was the development of a new legal concept, *zone à urbaniser en priorité* (zone to be urbanized in priority), or simply ZUP. Such zones had to be residential with a minimum of one hundred units.[58] The two ZUPs designated for greater Algiers were the satellite towns of Les Annassers, whose development had already begun under Mayor Chevallier, and Rouiba-Reghaia to the east. Their architectural "ideal" has been mocked as approximating a "match box," their urban design principles as relentlessly orthogonal, and their construction quality as "miserable."[59]

In terms of circulation, the corniche on the heights of Algiers (begun under Chevallier) was constructed, as well as six transversal roads intersecting it. This was in accord with the general principles of the Plan de Constantine, which specified the importance of freeways and bypasses, as well as the modernization of the transportation infrastructure.[60] For a parking garage that would hold as many as six thousand cars, reviving an earlier scheme from 1951, engineer Henri Côte proposed to lengthen the boulevards on the waterfront and use the spaces under the embankments, in an attempt to centralize parking as prescribed by the Plan de Constantine.[61] Public transportation was also addressed: aside from devising new tram and trolley routes, a subway system would connect the heights of Bab el-Oued to the lower part of the casbah and follow a route parallel to the coastline and reach all the way to Hussein-Dey; it would branch off at the Central Post Office and lead to Télemy on the hills, where the university is located.[62]

The intensification of the War of Independence forced the French authorities to halt construction activity in Algiers. All investment now concentrated in the creation of an administrative satellite in Rochet Noir, 50 kilometers to the east of the city, thus relatively protected from the war. Built in several months, the new center acted as the home of the provisional government for only a few weeks prior to the declaration of independence.[63]

Although the ambitious plans were not implemented, they had engraved a vision of the future for Algiers that was disseminated by popular media. The daily *Echo d'Alger*, for example, published a series of articles in 1959 titled " 'Grand Algiers': How Do You Imagine [It] in Twenty or

Thirty Years?" Without exception, the respondents agreed on an image determined by the architecture and urbanism of the *grands ensembles,* by huge building blocks, separated from each other by means of parks and gardens. Wide freeways, ample parking, and technologically advanced public transportation systems (such as elevated cablecars) complemented the vision of the modern metropolis.[64] This image would continue to haunt the city.

The daring interventions envisioned for Algiers under the guidance of the Plan de Constantine were, according to Deluz, products of a militaristic mentality, obsessed with quantification, regimentation, discipline, and control.[65] They constituted one front of the Battle of Algiers as well as a return to the first phase of colonial interventions to the city—again characterized solely by militaristic concerns. In addition to the militaristic mentality framing the beginning and end of French planning activities in Algiers, two other themes run through the French rule. First is the dichotomy between the lower city that grew along the waterfront and the settlements on the hills that made the upper city: they displayed different functional and physical characteristics, and creating connections between them remained a persistent issue. Second is the penchant for separating the European and Algerian populations. The initial division between the upper casbah and the French quarters translated from the 1930s onward to the designation of distinct zones to house Algerians—a pattern that worked in harmony with the urban design philosophy that treated each housing development as an independent unit.

CHAPTER 3

The Indigenous House

*Islam created numerous towns and left a characteristic
architecture that responds to the climate and to a way of life.
    The Arab house is particularly seductive; closed off from the
street, it developed around its interior court with its waterworks
and tiles, each house having its own square of the sky. The separation from the exterior, necessitated by custom, is enhanced by
irregular plans.*

                        Jean de Maisonseul, *Revue d'Alger*

      To Algerians living under French occupation, home car-
ried a special meaning as the private realm where they found refuge from
colonial interventions they confronted continually in public life. In the
words of social historian and former resistance fighter Djamila Amrane,
home was the "inviolable space" where Algerians recovered their identity.[1] A refuge for the family, it acted as a "buffer against the colonial
society."[2] It constituted, furthermore, an element in the "language of
refusal" created by Algerians, which involved "their behavior, their
clothing, and their whole way of life," in Pierre Bourdieu's words. Under the constant gaze of Europeans, Algerian society had chosen to remain tightly closed upon itself by developing innumerable barriers.[3]
Furthermore, the architectural qualities of the houses in the casbah facilitated defense against military aggression—an issue well understood
by the French. An official report in the immediate aftermath of the occupation stated that because it was possible to pass easily from one roof-
top terrace to the other, "during times of revolt, such communications
would come in very handy."[4]

The home was a most significant shell in this form of resistance. To the colonizers, the Algerian house represented the impenetrable aspect of Algerian life, centered around the family and women's activities. In the typical ambivalence that characterizes the colonial discourse, the house both nurtured Orientalist fantasies and signified opposition to colonialism, as perhaps the only realm of Algerian society protected from the French. To document and understand this realm in order to break it open was an important item on the colonial agenda, paralleled by a similar search regarding Algerian women. Like the domestic space, women represented the unconquered part of the colony. As women were considered to hold the key to Algerian society at large, clarifying and demystifying their status with the ultimate goal of changing it became a major preoccupation, intertwining the two projects of investigation.

The "traditional" Algerian house had been a romantic source of fantasy for European artists and literary figures since the beginning of colonial rule. Yet a disciplined inquiry into indigenous housing patterns did not happen until the 1880s, when ethnographers began to record and analyze the common dwelling as an expression of the material life of a community. The high point of ethnographic research on Algerian people and their culture occurred in the 1920s and 1930s. It is around that time, too, that architects started to express an interest in vernacular forms, in part stemming from their apparent affiliations with the favorite forms of emerging modernism. Ethnographic research, architectural analysis, artistic and literary depictions, and popular representations (such as postcards and movies) contributed to the definition of an "Algerian house." This definition played a primary role in the work of European architects who designed the collective housing projects for local populations in Algeria, and it served as an important resource in their attempts to respond to indigenous lifestyles and cultural sensitivies.

The Algerian House Defined by Ethnographers

French ethnography's first serious investigation into domestic vernacular architecture in Algeria is rightly attributed to the work of Emile Masqueray, a professor at the Ecole Supérieure des Lettres in Algiers involved in extensive field research.[5] In *La Formation des cités chez les populations sédentaires de l'Algérie* (1886), Masqueray undertook a survey of Berber societies of Jurjura, Aurès, and Beni Mzab, focusing on collective life and habitat and comparing Berber settlements with Roman towns. By studying a sector of the Algerian society until then deemed particularly "backward," at first sight Masqueray seemed to have gone "counter-current to the official ideology."[6] Yet around this time the government policy toward rural populations had changed, paralleling Masqueray's premise that Berbers were *assimilables*, in fact more so than Arabs, who lived mostly in the cities.[7]

Masqueray's work had long-term consequences because he set the method for the future of French ethnography in Algeria, which would focus predominantly on rural populations and the rural habitat. The culmination of French ethnographic discourse on the Algerian house is Pierre Bourdieu's well-known analysis of the Kabyle house, published at the end of the colonial rule. Described by Bourdieu as "the economic unit of production and consumption, a political unit within the confederation of families that make up the clan, and finally a religious unit," this house represents a cohesion of different aspects of life. Bourdieu, like other ethnographers before him, showed relatively limited interest in the urban house, although he dedicated a short section to the analysis of the sociophysical structure of the Algerian town.[8]

Much of the ethnographic discourse that followed Masqueray sought to pinpoint the causes for the supposed backwardness of indigenous people. The diagnosis identified two main issues, among others: the condition of women and the condition of housing.[9] Numerous studies commissioned by the French administration in the later decades of colonial rule attest to the importance attached to the sociocultural meaning of housing. The number of such studies increased in the 1920s and the 1930s, paralleling the growing deterioration in housing conditions and the first official undertakings to provide collective housing for local populations.

Auguste Bernard's *Enquête sur l'habitation rurale des indigènes de l'Algérie,* initiated by the governor general of Algeria and published in 1921, is the first inquiry into the typology of Algerian house forms. Bernard's classification involved two basic categories: mobile houses (tents) and fixed houses. The second category was further divided into the *gourbi* (considered the most miserable and most widespread type), the terraced house (with roof terraces), the tile-roofed house, and the European house. Bernard provided detailed descriptions of each type and its regional variations (Fig. 42). He included plans with extensive captions that explained the functions and rituals associated with each space and the utensils employed in various activities, often citing the terms in

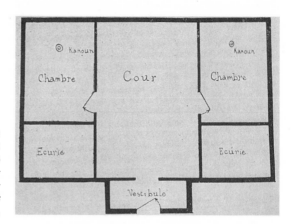

Figure 42. Plan of a house in Kabylia from Augustin Bernard's *Enquête sur l'habitation rurale des indigènes de l'Algérie* (1921).

Arabic and hence establishing an ethnographic glossary. Based on field-work and presented in a "scientific" language that avoided judgmental arguments, Bernard's book nevertheless offered in its two-page conclusion a solution for the inevitable "evolution" of indigenous society: transformation of its residential forms. The ongoing "slow decomposition" of the indigenous house, coupled with contacts with the modern world, would lead to its radical metamorphosis. If Bernard's *Enquête* did not bring groundbreaking interpretations to Algerian rural housing, it did establish a descriptive method and a rational classification that were pursued by other scholars. For example, in the 1930s Augustin Berque documented the changes he observed in the indigenous house since Bernard's findings and concluded that "fixed" housing was clearly replacing "mobile" housing in the countryside.[10]

In a short chapter, Bernard also attempted to classify the urban house. Tracing its origins to the Hellenic house, he described its essential feature as a courtyard open to the sky and often surrounded by beautiful colonettes. The main entrance would always be situated such that visual access was not allowed to the court. While the "terraced house" type dominated, others corresponding to his rural types, the "tile-roofed house" and the "European house," also existed in urban centers.[11] Bernard's reluctance to define a separate typology for urban housing would also orient future scholarship.

Ethnographic scholarship on Algeria thus established the habitat as an indispensable element of the indigenous culture, as a key to understanding the colonized people. The emergence of prominent women ethnographers in the 1920s helped broaden the field of exploration. Two pioneers in the field were Amélie-Marie Goichon and Mathéa Gaudry, authors of *La Vie féminine au Mzab* (1927) and *La Femme chaouia de l'Aurès* (1928), respectively. While they both considered their texts sociological studies, Goichon's subtitle being *Etude de sociologie musulmane* and Gaudry's *Etude de sociologie berbere*, the contents display a focus on daily life patterns and material conditions based on fieldwork, qualifying the books as ethnographic studies. Historically, the research and publication dates of Goichon's and Gaudry's books correspond to significant advocacy for fieldwork and to the establishment of the Institut d'Ethnologie in Paris in 1925.[12]

To look at "women looking at women" (French women looking at Algerian women) complicates the colonizer-colonized relationship and introduces additional perspectives into the power structure. As French women joined the scholarly community in growing numbers and as their visibility increased, they became identified with new roles that could not be played by their male colleagues. In the field of ethnography, their gender granted them easier access to private lives of indigenous women in Muslim cultures. The academic establishment acknowledged this fact wholeheartedly and capitalized on it. William Marçais, the well-respected historian of Islamic culture, emphasized the point in his preface to Goichon's *La Vie féminine au Mzab*:

> In reality we know very little about women's places in the Maghreb. We know only what men tell us, and they do not tell us very much: first, because they do not want to reveal to us all that they know, and then, because even they are ignorant of many things in these matters. It is the French women who must run to save us from our misery and undertake the necessary inquiries in this unexplored domain. To them, the access to the *Maghribines* that Islam denies us is not prohibited. The solidarity among members of the same sex, which is stronger than the antinomy between civilizations, will loosen the tongues and make the veils fall.[13]

The endowment of a special mission helped secure a place for women scholars in the discipline and welcomed them to an overwhelmingly male-dominated profession. Newly part of the establishment, French women ethnographers considered themselves full participants in the culture of ethnography—as revealed by their orthodox methodologies, formats, and references. However, their work also formed a bridge to early feminist writing on Algerian women, represented most prominently by Hubertine Auclert's book *Les Femmes arabes en Algérie* (1900). Written with clearly different agendas (Auclert's being overtly political as opposed to Goichon's and Gaudry's academic), these books share a concern with presenting an accurate picture of the women they study, as well as improving their lives and material conditions.[14]

Goichon's *La Vie féminine au Mzab* began with an exposé of the family structure and the status of women in Mzabite society, then analyzed the life cycle of women, paying a great deal of attention to the artifacts and material conditions at each stage, but also to the crucial role played by religion and magic. Goichon defined her thesis at the outset: in Mzab, women's lives were regulated by religious and social rules that gave a centuries-old "puritanism" to daily patterns. Hence, the preservation of culture owed itself entirely to the "element of stability" provided by women.[15] Furthermore, social rules prohibited women from leaving the land, thereby assigning them an essential role as social and cultural keystones. Paradoxically, the head of the family was the husband, and a woman's life was cloistered at home, in an excessively simple environment. Goichon described the Mozabite house in factual terms, referring to its materials, plan, light, ventilation, and built-in furnishings and linking it to women's routine activities. She used Arabic terms, expanding on the glossary begun by Berque.[16] As one of the first ethnographers to incorporate photographic documentation in a systematic format in her presentation of data, she organized her images thematically in groups (Fig. 43). Her photographs depicted characteristic parts of the domestic space that frame women's work and lives but also conveyed information on forms and materials.[17]

La Femme chaouia de l'Aurès, Mathéa Gaudry's published doctoral dissertation, dedicated more attention to the dwelling, presenting it as the primary frame for material conditions surrounding women. According to a scale of development Gaudry established, the women of Aurès were already at an "evolved social stage," because fulfilling multiple functions as housekeeper, worker, organizer of festivities, and religious leader made them true bearers of authority.[18] Yet the domestic spaces where women spent their lives were not worthy of their high virtues and needed much improvement.

Gaudry divided the houses of the region into three types: the *déchra* (houses attached to hill flanks, with the appearance of citadels), the house proper (*la maison*), and the tent. Her focus was on the house proper, which she first described from the exterior by dividing it into its individual elements such as the wall, the terrace, the balcony, and the windows. Each element was discussed in technical detail, with specific emphasis on materials and construction methods. Gaudry then examined the interiors in the light of functional and ritualistic uses. For ex-

Figure 43. A page of plates from Amélie-Marie Goichon's *La Vie féminine au Mzab* (1927). The top left photograph is titled "interior of a Mozabite house"; the top right and the bottom left photographs show young women of Ghardaia; the bottom right photograph depicts a young bride. Goichon notes that all faces are obscured by request of the women photographed.

ample, the poorest house had only one room with three large ritualistic blackened stones in its center. This room was the *kanoun,* the center of domestic life that sheltered the indispensable objects, such as the beddings piled in one corner, plates, pots, and other kitchen utensils. Gaudry presented a larger house with the help of a plan on which she marked the main furnishings, among them the weaving loom (Fig. 44). Like Goichon's photographs, Gaudry's also show women's work and activities in residential spaces, thereby complementing the text on houses (Fig. 45). Her grim closing observations echo Bernard: the "Chaouia house" was "poorly lighted, full of smoke [from cooking], irrational, unclean, without charm or comfort." In her conclusion, which advocated the need to improve women's conditions in Aurès to enable them to have a "better life," Gaudry emphasized the transformation of the habitat as a priority.[19]

Studying the housing patterns of Ouled Abderrahman Chaouia, a tribe from the south of the Aurès region, Thérèse Rivière, another

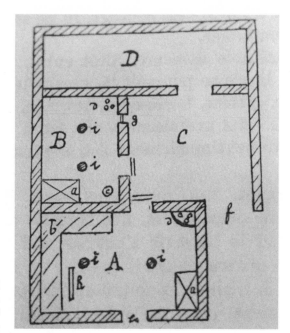

Figure 44. Plan of the ground floor of a house from Mathéa Gaudry's *La Femme chaouia de l'Aurès* (1928).

Figure 45. Photograph from Gaudry's *La Femme chaouia de l'Aurès* showing women weaving in a courtyard.

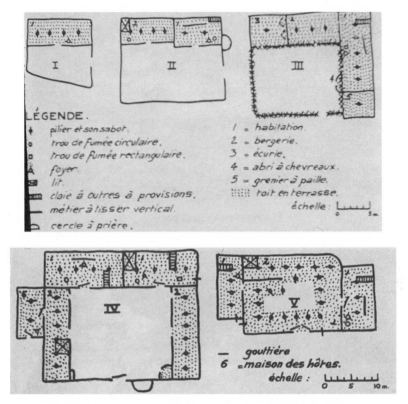

Figure 46. Plans of a terraced courtyard house from Thérèse Rivière's "L'Habitation chez les Ouled Abderrahman Chaouia de l'Aurès" (1938) showing the possible forms of growth around the courtyard.

well-respected ethnographer of the time, recorded three types: terraced houses, underground houses, and the much rarer tents or shelters under cliffs. In its simplest form, the terraced house, the most widespread type, consisted of a rectangular room (where all domestic activities took place and where goats were sheltered in winter) and a walled garden (Fig. 46). This scheme could be expanded by adding rectangular rooms around the court. Rivière's descriptions of building parts were accompanied by explanations of their ritualistic uses; for example, pillars and thresholds played important roles in marriage ceremonies.[20]

In her sociological and judicial analysis of women in Kabylia, *La Femme Kabyle,* Laure Bousquet-Lefevre, another woman scholar, included a description of the extended family compounds. In contrast to Gaudry's conclusive observations, for Bousquet-Lefevre the patriarchal system in Aurès was tyrannical, confining women to the unquestioned authority of the father and the husband and, consequently, to the house. Women, unaware of their oppression, were vehement guardians of the worst traditions, without the slightest desire for "revolt and emancipation." Living conditions reinforced their oppression. Different components of the extended family lived in separate small structures surrounding a communal courtyard. Women's activities and domestic work remained constricted to this "family village," while men worked outside, in agriculture.[21]

Another ethnographic analysis that concentrated on women's life in Kabylia, written by Germaine Laoust-Chantreaux, began with a chapter on housing. Limiting herself to the village at Aït Hichem in Upper Jurjura, Laoust-Chantreaux interpreted the house as "the symbol of the family born out of marriage, of the primitive social cellule." She observed only one type, consisting of a rectangular room that sheltered both humans and animals, though the barn that always occupied one-third of the space was divided off. Courtyards were essential and clusters of units typical. Like other ethnographers, Laoust-Chantreaux pointed to the symbolic and ritualistic importance of the threshold but also argued that the entire house was "a temple, a true sanctuary," reminiscent of the domestic cults of Greco-Roman antiquity. The women of the house took total charge of the "domestic spirits," the "guardians of the house." Echoing her colleagues, Laoust-Chantreaux concluded that this house hardly responded to most basic needs and that "the entire painful life of the Kabyle woman" was spent in severe and impersonal surroundings.[22]

Within the broader framework of French cultural politics that associated scholarship with policymaking, starting in the 1930s ethnographic research on domestic architecture, patterns of daily life at home, and the status of women in Algeria constituted an essential resource for new housing designs to shelter Algerians. It was argued that indigenous architecture in different regions of Algeria should be studied and understood properly to avoid the adoption of a standardized international architecture. In its efforts to elevate the "economic and moral" conditions of local populations, the government established the Committee of Indigenous Housing to research local housing patterns, rural and urban, from financial, technical, and ownership points of view.[23] Similarly, the administrators believed that without understanding the family structure and the role of women and without responding to the cultural specificities dictated by Algerian society, it was not possible to propose an architecture that could function well. At least some knowledge was required to design the housing units, as well as their conglomeration into urban-scale ensembles. The ethnographic literature thus served a practical purpose. Trusted for their academic authority, these books formed a respectable body of references. At the same time, and in part due to their abundant illustrations, they enjoyed a wide popular market and helped disseminate new information on Algeria.[24]

The official endorsement of research on the indigenous house was voiced in response to the growing need for more residential units in Algerian towns, which were just beginning to swell with waves of immigrants from the countryside in the 1930s. On the basis of the literature on "Muslim housing" that revealed "all imaginable kinds of habitats," uniform solutions to housing were criticized and difference emphasized, the concept of difference now translated into differentiating Muslim housing from European housing.[25] The ethnographic focus on rural domestic architecture was not questioned in terms of its relevancy to offer prototypes for urban housing, an attitude that may have derived from the homogenization of Algerian society. Furthermore, architects overlooked the typological diversity articulated in ethnographic literature and extrapolated a kit of parts from the most widely shared features of "traditional" Algerian houses.

The focus on cities inevitably broadened the boundaries of the field of inquiry to indigenous urban house types. In a formulation of the problem, and without any mention of aesthetic appeal or functional and urban design qualities, Lespès summarized the main deficiencies of indigenous urban housing around two points. First, massing was much denser than in the most crowded cities of Europe, as exemplified by the Algerian casbah with its densities reaching two thousand people per hectare. Second, sanitary provisions were almost always very poor. Algerians, "carefree and ignorant of the most elementary rules of hygiene, accommodate[d] themselves to slums and to least favorable conditions."[26] Lespès's viewpoint and concerns surfaced among the reformers in the following decades, and the new housing projects designated for Algerians made improved sanitary conditions a priority.

The Algerian House Defined by Architects

Architectural and aesthetic appeal of the houses in the casbah had already been highlighted during the centennial celebrations of the French occupation. Following the lead of ethnographic research

Figure 47. View of the Indigenous House of the Centennial, designed by
Léon Claro, 1930.

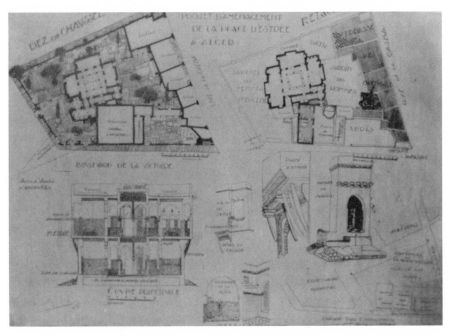

Figure 48. Léon Claro, site plan, plan, section, and details of the Indigenous House of the Centennial.

but focusing on the urban type, a model house was built at the intersection of the Boulevard de la Victoire and Rue de la Casbah, near the citadel, to "convey to tourists an idea of the habitation of Arabs in Algiers." Léon Claro, the architect in charge, designed the Indigenous House of the Centennial (*maison indigène du centenaire*) as a two-story structure in the middle of the irregular lot and surrounded it with gardens behind high walls and a row of shops facing the Rue de la Casbah, to incorporate a trace of the souks (Figs. 47 and 48). He replicated the colonnaded courtyard, organized the main spaces around it, separated men's and women's quarters and gardens, and mimicked all the elements of the "traditional" house. Details and ornamentation, realized with the help of old materials and fragments gathered from the casbah, accentuated the aura of authenticity. The architect's concern for authenticity was reflected in his drawings of details of the building considered especially significant.[27] Belonging more to the architecture of world's fairs than to Algiers, this building formed an uneasy relationship with the casbah.[28] Its location at the edge of the casbah signified its ties to the old city, but the unusual circumstances of its creation alienated it from its sociocultural context. The Indigenous House of the Centennial was a sanitized summary of the architecture of the casbah, intended for outsiders and accessible without necessitating contact with indigenous neighborhoods.

On the scholarly front, Berque's aforementioned survey had drawn some attention to urban housing in the 1930s. Bridging ethnography and architectural practice, Berque claimed the urgency of building in the cities and advocated temporarily abandoning rural housing programs. Accordingly, he praised the efforts of the Office of Low-Cost Housing (Office des Habitations à Bon Marché) for enabling the first schemes, the Boulevard de Verdun blocks built in 1930 and the projected Climat de France.[29] In a volume prepared for popular readership, Berque also undertook a systematic description of the "Algerian house." While the author's examination was initiated by his search for appropriate forms and styles for European residential architecture in Algeria, his characterization of the indigenous urban house contributed to the establishment of the "type." A "delicate jewel" from the exterior, the indigenous house stood out in its distinct separation of the public and private realms, its roof terrace as an "organ of respiration," and its interior-oriented decoration.[30]

The greatest credit must go to Le Corbusier, however, for calling the architectural profession's attention to the indigenous urban house of Algiers. Declaring the Algerian street an "anonymous corridor," Le Corbusier argued that life and poetry flourished inside the house. The narrow streets of the casbah, effectively sheltered from the sun by the projections of the buildings that lined them, were only public passages. Yet a "miracle" occurred when the door of an Arab house opened onto a lovely courtyard, one or two stories high, surrounded by sculpted arches (Fig. 49). Here silence reigned. "The street [was] abolished." By ignoring the street, that "violent passage," the Arab house afforded a life in coolness and tranquility. In addition, Arabs had "conquered the view of the sea for every house" by means of roof terraces that "created a roof over the city." Comparing the Arab city to the European, the "adorable courtyard" of the Arab houses to the "sinister courtyard" of the European apartment buildings, the protected passageways to the "jumbled streets," Le Corbusier concluded that Arabs enjoyed a higher quality of life than did Europeans. He juxtaposed his own housing proposals in Algiers with the patterns offered by the casbah and summarized the lessons he had learned: "terraces, suspended gardens, grand bays open to a landscape of dreams *conquered* by height."[31]

The Algerian rural vernacular also had many lessons for Le Corbusier.

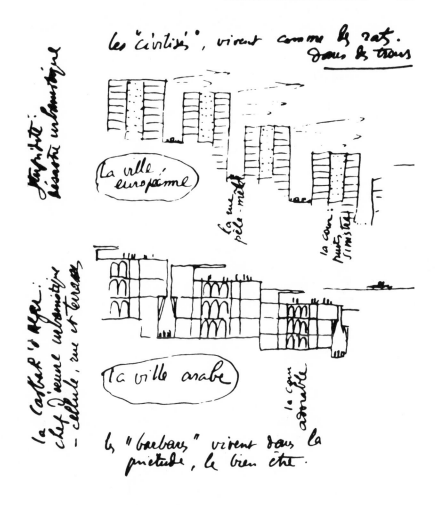

Figure 49. Le Corbusier, drawing comparing the houses of the Arab city with those of the European city.

The most important was a strong concept of unity, derived from a module, the square-shaped cell. He commented passionately on the cellular organization of Ben-Ishgem, a town in Mzab: "What an order, what a decision, what a sensible tool to the service of mankind." And he provided an architectural formula for happiness:

the key = the cell
      = men
      = happiness.[32]

Jean de Maisonseul, an architect, painter, and active voice among the intellectual circles in Algiers, had met Le Corbusier during his first visit to Algiers and had worked on the Obus plans. In an essay that called for "an art that would express our time and the country we live in" and would not tell lies, Maisonseul argued that the "purity" of a style resided in its "unity." In North Africa, this purity was to be found in the Arab house. Clearly referring to Le Corbusier's observations but expanding on them, Maisonseul provided an insightful analysis of the "Arab house" in an important article.[33] Even though he did not specify it, Maisonseul's "Arab house" was an Algerian urban type, a house from the casbah.

Like Le Corbusier, Maisonseul was enchanted by the blank facades of the Arab house on the street, by its development around an inner courtyard dotted with fresh water and ornamented with beautiful tiles. The courtyard gave each unit its own "square of the sky." Another distinguishing feature was a gradated use of light. While the entrance was dark, the hallway was lighted slightly from the small openings in the back, the galleries enjoyed a semi-light, the courtyard was bright, and the rooms were shaded. Such differences appealed to the senses and created a rhythm as one moved through the spaces. The individual thus felt that the architecture was modeled according to his own body, to a "human scale."[34]

Maisonseul then attempted to define a "Mediterranean" architecture that focused on the shared aspects of the "Oriental" and the "Occidental." Most striking was the relationship between planes and voids, and the "predilection for the austerity of grand nude surfaces." Ornamentation was localized, did not extend to the entire facade, and contrasted with the "naked parts." In general, the openings (porticoes, loggias) were deeply inserted to provide shelter from the sun. The square-shaped window remained on the human scale. Openings were further fragmented by *mashrabiyyas* (window lattices) to control the light, thereby modulating the shade as well.[35]

The Arab house, therefore, had much to offer to the development of a new architecture. Maisonseul maintained that even interiorization should not be given up despite the differences in French and Arab lifestyles. On the contrary, "this subtle arrangement of interior spaces, the delicious gradation of diverse scales that form the passage from one volume to the other," should be adopted in buildings intended for Europeans, too. Contemporary technology, in particular reinforced concrete, would permit a smooth application of the principles Maisonseul outlined without creating an appearance of "pastiche."[36]

If this interiorized architecture could easily be applied to individual houses, the problem became more complicated for collective housing, where true creativity would be needed to make meaningful adaptations. Maisonseul suggested duplex apartment units with interior stairs and a double-height living room. He argued that this room would function like "a patio absorbing in great quantities the light and the air from the exterior facade, itself protected by loggias." The other rooms would open to the living room. Such a solution would improve greatly on current apartment units, conveying a new feeling of space and freedom, bringing in the "charm" of the Arab house as well as its "truly varied plastic possibilities." [37]

Maisonseul was not isolated in his vision to include the Algerian vernacular, and especially the Algerian house, in a broadly defined regional style that adhered well to the formal principles of modernism, at least as practiced and advocated by Le Corbusier. A group of architects in Algiers subscribed to this viewpoint, and discourse on a "Mediterranean" architecture occupied the pages of professional and popular journals in Algiers for quite some time. For example, J. Scelles-Millie asked in 1946: "Does not the Arab house, with its patio [and] its marble basin, belong at the same time to the heritage of the Orient, Greece, and Rome?" He answered: "All this is the Mediterranean." Mediterranean architecture was characterized by its exteriorization toward the sea and the sun, on the one hand, and its interiorization onto courtyards and enclosed gardens, on the other. It was the "Oriental mystique" that had refined the interiorized qualities of Mediterranean architecture. The contemporary architect in Algeria was in a privileged position to find a "classical equilibrium" and apply modern technology to local elements that were "created in this country [Algeria] . . . for the enjoyment of this country." [38]

THE RESULTING PROTOTYPE

The cumulative analyses of ethnographers and architects produced a list of characteristics that defined the "Algerian house." With its courtyard as the key space, the Algerian house was interiorized. It enclosed itself to the street and the external world by its blank, planar facades with minimal openings. Yet it opened up to nature, to views by means of an ingenious use of roof terraces, considered one of its greatest assets. Decoration was used selectively and furniture was sparse. Sanitary conditions were poor and densities very high. This summary may not have expressed the depth of the research involved and the elaborate readings of built forms, but it provided a convenient checklist for future

Figure 50. Jean-François Rafaëlli, *La Charmeuse nègre* (1877).

designs. At least some of the "positive" qualities of the "Algerian house" surfaced in the work of many architects practicing in Algeria.

The establishment of a fixed image for the Algerian house was indebted to other cultural productions as well. Abundantly illustrated books on the places and people of the casbah, aimed at popular audiences, presented the urban house in its most exotic aspects and emphasized the collective forms created by the accretion of individual units. Lucienne Favre's *Tout l'inconnu de la casbah d'Alger* (1933), illustrated by Charles Brouty, and Robert Randau's *Sur les pavés d'Alger* (1937), illustrated by Henri Klein, are among the most successful representations of the surge of this literary genre at its peak in the 1930s. Le Corbusier's inclusion of Brouty's sketches in his own publications was not accidental; Brouty's lines depicted what modernism considered the best in the residential vernacular of Algiers (see Fig. 7).

Massing and interiority, the two aspects of the Algerian urban house that appealed to widespread sensibilities and that defined the concept generally, had also been incorporated by Orientalist painters, who were as much interested in the formal qualities of the casbah as in its lifestyles. A group of women on roof terraces, with the casbah in the background,

Figure 51. Jules Meunier, *Femmes d'Alger sur les terraces* (1888).

was a recurrent theme. Three randomly picked paintings present this theme: Jean-François Rafaëlli's *La Charmeuse nègre* (1877), Jules Muenier's *Femmes d'Alger sur les terraces* (1888), and Marius de Buzon's *Trois Algériennes* (1927) (Figs. 50, 51, and 52). In each of these paintings, Algerian women, clad in colorful clothes, are depicted against the con-

Figure 52. Marius de Buzon, *Trois Algériennes* (1927).

trasting white of the residential fabric that descends toward the dark blue of the Mediterranean beyond. If the exterior representations of the indigenous urban house conveyed the prevailing characteristics of the old town, interior views elaborated on more imaginary scenes. Continuing from Eugène Delacroix's *Femmes d'Alger dans leur appartement* of

Figure 53. Stage set from Julien Duvivier's film *Pépé le Moko* (1937).

1834 (see Fig. 103), the stage-set quality of women's interiors is striking in the exaggerated wealth of the decorative paraphernalia surrounding the central figures. In diametric opposition to ethnographic descriptions of stark interiors, such scenes belong to the broader themes of Orientalist paintings.[39] Nevertheless, despite their element of fantasy, they reinforce the introverted nature of the Algerian house.

The postcard industry that bloomed starting at the turn of the century duplicated the dual representation of the houses of the casbah. The exterior views focused on the terraces and the narrow, winding streets (postcards depicting such views were published by Le Corbusier to support his own arguments about a new urbanism and architecture), while the interiors were "assembled" in colonial postcards according to familiar Orientalist fantasies and as women's environments.[40] The postcard visions of Algerian interiors were reinforced by colonial cinematography. As in Jacques Feyder's *Atlantide* (1921) and Julien Duvivier's *Pépé le Moko* (1937), the Algerian house was presented to moviegoers during this formative period in a "cheap exoticism"—in the words of Algerian cultural critic Abdelghani Megherbi (Fig. 53).[41] Exterior views capitalized again on roof terraces, as observed, for example, in Raymond Bernard's *Tartarin de Tarascon* (1934), and the winding, tortuous streets lined with irregular buildings, as in *Pépé le Moko*.

The ethnographic scholarship (which focused on rural habitat) and the artistic tradition (which focused on most apparent forms and fantasies) both overlooked the transformations in indigenous houses caused by the French presence. Changes that took place in residential architecture were noted by those who studied social issues, most prominently the White Friars (Carmelites). A report that focused on the Algerian family and "modern social problems" in the 1940s noted that wealthier Arab families now commissioned European architects to design their houses, a phenomenon that resulted in buildings in a "modern tone— a serial product familiar to everyone." The greatest change was in the interiors, in furniture. The living rooms of upper-class Algerians became cluttered with "a heterogeneous mixture of furniture designed in very pure lines and a profusion of carpets, sofas, divans." A piano had become an indispensable part of a young bride's trousseau, which also had to include a collection of European trinkets (*bibelôts européens*). Even in the poorest houses, European-style chairs were common.[42] The much-revered purity of the Algerian house was disappearing fast, leaving in its place a hybridity characteristic of all aspects of a colonized culture.

The Squatter House

The squatter house was the response of new immigrants from the countryside to the housing shortage in urban centers. As such it displayed not only the economic, but also the sociocultural realities of these populations in flux (Fig. 54). The inclusion of squatter settlements into the French discourse on housing has a history that goes back to the 1930s, to the first *bidonvilles* in Algiers. The squatter house was qualified by Roland Simounet as a "traditional" house type with valuable lessons for architects and planners in the early 1950s—two decades before the publication of John Turner's influential book *Housing by People* (London, 1976), based on the same premise.[43]

According to Henri Alleg and his colleagues, the Cité Bisch, built between 1926 and 1930 near the cemetery of el-Kattar, was the first *bidonville* in Algiers.[44] In their comprehensive study of squatter settlements in Algeria, Descloitres, Reverdy, and Descloitres also fix the emergence of *bidonvilles* between 1926 and 1930 and discuss the official disregard of the problem at the time. It is significant, they argue, that Lespès, the leading scholar of Algiers, did not mention the issue in his monumental monograph on the city, published in 1930. Given the at-

Figure 54. A *bidonville* in Ravin de la Femme Sauvage, Algiers, 1961.

tention Lespès paid to the *insalubrité* of housing conditions in the casbah, this omission reveals the general impression that squatter settlements were not considered an urban problem at the time. Descloitres
and colleagues cite Berque as the first researcher to use the term *bidonville,* in 1936.[45]

   Immigration from the countryside to cities that swells the squatter
areas is not a pattern unique to Algiers, but has parallels in many coun-
tries. Nevertheless, the specific mechanisms of the colonial regime played
a crucial role in the surge of this phenomenon in Algeria. Descloitres
and colleagues gave three main reasons for the continuous demographic
flow to Algiers: the pauperization of the countryside, the breakdown of
traditional structures under the political and administrative campaigns
based on the European experience, and the attraction of Algiers as a locus
of employment. Bourdieu argued, in contrast, that the cause for this
immigration was the poverty in the countryside rather than the attraction of the city.[46]

The demographic growth of greater Algiers explains the housing crisis: a manageable city of 64,809 inhabitants in 1866, its population had increased to 266,268 in 1926, to 473,261 in 1948, and to 570,000 in 1954, making Algiers the fourth-largest city of "France," after Lyon. The growth in the urban population of Algeria was disproportionate, however: between 1926 and 1954, the European population had increased by 168,000 people, whereas this number was 889,000 for Muslims. Muslims constituted the overwhelming majority of *bidonville* residents. In 1954, out of the 41,000 squatter houses officially recorded in the urban zones, 39,500 were occupied by Muslim families. One Muslim out of every seven or eight lived in a *bidonville*. In Algiers 41.5 percent of the native population lived in squatter settlements.[47]

The residents of the *bidonvilles* had ceased to belong to rural society, but they were not integrated into the urban realm either. They formed what was called a "new proletariat" and "a new type of man," distinct from the Muslim urban population in terms of their skills, customs, lifestyles, and belief systems. Unlike Algerians who had lived in cities even before the French occupation, the newcomers had not been in constant contact with European "civilization." Neither were they familiar with city life. The cities, in turn, did not have sufficient employment opportunities, which resulted in the continued impoverishment of squatters. The fact that they did not own or rent the land on which they built their shacks further contributed to their status of "not belonging." In sum, the newcomers added a third element to the dual system of Algerian cities, one that would sharpen the contrast, and ultimately, the confrontation between Europeans and Algerians.[48]

Often situated in the valleys, the *bidonvilles* were hidden from sight. Focusing on one settlement, Bois des Arcades, Descloitres and colleagues described the formal characteristics of such clusters in Algiers in the mid-1950s. While the lower and relatively flat part of the site was filled with rectilinear shacks regularly lined up, the slopes had a more complex configuration, formed by terraces (Fig. 55). The doors of the houses on an upper level opened to the roof of those on the terrace below, and the entire site appeared like a "gigantic stairway," a familiar term from Le Corbusier's descriptions of the casbah. Almost all the shacks leaned on each other, forming dense clusters, often with a single winding pathway that provided access to a large number of units. The urban tissue displayed a similarity to that of the casbah, with its irregular and narrow streets, attached houses, and use of the sloped terrain in terraces. The houses of the casbah were larger, however, and each had a court.

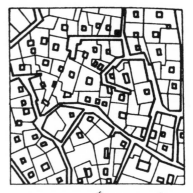

ÉCHELLE : 1/2.000ᵉ

Figure 55. Partial plan of the Mahieddine *bidonville* (left); similarities with the fabric of the casbah (right) are striking.

From nearby, the most striking aspect of the *bidonvilles* was the fragility of the structures, the variety and the poor quality of the materials used, and the scale of individual units. The units were often formed of a single room, a *pièce-logement* that sheltered an entire family. The discrepancy between European and native quarters had increased with the development of *bidonvilles;* while the overall occupation figure for Europeans in Algiers was 1.2 persons per room in the mid-1950s, it was 3.4 for Algerians. The cohabitation of several families in one unit was commonplace.[49] The mosque, the "unique luxury of the *bidonville*," was the only solid building in the compound and stood out from the rest. Shops were located at the borders of the settlement, in proximity to the mosque. The *bidonville* functioned like a quarter, with its comprehensive commercial facilities, Quranic school attached to the mosque, cafés, and public baths that were converted into dormitories to shelter the newest comers to the city.[50]

The first comprehensive analysis of a *bidonville* was done by a young architect, Roland Simounet, and presented by the Algiers Group to the ninth meeting of CIAM (Congrès Internationaux d'Architecture Moderne) in Aix-en-Provence in 1953. The Groupe CIAM Alger chose Mahieddine as its *bidonville* case study because this settlement had already been documented to some degree by aerial photographs and an overall site plan. Simounet's task involved documentation and analysis of the housing stock, as well as an inquiry into social conditions based on interviews with the residents.[51]

Simounet's analysis led to a proposal to adopt the principles of the settlement that corresponded to "the best conditions defined by modern urbanism," namely, principles concerning utilization of the site (based on a genuine respect for the site), topography, environment, greenery, provision of proximity to work, commerce, and recreation, as well as configuration of the main traffic arteries. Simounet and his colleagues especially appreciated the terraced use of land, the "organic" relationship between the buildings and the site (reminiscent of the casbah), the flexibility of spaces to accommodate diverse functions, and the changing needs of the users—all documented by Simounet's attractive sketches.[52]

Simounet recorded the dwelling unit as the only element of the *bidonville* that needed technical improvements. Construction methods used in Cité Mahieddine, however, did display some remarkable qualities, among them a high degree of standardization. In terms of aesthetics, Simounet observed here "the birth of a new art form," one that stemmed from the meeting of the Islamic and the European and that powerfully expressed the "instinctive and profound aspirations of Muslim populations." Customs, traditions, and beliefs had played an extremely significant role in achieving this synthesis. According to the report of the Algiers Group, Simounet's study showed the importance of situating plastic arts (which included architecture) on a "more social, even more ethical" platform. Firmly anchored in "human reality" and "social life," the Mahieddine settlement offered valuable lessons for "tomorrow's habitat."[53] Groupe CIAM Alger and Simounet personally influenced the debate on the *bidonvilles*. Architectural discourse of the 1950s and early 1960s frequently referred to the potential of squatter houses as models and to their "extreme sensibility and high human qualities."[54]

Despite the architectural and urbanistic qualities that opened vistas for housing design, *bidonvilles* in their current state were the most blatant manifestations of the inequality between Europeans and Algerians. The debates at the time emphasized the contribution of the growing contrast in material conditions to the revolts and predicted a worsening of tensions.[55] Helped by their dense and irregular siting that recalled the casbah, many squatter settlements became centers for resistance fighters during the war.[56] In retaliation and as part of the war strategy that bridged urban and rural policies, military forces bulldozed many squatter settlements, and army trucks transported the residents to dispersed locations to be rehoused.[57]

CHAPTER 4

Housing the Algerians: Policies

At this moment when the new generations reach out more and more to establish contacts with our culture, it is not conceivable to send them back to the gourbi. *In Algeria, this problem assumes certainly a human character, but also a political character, a dangerously political character.*

Dr. Montaldo, *Techniques et architecture*

The colonial administration's first radical steps to assume responsibility for improving the housing conditions of Algerians began in the 1930s, mainly in response to the rapidly accelerating need for more urban housing. In accordance with the comprehensiveness of the centennial reform package, however, housing policies were also extended to rural areas. Overlooking at first the emergence of semi-rural shantytowns on the peripheries of cities (especially Algiers), the administration devised separate rural and urban policies and ignored settlements that fell in between those two categories.

The conditions recorded by ethnographers gave policymakers the fundamental data on rural housing. Furthermore, their recommendations on how to improve it served as guidelines. The overall goal was to make it more hygienic, sound, and comfortable; masonry construction and tile roofs—"in the European manner"—were the first steps.[1] Within twenty years, this flexible proposal changed into enforced settlement policies in rural "camps" designed by the French. In the face of the growing armed resistance to colonialism, the *regroupement* policies of the 1950s aimed to establish strict control over rural populations. As the early rural policies are tangential to the main theme of this book, I do not deal with them here. I do examine the resettlement policies of the 1950s, however, because they depict a particularly revealing situation in which housing became a primary actor in the colonial confrontation.

In his book that aimed to refine French colonial policies to ensure the legitimacy and durability of the French empire, Albert Sarrault stated in 1931: "Colonization must remain faithful to the great task by which a spirit of civilization, compensating and correcting the injustices of nature, proposes to create . . . a state of material and moral progress, amplifying the means to universal well-being." Only then could the "historic reality" of early colonialism—characterized as "a unilateral and egotistical enterprise of personal interest, accomplished by the strongest over the weakest," and "an act of force" (not of "civilization")—be corrected. France had to develop a "precise colonial doctrine," relying on the "mirror of its conscience." It was not ethical to maintain two faces, the face of "liberty, turned to the *métropole*," and the face of "tyranny, turned to its colonies." It was indeed France's honor to acknowledge the "value of latent races" (*races attardées*) and to see the colonies not simply as markets, but as "creations of humanity." Behind this humanistic facade forwarded by Sarrault, the most important issue was the "control of local populations." To ensure the loyalty, fidelity, and attachment of the indigenous people was the prime responsibility of the colonizer.[2]

It was in this spirit championed by Sarrault that Lespès explained the political implications of housing in a colonial society. Raising the "material living conditions of our subjects will bring them closer to us," he argued. This was "humanitarian work, useful work, necessary work"; its neglect would result in grave consequences. Comparing the conditions in which Europeans lived with their own, the indigenous residents saw themselves treated as inferiors, despised, and kept at a distance; eventually they would develop strong sentiments, even hate, against the French.[3] Following a similar line of thought to gain the confidence of Algerians, the French administration included housing reform into the broader agenda of the centennial celebrations. For example, the president of the Chamber of Commerce in Algiers applauded the new vision of the Assemblée Algérienne that saw in the improvement of indigenous housing a means to bring a general "evolution" and emphasized the importance of creating among locals a "sentiment of trust in France." "Let us give them," he continued, "a taste of hygiene, well-being, and aesthetics." This way, people who "vegetated in despicable material and moral conditions will be elevated to a higher degree of civilization."[4]

Policies for Urban Housing

In terms of their architectural and urban design implications, policies regarding urban housing revolved around three issues: the choice between European and Algerian prototypes or a synthesis of the two, the physical separation of European and Algerian projects, and depiction of an appropriate style. While these discussions lingered until the end of French rule, their intensity diminished, and in time sociocultural aspects gave way to quantitative concerns.

In 1936, Albert Seiller and Marcel Lathuillière, two architects practicing in Algiers, asked a question that would preoccupy the technocrats involved in housing for many years to come: "Should we, like in Morocco, create new casbahs by improving the urbanistic qualities and by giving a relative degree of comfort to housing units, or on the contrary, should we create the same type of settlements as those reserved for Europeans?" The answer depended on the broader colonial policies and, in their opinion, was neither positive nor negative, but called for a middle ground. Although they defined the primary need of Algerian people as privacy and pointed to the importance of home in this culture, the architects argued against too much "respect" for the indigenous house. They advocated instead an architecture that would "prepare the way toward a progressive assimilation of European habits" by Algerian people, while prudently satisfying the old customs. Given the resources allotted to this sector, cost efficiency was a main practical issue; therefore, development of "very tight plans that would eliminate all unnecessary construction surfaces" and the employment of economical materials were essential.[5]

Housing advocates continued to reflect on the dichotomy of the "traditional" and the European and offered their perspectives on establishing a balance. Lespès argued against rigid prescriptions for housing designated for indigenous people in Algerian cities. He urged instead a careful study of living conditions, residential types, their groupings, and social categories that would prepare the foundations for designing appropriate architectural responses.[6] Other advocates of housing programs rushed to prepare solutions. For example, Jean Alazard, a professor in the Faculty of Letters at the University of Algiers, debated that courtyards did not function well in a multifamily housing scheme because of their public nature; the "swarming of all the women and all the children" in the galleries surrounding the court would result in "undesirable consequences" from the point of view of hygiene. It was, consequently, preferable to adhere to the type of collective housing built for Europeans. Meanwhile, each family should be given an interior loggia, protected by a *mashrabiyya,* for the use of women.[7] Alazard's argument on hygiene remained unconvincing and did not conceal his attempt to manipulate design in order to discourage social interaction, a potential threat to the political order.

The debate on the form of indigenous urban housing continued until the late 1950s and the unequaled construction boom initiated by the Plan de Constantine, when building fast and in great numbers became the sole concern. A report on "Muslim reforms" in 1944 stated that the rudimentary buildings worked against the "evolution already registered by the Muslim population." Therefore, it was essential to build housing complexes or garden cities, equipped with amenities for modern comfort, though still without ignoring "aesthetic and traditional" sensibilities. On the basis of the principle that the Muslim urban habitat should be distinct, the Commission for Muslim Reforms called for a revision of the legislation on HBMs (Habitations à Bon Marché, devised for France but applied in Algeria as well) that would accommodate the needs of Muslim residents and take into consideration local conditions.[8]

Tony Socard, an architect who worked in collaboration with planners and built low-cost housing for Muslims, argued for three types of residences, on the premise of separating Muslims from European settlements. For the "evolved" families that subscribed to the French lifestyle and values, European-type flats or villas were unquestionably the most suitable. Yet in some cities (for example, Blida, Tlemcen, and Constantine), "artisan" classes had maintained a preference for the "traditional courtyard house"; this type should be built, but not mixed with houses designed according to European formulas. The third category addressed the residents of the *bidonvilles* and approved a semi-rural pattern in specially designated quarters, such as Clos Salembier and Climat de France (where Socard himself had designed a low-rise *cité*).[9]

Another Algiers-based architect, J. Scelles-Millie, focused on the urban design qualities of the environments to be created for Muslims. Although he argued for the separation of the European and indigenous populations, he proposed to connect them by means of a commercial street and a public square, a "forum" with administrative offices. For the indigenous quarter, Scelles-Millie suggested as many "closed perspectives" as possible; appropriate monuments, such as public fountains or minarets, would be used to obstruct the streets. Whitewashed walls would protect the gardens of individual houses. The urban configuration of new Muslim quarters was to form a deliberate contrast to the European section, distinct with its orthogonal streets lined with clearly visible villas and gardens.[10] Scelles-Millie's proposal echoed the principles adopted by several schemes already projected for Algiers, as well as the *nouvelles médinas* realized under Marshal Lyautey in Morocco. With his emphasis on dual imagery, Scelles-Millie called for the replication of the ultimate colonial city paradigm, based on the difference of the local society from the European one.

The 1948 Plan d'Urbanisme emphasized another criterion for good housing design in Algiers: response to climate. Introducing one of the leading principles of the Athens Charter (established in 1933, but first published in 1941) and addressing the criticism that previous efforts overlooked the issues of orientation and ventilation, the authors of the 1948 plan called for absolute attention to local specificities, and most important, climatic factors. The plan clarified that all subsequent projects designated for Algiers would not be allowed to ignore such conditions.[11]

On the eve of Mayor Chevallier's tenure and the Algerian War, the housing problem was understood not only as a "human" problem, but more significantly as a "dangerously political" issue. In an attempt to smooth the relationships between the two communities, housing policies were revised. For the "evolved" Muslims, the "normal HLM [*habitations à loyer modéré*] formulas" in mixed settlements were seen as preferable to isolation, because a "politics of contact" would bring the indigenous people and the Europeans together. For the nonevolved sectors of the Muslim community (rural, but also urban—*bidonville* residents and newcomers to the casbah), low-rise housing was the best solution. On the basis of these overall considerations, the urban administration had devised guidelines for new housing. First, all units should have a degree of adaptability to accommodate changes in lifestyle and contribute to the "evolution" of the colonized. Second, highrise buildings were inevitable in large cities, but for "transitory" housing, intended to accommodate the newcomers to the city, low-rise developments were better, because they facilitated the rural immigrants' acculturation process. And third, "politics of contact" between different ethnic groups should be encouraged everywhere, whereas medina-style schemes should be rejected categorically because of their introverted quality.[12] In a shift from the previous policies, then, for the first time an experiment was proposed to bring the two communities together. However, this priority implicitly called for the total transformation of the Algerian house by turning it inside out and disturbing its inherent rationale. The policy was not put into practice, most likely because it proposed a radical step toward abolishing the physical distance between Algerians and Europeans.

In line with the growing trend that viewed housing as an urban design issue and as stemming from the ever-increasing need for large numbers of units, in the 1950s Mayor Chevallier's architects and planners treated new housing zones as totally independent units, each with its own design principles. Jacques Stamboul, a city planner in Algiers, articulated the validity of the trend to design fragments rather than a master plan: "The issue, in Algeria, is to practice true urbanism, and not reconstruction following a master plan. . . . Today, the most spectacular form of urbanism is housing," considered in conjunction with its social, commercial, and cultural "equipment."[13]

Summarizing the problems the city administration faced, Paul Messerschmitt, director of the Ecole Supérieure de Commerce in Algiers, highlighted the quintuplication of *bidonville* inhabitants between 1950 and 1954.[14] This "painful" and "anguishing" situation had to be addressed right away by buildings that were sensitive to financial factors (low construction costs and low rents) and social elements (traditions and customs of Muslims). Messerschmitt saw a distinct separation between the needs of "many Muslims . . . who had adopted the lifestyle of Europeans" and who lived at ease in European-type villas or collective housing, and those of shantytown residents. Yet he did not opt for a different housing type for the second group. Noting that despite the temporary solution the rural-type low-rise housing provided, he felt it was not a solution for cities. He thus agreed with the rejection of medina-style projects and pointed to the success of the recent Cité Boucle-Perez project and advocated designing new quarters with multistory blocks.[15] This point was reiterated in later official documents claiming that Algerians had lost their preference for low-rise units with courtyards and developed a new penchant for European-style multistory buildings. The "evolution" was considered a positive phenomenon that pointed to a future intermixing of Muslims and Europeans— one of the admitted goals of Mayor Chevallier's programs.[16]

Messerschmitt's formulation of the housing problem is indicative of the broader colonial policies of this period. He began his discussion by dissociating the administration's standpoint from a dual concept in housing: "In reality, we do not intend to discriminate between Muslims and non-Muslims. All citizens of Algeria can demand different construction formulas, be it an HLM or Algerian [type] habitat. Nothing prevents a Muslim, for example, from building a house that responds to his architectural conceptions and religious customs with a loan from the Crédit Foncier."[17] Although theoretically valid, this statement hardly conformed to the socioeconomic realities of Muslims in Algiers. It soon became evident that new legislative provisions had to be made in order to build the necessary quantity of low-cost units for Algerians. Until 1955, such housing could not be financed from the HLM funds, making it impossible to practice a "*politique d'urbanisme,* so necessary for harmonious development." The amendment of 7 July 1955, adopted by the Assemblée Algérienne, corrected this situation by expanding HLM funding to cover housing for "indigenous" populations.[18] Other provisions were made, too. For example, residents of shantytowns and government housing could now benefit from a financial assistance program to build better houses for themselves, provided they agreed to the plot assigned to them in a newly laid-out settlement and to construction supervision by the Commissariat à la Reconstruction; in addition, special loans were created for Muslims who had fought in the French army in World War II. In the late 1950s, it was an accepted fact that the "very great majority" of low-cost housing was occupied by French Muslims, in comparison to housing built according to "ordinary norms," where Europeans constituted the "highest proportion."[19]

During Mayor Chevallier's tenure, housing the Muslims gained priority, and it acquired a humanist, if paternalistic, dimension, clearly aimed at resolving the social unrest attributed to poor living conditions. The number of residential units built during this time was unprecedented although it still fell short of meeting the need. More striking than the quantity, however, was the attention paid to the quality of design and construction. Chevallier's principal architect, Fernand Pouillon, summarized the guidelines of the housing policy in three points: maximum construction speed, maximum comfort (because "equality in comfort reduces social resentments"), and minimal cost, with the goal of including a maximum number of units within the restrictions of a fixed budget.[20]

From 1954 onward, during the decolonization war, the French administrators and commentators viewed the construction of new housing projects as a weapon, basing their hopes on the pacifying powers of better living conditions. Yet as each completed project became another center of resistance, expectations began to dim. For example, in 1956 René Pottier, a member of the Académie des Sciences Coloniales, concluded his article praising Chevallier's architectural and urbanistic accomplishments on a negative note: the painful current events seemed to contradict the old saying, "Quand le bâtiment va, tout va" (If the building is right, all is right). Algiers, now proudly called a *ville-pilote* (model city), would perhaps remain so, but "was it possible for a pilot to fight against a tempest?"[21]

Nonetheless, the construction boom begun under Chevallier continued to escalate, preparing the ground for the statistic-obsessed period following De Gaulle's declaration of the Plan de Constantine. Of the 15-billion-franc credit allotted to Algeria in 1958, 2.6 billion went to housing construction and demolition of *bidonvilles* and 1 billion to urban infrastructure and roads. Only education had a higher allotment than housing, with 5.5 billion francs—being another area where the French had invested their hopes and money to sway the Algerians' loyalty.[22]

Expressed quantitatively as 5 percent growth per year in the income level of the Algerian population at large, the Plan de Constantine's goals were social and economic, but also political. The authors of the plan underlined that it was not possible to have "social policy without housing policy" and maintained that housing would be a key feature in the projected reforms. Between 1954 and 1958, twenty-eight thousand housing units had been constructed in Algeria, twenty-five thousand of which were in urban centers, still leaving a need for an estimated forty thousand units. To attack the problem effectively, the government decided to establish an office of housing in Algiers. Unique in France, this organization would provide administrative services to all parties involved in the construction of housing.[23]

In all of Algeria, 210,000 units would be built over a period of five years between 1958 and 1963, 134,000 of which would be lower-income dwellings, 62,000 middle-income, and 14,000 higher-income.[24] A precise schedule listed the numbers to be produced per year, gradually increasing from 22,000 in 1959 to 61,000 in 1963, when the cumulative goal of 210,000 would have been reached and 1 million people would have been housed.[25] Of this total, 53,000 units were projected for Algiers. The administrations to carry out the construction were already in place in the form of HLM offices, cooperative societies, societies of Crédit Immobilier, as well as non-HLM cooperatives. Of the three hundred architects working in Algeria, most were based in Algiers. Consequently, the architectural pool was insufficient in other cities. The plan strongly opposed the customary long-distance supervision by architects as far away as France and devised a mechanism to attract young architects to smaller cities and to the hinterland.[26]

The growing unrest dealt a blow to the construction industry, especially to middle- and higher-income housing, as Europeans began to question their future in Algeria. Still, according to official estimations, by the end of 1962 the sum of units built and under construction had reached 142,000—only 7,000 short of the original estimate of completed units.[27] Facilitated by the extensive use of prefabrication, efficient organization of construction sites, and the adoption of simple, formulaic schemes, new projects appeared all over the city. The settlement of *bidonville* residents en masse into apartment blocks rekindled the social aspects of the housing problem—almost forgotten in the technocratic and statistical frenzy of the production phases. The acculturation issue resurfaced: Was it "dangerous to create modern living conditions before promoting modern men"? Were these "semi-pastoral, semi-nomadic" people able to achieve their own development?[28]

At the outset of the Plan de Constantine period, Marcel Lathuillière, an architect involved in low-cost housing since the 1930s, endorsed the plan and explained the new reform agenda with a sentence taken from the social philosophy of the deposed mayor, Jacques Chevallier: "Human promotion will henceforth be linked to housing."[29] Social concerns remained superficial for Lathuillière in the 1950s, and he was not alone. The discourse on how housing would cure the social ills of Algerian society and turn the local people into docile members of a French-dominated system remained schematic throughout. The research and documentation branch of a low-cost housing agency stated in 1961: "We believe that the main obstacle to all evolution lies in the precariousness of living conditions. In contrast, we predict that improvement of his housing will likely give [the *bidonville* resident] the necessary momentum for his transformation." It was hoped that European-style apartments would endow the residents with a new spirit of collectivity and, once recovered from the rupture with traditional ways, the Muslim families would appreciate the advantages of modern comforts, of running water and electricity. New needs would generate "a new conception of work, a new organization of the family cell, a new mentality."[30]

The resistance of *bidonville* residents to displacement and resettlement in apartment blocks was sometimes interpreted as stemming from ignorance. According to one thesis, the former squatters did not know what was good for them and could benefit from "educators and guides" who lived by their sides, and allocation of low-income Europeans to every project could help enlighten Algerians on issues concerning family life and values. The most important lesson was the maintenance of the nuclear family; Algerians should not be permitted to open the doors of their new homes to relatives or fellow villagers as they were in the habit of doing in their *bidonvilles*.[31] If such social measures seem politically naive within the context of the war that affected daily life for everyone throughout Algeria, they display clearly the persistence of the *mission civilisatrice* until the end of French rule.

An issue that surfaced sporadically in the discussions on housing was style. Regardless of whether they opted for the neo-Islamic or the modern (or the neoclassical in the earlier phases of colonialism), colonial administrators and architects relied on sociocultural implications of style to enhance their agendas. In a monograph on Algiers in 1938, Louis Bertrand took a popular stand among architectural circles and mocked the neo-Moorish style favored since the turn of the century in administrative and educational buildings as an "architecture of the Universal Expositions." Yet he qualified his criticism by praising the noble intentions behind the neo-Moorish style, which honored the taste of Algerians. In Algiers, the French sensibility had tempered African exuberance and turgidity, as opposed to the "carnival-like cartoons and frippery" seen in Cairo and Alexandria. While it was high time to create a "new style" in Algeria, this style should learn some lessons from the previous experimentations, but reveal a "truly Algerian" character, in accord with the climate, customs, and comforts of modern life.[32]

The question of finding an equilibrium between modern and local styles dominated the discourse. While some architects argued for the "truly Algerian" character, others proposed a more universalist solution, with references to the classical Mediterranean house (Greek or Roman) in the spirit of Tony Garnier's housing schemes for the Cité Industrielle. For architect Scelles-Millie, for example, a synthesis of the classical, modern, and Arab styles was the most reasonable alternative for Algeria, because the Arab house, with its patio and whitewash, belonged as much to the great Mediterranean tradition as to the heritage of the Orient.[33]

The shift in the 1950s from low-rise schemes to apartment blocks brought an opposition to neo-Moorish experiments and direct stylistic references to the Arab house while introducing new considerations for appropriate styles. If in the past inspiration from Moorish architecture had produced "charming villages," now great vertical lines had to dominate the surfaces. The architecture of modern Algiers, the *ville-pilote,* should adopt a new style that responded to current needs and relied solely on the African sun as the "subtle decorator" that enlivened the "restricted and severe" surfaces.[34]

The debate on the choice of an appropriate style, as illustrated here with three mainstream arguments from three decades, corresponds to the actual building scene at large and to the stylistic experiments undertaken in the housing projects designed for Algerians. As the discussion of individual projects will reveal in the next chapter, while the few schemes built between the centennial and World War II opted for a strong *couleur locale,* the postwar housing turned to a more universalist vocabulary, convenient to the scale and construction rationale of the building types.

Policies for Rural Housing

Although the focus of this book is the city of Algiers, a detour to rural housing policies sheds much light on the colonial endeavor to use housing as an instrument of control over the local populations. If mention was made of improving the housing conditions of the rural masses, not much was done prior to the beginning of the Algerian War. A report from 1939 summarized the approach to new rural housing and specified the building and configuration types considered suitable for rural areas by early reform proposals. According to this model, a school, a post office, a community center, and a market would constitute the core of the settlement; a public fountain would serve as a gathering place for women; across from the fountain, a "Moorish café" would be frequented by the male population. The surrounding houses, "rustic and improved *gourbi*s," would be shaped after the "indigenous rural house" and respond to climate and customs; "exaggerated prescriptions" for hygiene and comfort were to be avoided, as they called for a certain degree of maturation not yet achieved by Algerian peasants.[35]

The policy aimed at the education of the peasant by improving the living conditions was established as early as 1836 by Marshal Thomas-Robert Bugeaud. He initiated the construction of two model villages with "simple, tile-roofed houses," the provision of certain tools and equipment, and the distribution of some land to the inhabitants. It was hoped that better conditions and the introduction of European agricultural methods would reinforce the peasants' attachment to the land. To this end, two villages were built, the first near Oran in 1838 and the second in Haouch Guerroeaou in Mitija in 1845. Without a rigorous policy, scattered experiments based on hypotheses were conducted in the following decades.[36]

A discussion of the new form of rural housing also helps to highlight colonial priorities in critical situations. The elaborate academic discourse on the form of the rural house and its accommodation of the Algerian peasants' daily life patterns was ignored totally in the design of the new resettlements (*regroupements*), whose architecture depended solely on militaristic considerations. The massive resettlement policy of the 1950s was the direct outcome of the struggle against colonial rule. The intensification in the relocation of Algerian peasants corresponded directly to the degree the war had penetrated the countryside and to the growth in the popularity of the FLN.

The launching of the resettlement policy in 1954 immediately followed the beginning of the "insurrection," with the rationale that the rural masses formed the "engine of the revolution" because of their "extreme misery." Soon after 1 November, the term *zone of insecurity* was coined, and the inhabitants of villages deemed "insecure" were forced to vacate even though they were not provided with alternative shelter. Surveying the countryside systematically, the military command hoped to isolate the rebels by the end of the year. Each zone of insecurity became a "banned zone," and between 1955 and 1957 the entire country was dotted with "banned zones."[37] The process was described in *El Moudjahid:* "Such initiatives were due to the diligence of the local French commander to claim vengeance for an ambush by the ALN [Armée de Libération Nationale]. After each ambush, the custom became to raze the nearest village, certainly an accomplice, and declare it a 'banned' zone. . . . People chased from their village roamed for days and nights hungry and aimless."[38]

Although a few centers of *regroupement* had been built in 1955 in Aurès, it was not until 1957 that the military commanders enforced a policy of resettling the peasants in environments that could be easily controlled—in order to disrupt communication between peasants and FLN fighters.[39] New housing was not necessarily provided for the "refugees," and more often than not they were encouraged to build their own dwellings with special funds and under the supervision of government-appointed experts on allocated lots.[40] Next to militaristic concerns, economic efficiency played an important role in shaping the *regroupement* policies. A government report that outlined the measures taken after the big earthquake in the Chelif region in 1954 (where sixteen hundred people had died) set the guidelines for later projects. It argued that the vast dispersal of dwellings throughout the countryside, often at places difficult to reach, increased construction costs and maintained that the new structures should be concentrated in "rationally conceived" settlements, where people could benefit from collective services.[41]

The Plan de Constantine refined the resettlement policy under the catchy title of *mille villages* (one thousand villages). While *regroupements* were acknowledged as the "most efficient ways to fight the rebels," they should only be seen as a step toward the creation of villages, the main sociological unit. The resettlement centers would be considered temporary and disappear progressively. According to one viewpoint, the new villages would act as centers of a revitalized agricultural economy and as catalyzers of a "rural revolution" under the supervision of the army. The rejuvenation of the countryside would also help to put a brake on the immigration to cities. Added to the provision of housing and educational and health services, attachment to the land would help keep the rural populations in the countryside. The humanistic terminology aimed to soften the harshness of the resettlement strategy and used a familiar phrase promoted earlier by Albert Sarrault: "the conquest of hearts" was preferable to "the conquest by force."[42]

Militaristic or humanitarian, the resettlement policy, coupled with the voluntary immigration to cities and to France, subjected Algerians to "a veritable diaspora," in the words of Pierre Bourdieu. He stated that in 1958 three million Algerians did not inhabit the home in which they had been living in 1954, this figure amounting to one out of every three Algerians.[43] With the systemization of the resettlement policy, during 1959 and 1960 the displacement reached alarming proportions. By the summer of 1959, one million "mountain people" were deracinated from their villages. *El Moudjahid* summed up the situation: "150,000 Algerians in jail, one million in resettlement centers, nearly 300,000 refugees in Tunisia and Morocco, and the rest at the mercy of the French military machine. Here is the first assessment of 'the pacification.'"[44]

The permanent villages were built at a record pace after 1959. Five months after the launching of the *mille villages* program, 160 settlements were already in place. "Traveling teams" that consisted of an army officer, an agricultural expert, a hydraulics specialist, and a doctor had toured the countryside the entire summer, inspecting the resettlements already under construction and choosing sites for new ones. Within a year, the number of villages under construction reached 602.[45]

The "teams" decided everything about the *regroupement*, from the choice of the site to the layout and the design of dwelling units, with little, if any, consultation with the users. Bourdieu summarized the prevailing mentality:

> Convinced that they must make men happy in spite of themselves, persuaded that they knew the real needs of others better than the latter did themselves, assured of belonging to a superior civilization that was absolutely good in itself, the officials were unable to conceive of the customary life of the people as being anything other than a primitive and barbarous survival, and concluded that any resistance offered to the order they wished to impose was the mere expression of an obstinate and absurd routine way of thinking.[46]

The teams thus "disciplined" the sites with orthogonal plans—with straight streets lined by uniform dwellings whose entrances could be supervised easily (Figs. 56 and 57). In the center was an oversized square with public amenities such as a clinic and a school. The Reconstruction and Rural Habitat Board (Commissariat à la Reconstruction et à l'Habitat Rural) had developed a type of unit that was cheap and could be assembled quickly. It consisted of two minuscule rooms and a kitchen, altogether less than 20 square meters, and a small courtyard of about 5 by 6 meters. No provisions were made for sheltering animals or storing the harvest, and the 20-centimeter-thick cement-block walls were not insulated, and so gave the inhabitants no protection from heat or cold.[47]

According to Bourdieu, the enforced distance between the peasants' home and their land, animals, farm implements, and agricultural products caused a dramatic rupture in lifestyle. Prior to the resettlement, the Kabylian peasant had integrated all aspects of life and placed the home at the center of everything. Family life and production processes were attuned; the peasant enjoyed autonomy and independence.[48] The resettlement interrupted both domestic and community order—the structure of the village and the relationship between peasants. The standardization of site plans added to the homogenization of the unit, the creation of monotonous patterns, and the inevitable loss of individuality; the policy was criticized even in government publications. According

Figure 56. *(above)* A *village de regroupement* in Aumale, October 1960. On the left is a farm compound razed by the French army. Figure 57. *(below)* Le Mezdour, a *village de regroupement*, built à la Vauban, October 1960.

to an official report from 1961, the *mille villages* did not merit their name (which implied diversity), because their "serial fabrication" ignored the originality of each region.[49]

Even the much-boasted improvement in the housing conditions remained unsatisfactory. For example, the standard dwelling unit erected throughout the country ignored climatic differences, resulting in physically uncomfortable environments. Site selection was random, often without taking into consideration topographical factors, exposure to sun and strong winds, and availability of water. Michel Cornaton maintains in his extensive study of the *regroupements* that the popular formula given to tourists, "Algeria is a cold country where the sun is hot," was completely overlooked in these projects. Some settlements were exposed to cold winds or sand storms, whereas others were placed in valleys that frequently flooded. As the water situation was not always carefully checked prior to site selection, many settlements ended up with very little or no water at all.[50]

Misery was rampant in the resettlement centers. *El Moudjahid* regularly referred to the centers as "resettlement camps" (*camps de regroupement*), evoking the memory of Nazi concentration camps. A Swedish journalist reported on the "tens of thousands" of children "dying of hunger and sickness . . . in internment camps"; she summarized the living conditions, where feverish children had to sleep on dirt floors, with no blankets to cover them.[51] Furthermore, continuous supervision and loss of freedom caused "moral misery" among the resettled people. Only in rare cases were entry and exit unsupervised; the residents and their guests customarily carried permits. In some "villages," the beginning and the end of the work day were announced by the sound of a clarion and the residents were taught how to salute the military officers. The attempts of a few officers to introduce recreational activities, such as theater, movies, and sports, were met with a determined hostility.[52] As expressed in the words of an older woman, the residents of *regroupements* regarded themselves as being in prison: "They threw all men in jail. This was not enough, because the war continued. They thus had to imprison women, children, and the elderly. There is no more room in prisons. It is easier to demand that we build our own prisons with our own hands. This costs nothing and they will not even have to serve us the prisoners' soup."[53]

The *regroupement* policy failed entirely because it only aggravated resentment against the French officers. The FLN found strong support in the settlements, where resistance cells mushroomed, often under the leadership of women, who were considered "the most engaged in this particular form of struggle."[54] Critics of the project declared it a complete failure, as well as "a terrible threat to the future" on the socioeconomic front: by 1960, 1.5 million peasants were uprooted and relocated; it was reasonable to foresee that the majority of these people would never return to their villages, but immigrate to cities.[55] If there was any success at all, it remained restricted to a short-term economic gain: under the protection of the army, the colons benefited from the captive cheap labor concentrated in the *regroupements*.[56]

CHAPTER 5

Housing the Algerians:
Grands Ensembles

Construction of housing responds to an urgent social need. . . .
Housing is a decisive factor in social evolution: the modification
of habits and familial needs that it instigates broadens the
possibilities for industrialization and general development.
République Française, Délégation Générale du
Gouvernement en Algérie, *Plan de Constantine*

In the wake of the modernist practices that had become
commonplace in Europe, social housing made its debut in Algiers in the
mid-1920s. Between the years 1925 and 1933, seven complexes were built
for Europeans.[1] Situated on the outskirts of the city proper as independent enclaves, these early experiments were the model for future trends.
From then on, housing complexes in Algiers dotted the unbuilt zones
on the edges of the city and played an instrumental role in its growth
pattern (Fig. 58).

Promotion of modern low-cost housing for the Algerians followed
in the footsteps of the projects built for Europeans, but incorporated
another set of sociocultural criteria that maintained the separation of the
two communities. As discussed in the previous chapter, the first serious
discussions on the urgency of promoting such housing took place as
part of the attempts to renovate Algiers on the centennial of the occupation. Not only were policies and legislations developed, but also questions of lifestyle and cultural differences were addressed, incorporating
debates on the form of the traditional house, the nature of the Algerian
family, the role of women, and the adoption of appropriate architectural
forms and styles. Owing to former practices in Lyautey's Morocco and

the experimentations with Islamic forms in the colonial pavilions of the universal expositions, the first housing schemes reflected strong "arabisance" traits.[2]

At the same time, the architects of the first phase of indigenous mass housing relied on the puristic white plasticity of modernism, also favored by the North African vernacular. Two theoretical Cité Musulmane projects from the 1930s crystallize the idealized qualities of the "traditional" Algerian vernacular, although tamed according to French rationalism. In François Bienvenu's 1933 proposal for a modern indigenous quarter in Climat de France on the heights of Bab el-Oued, the whitewashed, cubical volumes recalling the casbah are regimented by straight streets; to reinforce the casbah association, the drawing depicts veiled women in white robes crowding these streets (Fig. 59). Individual houses are interlocked with each other and each house is introverted by means of a courtyard with only one main window to the outside. In Louis Bérthy's 1939 *cité*, again an iron grid organizes the abstract site, creating a straightforward street network (Fig. 60). Within the grid each block is divided into individual houses with courtyards that share walls. The street facades are blank except for the entrance doors, whereas the houses open up to the courts, which display miniature havens planted with exotic plants and trees.

Only three housing projects were built for indigenous people during the 1930s. They were stylistically conscious undertakings that emphasized the cultural differences between the two communities in Algiers. This trend was gradually overshadowed by the more universal architecture of the second and third periods of massive housing construction—the second under Mayor Jacques Chevallier between 1954 and 1958, and the third corresponding to the implementation of the Plan de Constantine between 1959 and 1962. While "statistical" concerns would gain priority in the 1950s, a nod would always be given toward the sociocultural norms of Algerians, and in a few cases, architecturally intriguing solutions would attempt to reinterpret local lifestyles.

The First Phase: The 1930s

The first *cité indigène* by François Bienvenu was an HLM that consisted of sixty-two apartments. Located on the Boulevard de Verdun, which defines the northern boundary of the casbah, it sits on

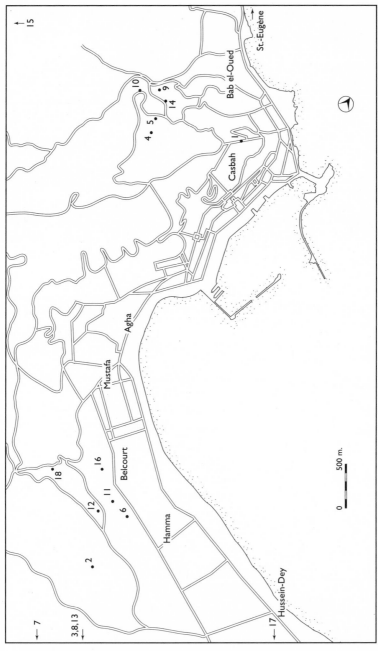

Figure 58. Schematic plan of Algiers showing the location of housing projects discussed in this chapter. The numbers correspond to the order in which the projects appear in the text. (1) Boulevard de Verdun, (2) Scala, Clos Salembier, (3) Ste.-Corinne, (4) Climat de France, (5) Boucle-Perez, (6) Diar el-Mahçoul, (7) La Montagne, (8) Dessoliers, (9) Carrière Jaubert, (10) Djenan el-Hasan, (11) Cyclamens, (12) Nador, (13) Eucalyptus, (14) Taine E, (15) Asphodèles, (16) Mahieddine, (17) Dunes, (18) Diar es-Shems.

Figure 59. *(above)* François Bienvenu, *cité indigène* project, Climat de France, 1933. Figure 60. *(below)* Louis Bérthy, *cité indigène* project, 1936.

Figure 61. Bienvenu, Boulevard de Verdun housing, view, 1935.

the ramparts of the Ottoman fortifications (Fig. 61). Its placement at
the very edge of the old city and its architectural qualities—"rationalized" from the houses of the casbah—allude to its symbolic ambivalence: the Verdun housing belongs and does not belong to the casbah.
The *cité* consists of three blocks, separated from each other by interior
passageways and courts. Multiple entrances, marked with horseshoe
arches, provide access to various levels, but only from the Boulevard de
Verdun side; the complex cannot be reached from the casbah. The massing and the height of the blocks (which reach seven stories at their highest) form a contrast to the scale and fabric of the casbah and further
accentuate the "in between" quality of the project. The complex topography of the site helps enliven the volumes and spaces; while the facades
on the Boulevard de Verdun are from six to seven stories high, the back
facades remain only three stories.

The architecture of the Boulevard de Verdun blocks aimed for a new
urban image that combined the "traditional" with the European and a
new housing type that responded to the customs of Muslim residents
while giving them the amenities of modern habitation. With their clean,
modernist lines, white surfaces, sparse openings, crenellated rooflines,
and flat roofs, the new buildings complemented the old quarter in their
picturesque appearance, but their exaggerated height on the Boulevard
de Verdun acted as a clear-cut boundary. The plans were derived from

the courtyard houses of the casbah, but what was private in the latter was made public in the former: apartment units now faced the courtyard, not the rooms of the same house. A continuous hallway surrounded the courtyard and gave access to individual units. The concept remained a simple enlargement of the casbah-style house into a communal type, despite the emphasis on "conform[ity] to Muslim customs."[3]

As it was the first housing project built for Algerians in a prominent location, the Boulevard de Verdun apartment complex enjoyed great publicity. Yet it failed to serve as a model for other complexes in the 1930s, because the predominant characteristics of the "traditional" Algerian house (as studied by the French) dictated that "horizontal" housing met the needs of Algerians better than "vertical" schemes. The choice for low-rise single-family patterns called for ample space, and the subsequent low-cost projects were not built in the center of Algiers, where land was scarce and expensive.[4] The Boulevard de Verdun housing thus remained a unique experiment.

In contrast to the Boulevard de Verdun blocks, the other two schemes realized in the 1930s were horizontal developments located away from the center of Algiers and consisted of attached individual units, each with its own courtyard or small garden behind high walls. Architects Albert Seiller and Marcel Lathuillière designed the Cité Scala (also known as La Madania), on the Clos Salembier hill, near Belcourt. Covering an area of 8 hectares, this settlement was intended to house six thousand residents with diverse social origins, including "the poorest . . . families and bachelors who had just arrived from the countryside." The project was considered an excellent social and political solution to the pressing problem of hygiene, commonly attributed to old indigenous quarters of the city.[5]

Lathuillière's sketch, published in *Chantiers* in 1935, shows a compact settlement nestled against the hill and consisting of cubical, flat-roofed, low-rise houses with very small windows (Fig. 62). The rooflines of the houses are broken by chimneys and, on the larger scale, the domes and minarets of the religious and social centers animate the entire built fabric. A central axis divides the quarter in two and is stepped to conform to the topography. On this axis is a public square faced by a large institutional building with neo-Arabic facades and a courtyard. Lathuillière's idealized drawing borrows from the picturesque Islamic villages of the world's fairs, especially from the 1931 Colonial Exposition with its extensive Tunisian village and from Morocco's *nouvelles médinas* of the 1910s and 1920s. Nevertheless, it also displays a similarity to Tony Garnier's

Figure 62. Albert Seiller and Marcel Lathuillière, housing project in Clos
Salembier, initial scheme, 1935.

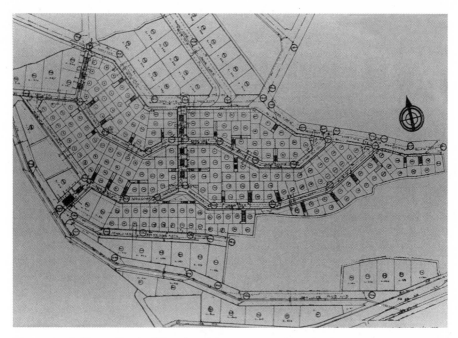

Figure 63. Seiller and Lathuillière, housing project in Clos Salembier, site plan, 1936.

Cité Industrielle in the cubical white masses of the housing, the courtyards, the placement of communal facilities, and the clear hierarchy between main streets and residential ones. If the "arabizing" details were
erased from the drawing, the references to Garnier's vision would be
truly striking in the resulting image—not a surprising influence given
Garnier's reliance on an abstract Mediterranean residential type. Garnier's socialist agenda is absent from Lathuillière's design, however, as
utopia is a tricky notion when building for the colonized.

Seiller and Lathuillière's preliminary design underwent changes as
the construction was executed. The built scheme followed the initial
site planning principles, which adhered to the topography in creating a
terraced settlement pattern (Fig. 63). The main axis with its central spine
of stairs was also kept. The architects diluted the architectural vocabulary by deleting the overt neo-Islamic references and by opting for a
pure and modernist vocabulary. In its final form, the overall appearance
of the Clos Salembier project ends up displaying strong formal affinities
to Garnier's early modernism. Yet the spatial organization of each unit
recalls the rural housing types studied by ethnographers (Fig. 64). With

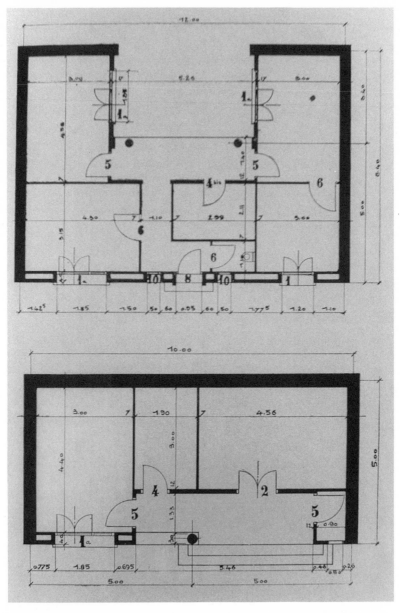

Figure 64. Seiller and Lathuillière, housing project in Clos Salembier, plans of two house types, 1936.

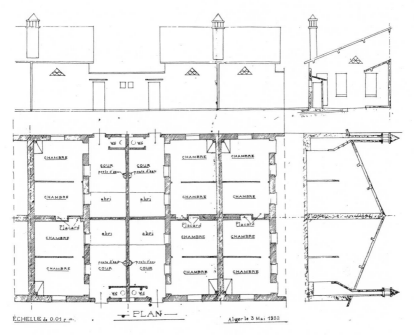

Figure 65. Louis Bonnefour, indigenous housing project in Maison-Carrée, plans, sections, and facades, 1932.

few exceptions, direct communication between rooms was not provided for. The attached single-story houses had prototypical U-shaped plans, with courtyards that gave access to all interior spaces. The overall plan thus recalled an extended family compound, as studied by Thérèse Rivière, for example.

The last housing project from this period is the *cité indigène* in Ste.-Corinne in Maison-Carrée, an industrialized suburb of Algiers. In 1933, an official document recorded two *quartiers insalubres* in Maison-Carrée: a "village of negros" (*village nègre*) and Ste.-Corinne, both deemed "unacceptable." Several measures were taken to reorganize the quarter, in addition to building a new housing project.[6] An early scheme prepared by Louis Bonnefour, an architect practicing in Algiers, proposed a continuous framework of houses with shared side and back walls (Fig. 65). The exterior facades had minimal openings— an entrance door, a bathroom window, and a triangular ornamental window for ventilation. One pitched roof sheltered two units, back to back. Organized by an ever-extendable grid, each unit consisted of two rooms, a court with a water outlet, a separate toilet, and a sheltered area.

Figure 66. Socard, low-rise *cité indigène*, view, 1951.

The rooms opened onto the courtyard, intended as the heart of the house. There was no separate kitchen or facilities for cooking, most likely justified by studies of traditional housing and women's domestic work. The fireplace in the main room could be used for cooking as well as heating the house. Because the water outlet was in the courtyard, accommodations for cooking were not coordinated, setting a precedent for future kitchen designs, which remained problematic.

A couple of years later, in 1935, architects Guérineau and Bastelica reinterpreted this scheme and increased the density by superposing another unit on top of two neighboring units while maintaining the internal organization of each unit. The *cité indigène* in Ste.-Corinne did not resolve the hygiene problem in Maison-Carrée outlined in the 1933 report, but it did introduce a long-lasting typology. As argued by Deluz, the minimal living spaces and the inner private courtyards with water outlets and toilets, derived from "traditional" houses and supposed to answer the needs of Algerians, were later incorporated into high-rise blocks.[7]

Another scheme to shelter two thousand Muslims in the Climat de France area to the west of the casbah also dates from 1934, although its execution had to wait until the end of World War II. By the early 1950s, two new settlements were built here: a "horizontal" development, consisting of parallel rows of two hundred single-story units, and an apartment building complex known as Boucle-Perez. The first, also referred to as Cité Climat de France, was later extended to incorporate ten thousand units. Architect Tony Socard designed the core settlement with groups of two houses whose courts shared a party wall. Constructed in a prefabricated system, they could be reproduced easily (Fig. 66). Each house had two or three rooms under a tiled, pitched roof, and there was

Figure 67.   Bienvenu, Boucle-Perez housing project, overall view, 1952.

a toilet in the courtyard, repeating the pattern set by the Ste.-Corinne housing and referring back to the "traditional" house.[8] The ornamental framing of the windows facing the streets was intended to secure privacy for the family. The bold expression of the geometric patterns generated by the prefabricated elements and the formal qualities of the window and ventilation frames, derived from the rural vernacular, enlivened the facades in a vocabulary familiar to the modernist architecture of Algiers—showing particularly the influence of Auguste Perret. Some communal facilities, such as a clinic and a nursery, were also projected for this neighborhood, in addition to eight shops. The site plan formed

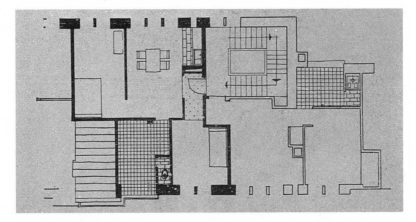

Figure 68. Bienvenu, Boucle-Perez housing project, plan of a unit, 1952.

a grid, with stepped streets which climbed the hill and were interrupted by platforms at individual entrances.

The Boucle-Perez housing block, designed by François Bienvenu and intended for the resettlement of the populations evacuated from the Marine Quarter, was situated on Avenue Ahsan. While it belongs to the same typology as the Boulevard de Verdun project, its relative distance from the casbah freed the architect from stylistic references to the architecture of the old city (Fig. 67). Bienvenu organized the project as one building, a perimeter structure that surrounded a communal court. The court was reached from Avenue Ahsan by a monumental stairway; a new mosque on the other side of the road, but on the same axis as the stairway, provided the community with an essential amenity and created an architectural vista. A secondary street that cut through the lower part of the project and ran parallel to the avenue activated the inner landscape of the complex. The communal court acted as the main focus with shops on the ground floor. The overall symmetry of the composition around the court was broken up by the varying heights of the buildings, the tallest reaching six stories. The density and the "picturesqueness" of the resulting cluster referred to the casbah without mimicking it. The individual units consisted of two or three rooms with a kitchenette in the living room, and a deep and sheltered "patio," intended to duplicate the traditional courtyard, where the toilet was located (Fig. 68).[9]

This configuration, based on adapting a rural pattern into an urban typology, had serious shortcomings. Mainly, it worked against the intended use of the patio as an open-air living room and turned it into a secondary space as an extended bathroom and storage area. In some cases, the residents enclosed it to gain an extra bedroom. Two problems contributed to the transformation of the patio: the fact that the apartments were often inhabited by more people than intended and the poor quality of the plumbing, which stemmed from corners being cut during construction. Despite the obviousness of these deficiencies from the first, the same pattern was repeated in many housing projects.

The Tenure of Mayor Chevallier: 1953–58

"He builds for Arabs . . . he is the mayor of Arabs, the mayor in fez [*chechia*], he does everything for them." Such were the accusations Jacques Chevallier would have to defend himself against continuously during his tenure as mayor between 1953 and 1958.[10] These years marked an intense housing construction program, much of which was geared toward the local populations, in direct response to their ever-deteriorating housing conditions and the growth of squatter settlements around Algiers. Based on more than a personal love for Arabs, however, Chevallier's campaign expressed a policy to secure the future of French rule in Algeria by addressing a crucial problem that, in the mayor's mind, lay at the heart of the unrest among local populations.

In a speech Chevallier delivered during the groundbreaking ceremony of the Diar el-Mahçoul project on the eve of the War of Independence in 1953, he emphasized that the main goal was to assure "the triumph of human dignity, of French liberties, and of the future of French-Muslim civilization." Reiterating Sarrault's proposals to revise and humanize colonial policies and Lyautey's dictum that "each construction site is a battleground," he argued that "France had to build in Algeria, day and night, as much as possible, so that she would not have to worry any more about the political problem." Addressing himself to Maurice Le Maire, the minister of reconstruction and urbanism who laid the first stone of the project, he criticized the French Parliament for developing grandiose political ideas for North Africa without comprehending the real problems, without seeing the *bidonvilles*. For Chevallier, the drama of North Africa was not political, it was social—it was about human dignity. Nonetheless, this social drama would shape the political one if not addressed effectively.[11]

Chevallier's chief architect, Fernand Pouillon, would later recall the acuteness of the mayor's sociopolitical concerns. Pouillon recorded in his *Mémoires* his initial encounter with Chevallier, during which the latter articulated the essence of the problem as he saw it. The mayor also made an urgent call for immediate measures:

> I want to take care of my city. She needs it. First, we must provide shelter for the inhabitants. The crisis is terrible. You will see the *bidonvilles.* Awful. Nothing has been done for these poor people for the last twenty years. . . . Here, everything belongs to Europeans. There is nothing for Muslims and for little people. I would like to build one hundred thousand housing units. Then we will see more clearly.

Pouillon interpreted Chevallier's long-term vision for Algeria as separatism: Algeria should be independent with a federal status, but maintain a cultural and economic link to France.[12] The housing projects built under Chevallier's leadership reveal a wide range of experimentation and a great deal of architectural ambition. The principal architects of the time were Fernand Pouillon and Roland Simounet. The following discussion focuses on their work and glances at several complexes designed by other architects.

FERNAND POUILLON

The year Chevallier became the mayor of Algiers, he named Pouillon the chief architect (*architecte en chef*) of the city and commissioned him to design the Diar el-Mahçoul housing development. First educated at the Ecole des Beaux-Arts in Marseille, then the Beaux-Arts in Paris, Pouillon had established himself in Aix-en-Provence and Marseille; by the early 1950s he had an impressive record of public and private buildings. It was most likely Pouillon's Mediterranean sensibilities and his experience in southern France that had appealed to the mayor. Unattached to any school, Pouillon's architecture represented a modernistic hybrid, learned from the local heritage as well as classical antiquity. His career in Algiers would be prolific and outlive Chevallier's, extending not only into the building frenzy of the Plan de Constantine period, but also well into the postcolonial era.

Diar el-Mahçoul, purposely named in Arabic, means "land of plenty." Its topographically complicated site on the hills above the Jardin d'Essai necessitated terracing 100,000 square meters and constructing massive supporting walls in concrete. The development was divided in two by means of a main road, creating two distinct quarters: *cité confort normal* and *cité simple confort* (Fig. 69). The former was to the south of the corniche; it afforded good views of the bay and was reserved for Europeans. The *simple confort,* designated for the Muslims, faced the highway and the valleys. Although first intended as 1,200 units, in its

Diar el-Mahçoul, *cité simple confort*   Diar es-Saada (second plan)   Diar el-Mahçoul, *cité confort normal*

Figure 69. Fernand Pouillon, Diar el-Mahçoul and Diar es-Saada, view of the entire development, 1957.

completed version Diar el-Mahçoul had 1,454 units, 912 of which were *simple confort*.[13]

Pouillon summarized his design philosophy in his *Mémoires:*

> I work for the pedestrian, not for the airplane captain. . . . I walk around . . . imaginary spaces and I modify them if I do not get the sensations that I want. It is them [the sensations] that come to me first, together with various geometric plans that delimit them: facades, porticos, without forgetting that other important facade formed by floors and gardens. A space is surrounded by walls, grass, trees, pavings. Everything takes on importance: materials, proportions of openings create the complement of an indispensable harmony. The architect, the urbanist, must think like a sculptor, not like a surveyor who distributes buildings alongside a street.[14]

Pouillon thus designed his housing projects with direct reference to cities. He understood the city as a network of public spaces, each public space bearing a different character that could not be explained by clear-cut typologies. A crucial issue for the architect was to establish the right relationship between buildings and public spaces as one defined the other.[15] The ambiance the architect wanted to create in Diar el-Mahçoul was culturally multilayered. In his view, historic Algiers expressed the presence of two cultures strongly: Ottoman and Islamic Spain. In Diar el-Mahçoul, the monumental quality of the walls referred to the Ottoman ramparts, whereas the interior squares, gardens, and patios were inspired from Seville and Granada in their porticos, fountains, and cascades.[16] The architect implicitly stated that the technical ingenuity and design synthesis were French.

The "Islamic" qualities were expressed more strongly in the *simple confort* quarters, where the placement of blocks and the smallness of openings enhance the fortification-like effects and where the public squares—some planted with palm trees—are more numerous (Fig. 70).[17] The terraces on which the public squares are located interlock with each other by means of monumental stairways, fragmenting the site into more intimate zones, and the composition of volumes allows for visually active perspectives. The varying dimensions and heights (two to ten stories) of the blocks and their open staircases enliven the massing of Diar el-Mahçoul further, in both *simple confort* and *confort normal* sections. In addition to the dynamism of the massing, based on a manipulation of cubical volumes, the accessibility of the roofs referred to the architecture of the casbah in a "typological search" for an Algerian habitat.[18] Pouillon continued to explore the potential of rooftops as the women's realm in Climat de France, thus separating men's and women's public spaces and following the pattern set by the old town.

At the completion of Diar el-Mahçoul's construction, it was proudly noted in the architectural press that "nowhere could one feel any impression of repetition, of the sad monotony of barracks." Pouillon's choice of materials played a crucial role in the subtle effects he desired to create. All the walls are of a cream-colored stone, transported from the Fondvieille quarries in Provence.[19]

The communal facilities, such as the markets and the church (now transformed into a mosque), bring a deliberate contrast to the architectural unity of the housing blocks. The market in the *simple confort* quarter is a rectangular space surrounded by a low brick arcade, formed by cross-vaulted units; its center is planted with palm trees (Fig. 71). The market of the *confort normal* area again uses the arch to mark its difference from the residential functions, but here the arch is less accentuated, less "vernacular"; it is a stylized low arch that sits on an orthogonal arcade. The church, the former St.-Jean-Baptiste, was placed in the European section. A concrete structure defined by vertical thin elements, it was covered by four cross-vaults, open at the sides. Its bell tower referred to North African minarets with its square form and tripartite organization. No provisions were made for a mosque.

Figure 70. *(above)* Pouillon, Diar el-Mahçoul, view. Figure 71. *(below)* Pouillon, Diar el-Mahçoul, view of market square, 1957.

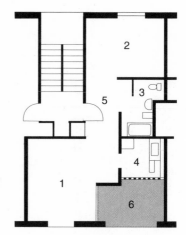

Figure 72. Pouillon, Diar el-Mahçoul, plan of a one-bedroom *confort normal* apartment. (1) living room, (2) bedroom, (3) bathroom, (4) kitchen, (5) entry, (6) patio.

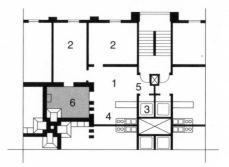

Figure 73. Pouillon, Diar el-Mahçoul, plan of a two-bedroom *type évolutif* apartment. (1) living room, (2) bedroom, (3) water closet, (4) kitchen, (5) entry, (6) patio.

The units ranged from two to six rooms, with the larger ones in the European quarter. In accordance with the search for a new dwelling type that would adapt and modernize the "traditional Algerian house," Pouillon cited its most prominent element, the interior courtyard, as his primary concept. The organization of the apartments incorporated considerable variation. For example, a one-bedroom *confort normal* apartment had an entrance hall, a living room onto which a large patio opened, a separate kitchen, and a separate bathroom with sink, tub, toilet, and bidet (Fig. 72). A two-bedroom *type évolutif* unit in the Muslim quarter, in contrast, had an interior patio without a view, a living room with a kitchenette in one corner, and a Turkish-style toilet with a small sink (Fig. 73).[20] One of the main deficiencies in the housing provided for Algerians was the poor quality of sanitary services, ironically betraying the French concern with reforming the habits of hygiene among the indigenous people. Nonetheless, it was reported at the time that even the most modest apartments were well built; they had good ventilation

Figure 74. Diar el-Mahçoul during the Algerian War.

and light. In contrast to the "horrible aggregates" of *bidonvilles* as well as the "not very brilliant" previous social housing experiments, Diar el-Mahçoul should be considered a success, because it was not as crowded, and it was constructed well.[21]

Pouillon remained ever proud of the "humanism of [his] contemporary 'casbahs.'"[22] The project was also hailed enthusiastically by those who believed in the power of social reforms to overcome the problems France faced in Algeria. According to this view, Diar el-Mahçoul could even serve to pacify its inhabitants: an editorial in *Travaux nord-africains* maintained it was "highly probable that Diar el-Mahçoul would never become a recruitment center for rebellion against the established order." It was acknowledged that the scheme diverged from common practice by taking certain risks, mainly by not entirely segregating the Muslim population. Nothing could be taken for granted, however, and the future would depend on the behavior of the residents, as well as the vigilance of their guardians.[23] In fact, the War of Independence transformed the social atmosphere of the settlement, turning the public squares and gardens into proper battlegrounds and army stations (Fig. 74). For example, on 11 December 1960 about five thousand residents of Diar el-Mahçoul and the Mahieddine *bidonville* descended the hills, joining the demonstrations downtown.[24] Hostilities toward the French had already surfaced much earlier. As reported by *L'Echo d'Alger* in March 1957, a visit by Mayor Chevallier and a group of schoolteachers to the construction site of Diar el-Mahçoul had ended with the "salutations of about one hundred little Muslims who shouted 'Algeria is ours' and who threw stones at the visitors."[25] A couple of years later, military forces would be installed in the school buildings of Diar el-Mahçoul and Diar es-Saada, as well as the high-rise structure in Diar es-Saada.[26]

Pouillon conceived Diar el-Mahçoul together with Diar es-Saada ("land of happiness"), the latter reserved exclusively for Europeans and at a good distance from the former. The construction of an artery between the two projects, however, emphasized the interrelationship of Diar es-Saada and Diar el-Mahçoul in accordance with the new mentality, advocated by Chevallier, that did not separate the indigenous population from the European.[27] Pouillon organized the site of Diar es-Saada along a main pedestrian street that turned into sets of stairs at higher slopes. A series of rectangular and L- and U-shaped blocks of various heights defined communal courts, some paved, some planted with palm trees. A twenty-story tower added to the silhouette. The project housed about eight hundred families. Here Pouillon's prototypes were European, with no reference to Algerian forms and spaces (Fig. 75). The differences from the Muslim housing units were also blatantly evident in the separation of the kitchens from the living quarters and in the design of the bathrooms with full facilities.[28]

In addition to Pouillon's project, there were three other housing types in the area, to the west of the *cité simple confort*. The farthest from the new development was a *bidonville*, a trace of the original pattern before municipal interventions. The second, situated above the shantytown, consisted of minimal barracks for "emergency rehousing" (*recasement d'urgence*). The third, the "transit housing," was formed of two-story longitudinal buildings. Both emergency housing and transit housing were considered temporary solutions to the *bidonville* problem.[29] Therefore, this site revealed all stages and forms of low-cost "mass housing" for Algerians: spontaneous, temporary, and permanent, the last in its most ambitious format. Farther away, although still part of the same complex, were the "better" collective housing developments for Europeans.

Pouillon also designed the most spectacular and extensive project of Chevallier's tenure, the Climat de France complex. On a sloped site to the west of the casbah with views toward the Mediterranean, its

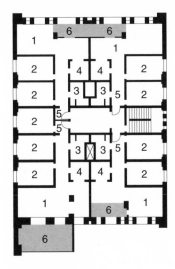

Figure 75. Pouillon, Diar es-Saada, plan of two- and three-bedroom units. (1) living room, (2) bedroom, (3) bathroom, (4) kitchen, (5) entry, (6) patio.

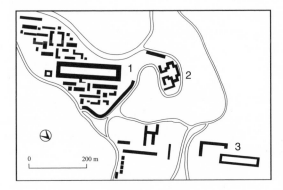

Figure 76. Pouillon, Climat de France and vicinity, site plan. (1) Pouillon, Climat de France, (2) Bienvenu, Cité Boucle-Perez, (3) Simounet, Daure, and Béri, Cité Carrière Jaubert.

most memorable structure, the 200 Colonnes, defines its focus. The site is like an island, surrounded by major roads—Boulevard Mohamed Harchouche to the west defining the highest boundary, Avenue Ahsan marking the lowest area to the north, and Boulevard el-Kattar to the east. This tight circumscription allowed Pouillon to treat the development as a small town with its own hierarchy of streets, squares, monuments, and residential zones.

Pouillon conceived the 4,000-unit development covering an area of 30 hectares as a conglomeration of distinct nodes, each with its own streets and open squares (Fig. 76). The northern boundary was fixed by an Aaltoesque building whose curvilinear lines followed the contour of Avenue Ahsan. The pedestrians were to walk between the buildings (and sometimes cut through the buildings), following narrow, often

stepped, paths interrupted by paved and planted public squares of varying sizes. The two main arteries ran perpendicular to the slope in the
northeast-southwest orientation and connected Avenue Ahsan with the
200 Colonnes and Boulevard el-Kattar with the second largest plaza.
Lateral connections were provided mainly from the east. The blocks
were carefully placed with respect to each other to allow for uninterrupted perspectives to the sea. They were grouped in four types: linear
buildings, those with interior courtyards, a series of buildings linked to
each other, and single towers. Like in Diar el-Mahçoul, Pouillon varied
building sizes greatly and sought for a compositional balance in the
placement of large and small structures. Terracing of the terrain to manipulate its 25 percent natural slope helped animate the massing.[30]

The siting of the Climat de France was applauded by Jacques Berque
(writing on housing issues in Algiers at the time), who labeled it "geo-
logical urbanism" because of its sculptural treatment of large blocks. He
suggested that Pouillon's approach to landscape, characterized by the
"petrification and crystallization" of the site, paralleled the former aspects of *médinas,* which had evolved spontaneously. The resulting image is so multivalent that G. Geenen, A. Loeckx, and N. Naert argue
that there are three distinct images: viewed from the northeast, Climat
de France evokes the image of a new casbah; from the northwest it re-
sembles a small fortified town; and approaching the development closer
from the northwest, it appears like actual fortifications.[31]

The massing and architectural vocabulary of Climat de France was
similar to Pouillon's experiments in Diar el-Mahçoul: his crisp, geometric volumes were pierced by small modular openings (windows and ventilation holes); the bold expression of bricks and stones enhanced the
architectonic qualities of the facades; the rectilinear arcades of the
ground floors complemented the series of square openings that defined
the roof terraces. Although not acknowledged by Pouillon, the influence of Italian rationalist architecture is clear on this formal language,
making the architect a pioneer neorationalist. As such, he is a predecessor to Aldo Rossi, whose work would display a striking similarity to
Pouillon's fifteen years later. Pouillon's affiliation with Italian rationalism did not carry political undertones, but should be understood within
the context of his broad search for a contemporary Mediterranean architecture that brought together modernism with local forms, needs,
and sensibilities.

The apartment units of Climat de France can be grouped into three
main categories: "double-exposure type," "single-exposure type," and
"particular solutions" that also included "buildings with patios."[32]

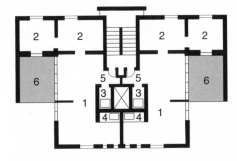

Figure 77. Pouillon, Climat de France, plan of a "double-exposure type" unit with two bedrooms. (1) living room, (2) bedroom, (3) water closet, (4) kitchenette, (5) entry, (6) patio.

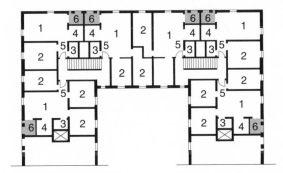

Figure 78. Pouillon, Climat de France, plan of apartments in a "patio-type" building. (1) living room, (2) bedroom, (3) water closet, (4) kitchenette, (5) entry, (6) patio.

Units with double exposure (40 to 50 square meters) occupied the entire width of the building, and a staircase served two units on every floor (Fig. 77). In general, the units consisted of one or two bedrooms, a living room with an open kitchen corner, and a toilet-shower closet immediately off a small entry hall. Units with single exposure were grouped in fours around a "sanitary core." Smaller than the first type (about 30 square meters), some had one bedroom and a living room, while others accommodated the two functions in a single space. The kitchen was again in a corner of the living room and the toilet-shower area off the entrance. Of the third type, the "particular solutions," the "patio scheme" allowed for the grouping of twelve apartments around an inner court and facilitated cross-ventilation (Fig. 78).

With few exceptions, each unit was equipped with a deep balcony protected by a perforated wall, by now the customary substitute for the courtyard. Aside from providing privacy and shade, these walls made a formal reference to *mashrabiyyas* and integrated an element of the "traditional" urban house into the facades. The arrangement of the entrance hall so that direct views were obstructed from the main door into the living spaces by the careful placement of the toilet-shower closet was another attempt to respond to local forms and customs.[33]

Figure 79. Pouillon, 200 Colonnes, overall view.

In the center of Climat de France sat the 200 Colonnes, a vast rect-angular housing block with a monumental agora, 233 meters long and 38 meters wide, as its court; the similarity of its size to the Palais Royale in Paris was a matter of pride (Fig. 79).[34] The courtyard was surrounded by a three-story-high colonnade made up of two hundred square col-umns that gave the project its name. In addition to apartments, the complex was to shelter two hundred shops and act as the heart of the entire settlement, considered an "absolutely autonomous" area com-plete with its own educational, commercial, and health services.[35]

Aside from the obvious references to Hellenistic agoras, Roman fora, the Place des Vosges in Paris, and the Court of Myrtles and the Court of Lions in the Palace of the Alhambra, the 200 Colonnes also displayed several obscure influences. With this building, Pouillon admittedly turned away from the "charming" effects he had achieved in his former projects in order to create a "more profound, more austere plasticity." He thus moved from the "arabesques of Algiers" and toward the south, to the Sahara, the towns of Mzab and the ruins of el-Goléa and Timi-moun—all of which, he wrote later, gave him a lesson in formal auster-ity, as well as a new sensibility with numbers and proportions.[36] Greatly revered by modernist artists and architects, the architecture of the Mzab is characterized by its simple rectilinear geometries and blank walls; furthermore, the two villages Pouillon specifically refers to have rectilinear, "rational" street plans.

Two years before Pouillon started working on 200 Colonnes, he had visited Isfahan, a very different Islamic city. Isfahan's seventeenth-century Maydan-i Shah had made a great impression on him.[37] Maydan-i Shah is an introverted public space, surrounded by a continuous two-story colonnade. Its longitudinal axis linked the Masjid-i Shah, built at the same time as the Maydan, with the preexisting markets. The Maydan has two axes in the other direction; the major one connects the Lutfullah Mosque to the Ali Qapu Palace, while the other axis simply opens into the existing fabric on each side. The axiality in Pouillon's "maydan" echoes this pattern: the main axis, marked with hypostyle hall-like entrances, crosses the court lengthwise while the short axis is off center, as in Isfahan. The other gates to the court do not define axial connections and, devoid of columns, assume a secondary role.

The main entrances to the 200 Colonnes (on the shorter facades) were delineated by protruding propylaea that mirrored a fragment of the interior colonnade on the outside. Monumental stairs adjusted the gates on the longitudinal facade to the sloping site, meanwhile enhancing the differentiation between entrances. The variation in their size and monumentality alluded to the two scales the project combined: urban and residential. The contrast between the exterior and the interior facades turned the building inside out, making the interior public and urban. With its small, receded openings and dominant planar quality, the exterior facade made reference to city walls—a theme dear to Pouillon, as observed in Diar el-Mahçoul. In addition, the treatment of the facade as a modular tapestry was inspired by the carpets made in southern Algeria,[38] and the emphasis on crisp geometry evoked the flavor of the casbah. The inner facade, in contrast, was and remained the "austere" and open one, its public nature expressed by the colonnade behind which the vaulted entries to the shops were lined.

The roof terrace was a major feature of the 200 Colonnes. Pouillon borrowed the concept from the casbah rooftops, appropriated by women as their own public and private spaces. He made the stairs climbing up to the roof particularly narrow to emphasize the domestic and private nature of the passageway and as a reminder of the stepped streets of the old town. The immense roof terrace—dotted with small, domed washhouse pavilions placed at regular intervals—was intended as a place for work and socialization for the women who lived in the building. The drying laundry would add a colorful background to the picturesque scene created by groups of women and children. The women of 200

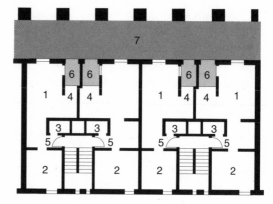

Figure 80. Pouillon, 200 Colonnes, plan of units. (1) living room, (2) bedroom, (3) water closet, (4) kitchenette, (5) entry, (6) patio, (7) public hallway.

Colonnes, however, refused to climb up the narrow stairs with basketfuls of laundry and, despite the inadequacy of the provisions, chose to wash their clothes in their apartments. To dry the laundry, they projected rods from the windows, thus adding unintentionally to an atmosphere of "authenticity," so cherished by Pouillon.

The units of 200 Colonnes were of the "double-exposure"/one-bedroom type, according to the formula described earlier (Fig. 80). Albert-Paul Lentin, a critic of French colonial policies in Algeria, contrasted the "futurist ridicule" (*tantinet futurist*) of the building's exterior appearance with the design of the apartments, clearly conceived for the "underdeveloped." He described them as having "two rooms with low ceilings (2 meters high), one 2 by 3 meters, the other 3 by 3 meters large, a tiny kitchen, a water closet, narrow windows." [39]

Pouillon defended his scheme not only as architecture but also as agent of social reform catering to the Muslim, who had been acknowledged until then as only an *indigène*—a term loaded with "pejorative and humiliating" undertones. The architect proudly announced that here, "for the first time [and] thanks to Mayor Chevallier, Algerians would live in a real city." Intended for the lowest income groups, 200 Colonnes met all the requirements for a monumentality commonly reserved for official buildings of prestige. Pouillon himself referred to this building as "the monument of 'Climat de France'" and argued that he had "installed men in a monument . . . perhaps for the first time during modern times." Furthermore, he continued, "these men, the poorest in poor Algeria, understood it. It is they who baptised it 'Two Hundred Columns.'" [40] In tune with Mayor Chevallier's paternalistic benevolence aimed at engraving a sense of pride in the residents, Pouillon saw himself bringing a new urbanity to this chaotic fringe of Algiers.

It was reported repeatedly that the apartments in Climat de France seemed like "paradise" compared to the shantytowns. Relying on this assumption, an administrative report quoted by Lentin stated that "the settled, well-housed population of 'Climat de France' is less fidgety than that of the neighboring casbah." Lentin ironically noted, however, that this population had decided to "move" too, and had joined the rebelling crowds. To cite one incident, sixty people from the 200 Colonnes were killed by the French forces in the massive demonstration on 11 December 1960.[41]

ROLAND SIMOUNET

Pouillon's sweeping approach to architecture and urban design and his radical interventionism vis-à-vis site conditions present a contrast to the architecture of Roland Simounet. Simounet's responsive and imaginative buildings gained him respectable status and a place among Chevallier's leading architects, despite his relative youth and his blatant disapproval of the aesthetic sensibilities of Pouillon, the mayor's chief architect.

Simounet was greatly inspired by the work of Le Corbusier, but he was also a careful student of Algerian architectural culture, with a focus on the Algerian vernacular. His architecture was shaped by the lessons he learned from European modernism, his respect for the site, and his inquiry into vernacular residential forms (including squatter houses) and patterns of daily life and ritual.[42] In a retrospective evaluation in 1980 that maintained the fervor of the debate of the 1950s positing Pouillon and Simounet as polar opposites, Pierre-André Emery, another Algiers-based architect of Le Corbusier's school, criticized Pouillon's urbanism by suggesting that he could have learned a thing or two from the contextual approach of the turn-of-the-century Austrian architectural theorist Camillo Sitte and dismissed Pouillon's architecture for being "very personal" and not relating either to the site or to the local context. Simounet's work, in contrast, stood out with its "plastic language that had evolved *naturally,* allowing [the architect] to resolve new problems *simply*"—in the words of Jean de Maisonseul, another member of the same circle.[43]

Simounet's first housing project was a collaboration with Parisian architects A. Daure and H. Béri, who had won a competition to design the vast complex of La Montagne, intended solely for Muslims in 1955.[44] Located above Bel-Air and to the west of Maison-Carrée on the hill of the same name, the settlement consisted of two parts: "col-

lective" housing (walk-up apartment blocks) on the summit and individual houses on the slopes (Fig. 81). Communal facilities, namely a
market, shops, baths, and "Moorish cafés," constituted the rest of the
program.[45]

The architecture of La Montagne displayed Simounet's respect for
the customs and habits of the future residents, especially in the design
of individual units. The apartments in the longitudinal blocks of the collective housing had an unusual plan type, with two loggias facing opposite directions (Fig. 82). The living room (with a kitchenette) was sandwiched between the loggias, and the two bedrooms were interconnected,
resulting in a peripheral circulation pattern. The architect separated the
elementary functions that occurred in the courts of the "traditional"
houses: the narrower loggia in the back acted as the entry zone, whereas
the front loggia housed the water closet. Cross-ventilation, "indispen-
sible in Algeria," was provided in all spaces. The tiny kitchenette, however, squeezed in a corner of the living room, was not adequate for
cooking for large families.

The architectural conception of the individual house stemmed from
the "independence of the entrance from the kitchen and the patio—
both reserved for women."[46] Units with one or two rooms were placed
in rows, and the topography of the site was utilized to energize the overall massing of the settlement. The entrance of each unit was through a
small court, to which a general room, the bathroom, and the *abri* (a
sheltered but not enclosed space where the kitchen was placed) opened
(Fig. 83). Separated from the entrance, the garden became a private
place. In the larger units, a second room, in line with the first, connected
to the garden. The "horizontal" housing in La Montagne was developed on the basis of a prefabricated construction system consisting of
load-bearing walls and double-shelled (ventilating) vaults. Responding
to the irregular topography, the siting of the rows allowed for the vaults
to be oriented in three directions, thereby introducing a subtle plasticity
to the overall composition. Two reasons dominated the choice of vaults:
to evoke the picturesque character of indigenous forms and to discourage vertical additions that would increase densities and damage the
unity of the nuclear family. In the housing discourse of the time, overcrowding and cohabitation were considered "destroyers of family life."[47]

The architecture of the shops and workshops echoed that of the
"horizontal" housing in its attempt to create an "indigenous" environment (Fig. 84). Rows of shops under vaults repeated a regular pattern
that accommodated prefabricated construction techniques in four types
responding to different needs. Capitalizing on his knowledge of local

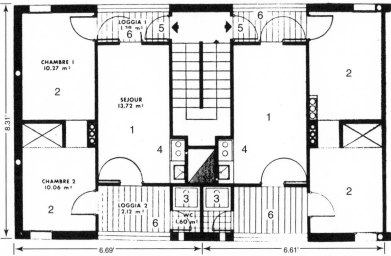

Figure 81. *(above)* Roland Simounet, A. Daure, and H. Béri, Cité La Montagne, model, 1955. Figure 82. *(below)* Simounet, Daure, and Béri, Cité La Montagne, plan of units in an apartment block, 1955. (1) living room, (2) bedroom, (3) water closet, (4) kitchenette, (5) entry, (6) loggia.

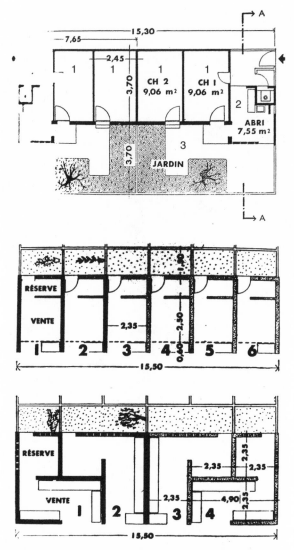

Figure 83. *(above)* Simounet, Daure, and Béri, Cité
La Montagne, plan of low-rise unit, 1955. (1) room,
(2) shelter, (3) garden. Figure 84. *(below)* Simounet,
Daure, and Béri, Cité La Montagne, plan of shops,
1955.

lifestyles, Simounet created sitting areas for informal socialization in front of shops, as well as inside some, and gave the majority of shops a private court in the back.[48]

"Horizontal" housing, now considered most appropriate for the most recent immigrants to Algiers because they had the strongest ties to rural living, was also envisioned for Cité Dessoliers in the Ste.-Corinne quarter of Maison-Carrée. Roland Simounet's contribution to this settlement, commissioned to several teams of architects, was a cellular scheme that attempted to relate to the slight slope of the site. Consisting of two rooms, courtyard, kitchen, *abri*, and water closet, the individual unit duplicated many characteristics of La Montagne.[49]

Despite their problematic initial collaboration, in 1957 Simounet worked with Daure and Béri on another housing project, the Cité Carrière Jaubert, named after the stone quarries nearby.[50] Carrière Jaubert was part of an experiment in "transit housing" to provide temporary shelter for the residents of demolished *bidonvilles*, who would eventually be moved to newly built permanent housing projects. Considered as a "transit hotel," a caravansary around a vast courtyard, the complex would shelter sixteen hundred apartments in a tripartite composition. Of this ambitious scheme, only the central unit was realized, reducing the original program by half.[51]

The result was a huge, fortresslike structure, a long rectangular building around a narrow courtyard that maintained its references to a large caravansary (Fig. 85). The regularity of the plan was deceptive, as the architects used several devices to animate the massing. The building adhered to the topographic conditions, with the heights of different sections varying along with the sloping site. The fragmented silhouette attempted to inscribe the building into the site in a manner reminiscent of the old stone quarries.[52]

The units were kept small, with the majority consisting of two spaces, an 18-square-meter living room and a 7-square-meter loggia. Simounet's drawings of the interiors revealed the architect's vision of life in these units, where nothing was permanent and the sparse furnishings were transportable (Fig. 86). Two variations accommodated larger families: a "twin" unit, formed by combining two neighboring units, and a duplex. Every unit received light and cross-ventilation. There were, however, no washing and toilet facilities in individual apartments, but a communal lavatory could be reached by means of the back corridor, the latter considered an inner "street" that periodically opened up onto a "communal space." The concentration of hygienic facilities

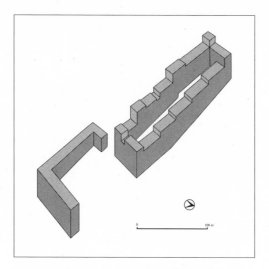

Figure 85. Simounet, Daure, and Béri, Carrière
Jaubert housing, axonometric view.

stemmed from economic considerations but also fit the idea of a caravansary and could be easily justified as communal places derived from
local culture. References to traditional living patterns were reiterated by
drawing parallels to the public fountain and the bath, the *hammam*. Issues of privacy related to gender differences—a recurrent theme in the
discourse on the Algerian home life—were totally ignored.[53]

Following his architectural collaborations, Simounet had the opportunity to work independently on a housing project, the Djenan el-
Hasan. Widely published and discussed, this project established Simounet's reputation as one of the most talented architects in Algiers. In the
vicinity of Climat de France, on the southern slope of M'Kacel Valley,
the 210 units of Djenan el-Hasan were intended to rehouse temporarily
one thousand former residents of the demolished *bidonvilles* in the area.
Confident in his knowledge of the residents' lifestyles and former living
conditions, and experienced in low-cost housing issues, Simounet accepted the challenges of the project—the difficulty of the site and the
economic restrictions—with great enthusiasm.[54]

The scheme, described as "between vertical and horizontal," accommodated eight hundred inhabitants per hectare, compactly settling as a
series of terraces on the steep slope of the terrain (Figs. 87 and 88).[55] The
superimposed uniform, vaulted units reinterpreted, rationalized, aes-
theticized, and synthesized the lessons Simounet had derived from the

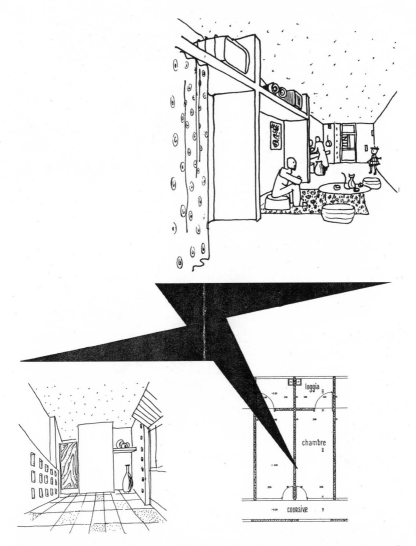

Figure 86.   Simounet, Daure, and Béri, Carrière Jaubert housing, sketches and plan of units, 1957.

casbah and the *bidonville*. The overall image borrowed at the same time from the architecture of Le Corbusier, in particular the 1949 Roq et Rob project in Cap St. Martin—a particularly relevant scheme in the "Mediterranean" tradition and on a dramatically steep site. Rationalizing the street network of the casbah, Simounet developed here a complex circulation system that responded to the site and opened up to communal

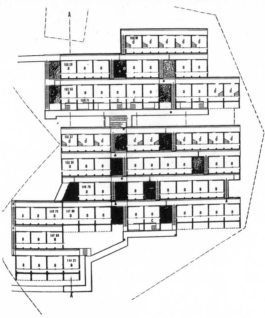

Figure 87. *(above)* Simounet, Djenan el-Hasan, overall view, 1959.
Figure 88. *(below)* Simounet, Djenan el-Hasan, partial site plan, 1958.

spaces. It consisted of two interconnected networks: single-level paths and stepped paths. Horizontally laid out paths on leveled terraces served the individual units, as well as separating them from the concrete foundation walls of the neighboring terraces above. Stepped paths in staggering rows ran perpendicular to the horizontal ones and the contours of the land. A public patio was placed next to each staircase for ventilation and good views. All existing trees on the site were preserved and "productive trees" (mainly fig trees) were planted in the communal zones.

Siting principles and the circulation system made the units "strictly independent" and gave them "absolutely uninterrupted views." A strictly modular system, derived from Le Corbusier's Modulor, organized the complex and the two types of apartments. The first type consisted of a single room, about 12.4 square meters large, and a loggia of 4 square meters; a water spigot and the toilet were located on the loggia. Each room boasted "a well-lighted corner" and "permanent ventilation" from the French windows (*porte-fenêtres*) that connected the living room to the loggia, and the door that opened to the alleyway behind. The second type was a duplex. Its upper level replicated all characteristics of the first type, while its lower level was made up of a single room; an interior stairway linked the two stories.

The load-bearing walls in concrete masonry blocks carried the vaulted, tile-covered roof. The blocks were deemed to provide good thermal insulation and resistance to rainwater and wind. On both the interior and the exterior, the walls were whitewashed. The sanitary system was enclosed within the construction, with access doors at the top for easy repairs. This avoided the previously common practice of breaking open the walls to get at the pipes.[56]

Simounet's apartment designs recalled closely the ones he had developed for Cité Carrière Jaubert, both projects intended for the most destitute members of the Algerian population. Aside from the gridlock of their economic situation as recent immigrants to the city, these people were confronted with a new lifestyle, in their encounters not only with urban colonial culture, but also with an Islamic urban culture. As recorded over and over by French ethnographic studies, life and the forms that accommodated life were drastically different in the Algerian countryside—a phenomenon whose correspondence to the differences between Arabs (urban) and Berbers (rural) was insistently stressed. The housing developments of Djenan el-Hasan and Carrière Jaubert focus on this difference as well as the transitional situation of the immigrants which Simounet had studied in the *bidonvilles*.[57] fitted within a strict matrix, the residential units themselves resemble nomadic structures. They provide basic shelter, and their grouping reinterprets and regularizes the "organic" quality of *gourbi*s. In these projects Simounet developed a new dwelling type distinct from the "horizontal" schemes and the multistory blocks with apartments essentially based on European precedents. Despite their intended "temporary" status, the buildings embodied a powerful permanency due to their architectural imagery and construction techniques—in contrast, for example, to the single-story barracks next to Diar el-Mahçoul built as temporary housing, which seemed ready for dismantling at any time.

Another issue raised by Djenan el-Hasan and Carrière Jaubert is the degree of commitment to the "civilizing mission" of French colonialism. A consideration of the sanitary facilities in these projects—as well as all other projects to varying degrees—reveals conflicts between enforcing hygienic reforms and considering economics. Given that the sanitary amenities of indigenous housing had been a major point of criticism by the French, the provisions in the housing built for new immigrants cast doubts on the sincerity of efforts to improve the living conditions of local populations. In view of the resulting hygienic facilities (bathrooms and kitchens, but especially bathrooms), the elaborate lip service paid to the "customs and needs" of "indigenous people" seems in conflict with the agenda to "civilize." The residents were persistently denied the most basic technological comforts of European "civilization" in the very projects intended to ease their transition to a better life.

Like Carrière Jaubert and other "transitional" housing projects, Djenan el-Hasan eventually became permanent shelter. Nevertheless, lack of space had turned into a major issue immediately after completion of the settlement. According to projected figures at the time of the development's conception, an average of five people would live in each unit in Djenan el-Hasan.[58] Mainly due to the continuous flow of new immigrants joining their extended families, this number turned out to be much higher. As the tight site plan did not allow for any incremental growth—an essential characteristic of squatter housing—the only answer to lack of space was to turn the loggia into living quarters. This intervention robbed each apartment of its breathing space and transformed both the quality of the well-lighted and well-ventilated interior and the plastic integrity and aesthetic rhythm of the exterior. The numerous materials employed in the later additions were chosen for their cost and availability, rather than in light of the original construction. The result was an overall patchy appearance that again disrupted the formal purity of Simounet's design. Finally, to make up for the loss of the loggias, the residents installed horizontal rods from their windows to dry their laundry, pushing the limits of their units into the open air, as the residents of 200 Colonnes and other new housing projects had done.[59]

CHEVALLIER'S OTHER ARCHITECTS:
A SAMPLE

Mayor Chevallier's massive campaign for housing created opportunities for numerous architects, some based in Algeria, others in France. Restricted by economic considerations, focused on quantities, and built in haste, these projects were not memorable architectural creations and their success in providing decent living conditions was limited. However, their impact on the city of Algiers was significant. They played an important role in the shaping of the outskirts of Algiers in a process that recalls many cities throughout the world. Islands of new structures surrounded the city and contrasted with the congested architectural pluralism of Algiers proper. Because each housing project was treated as an individual unit without much consideration of its context and its links to neighboring settlements or the city itself, the resulting conglomeration lacked an urban cohesiveness. The projects themselves displayed a range of experimentation in their massing, architectural vocabulary, and unit plans.

The majority of housing complexes were high-rise *ensembles,* with low-rise projects few and far between. In the Cité Dessoliers in Maison-Carrée, the team of Barthe, Cazalet, and Solivères designed 250 "cells" of one, two, or three rooms that were covered by cement vaults and organized in six groups (Fig. 89). Each unit boasted a simple kitchen corner and a patio where the water closet/shower was located. The stated goals were "light, comfort, independence, and low cost."[60] Architects Georges Bize and Jacques Ducollet, responsible for another six hundred units in the same location, stated proudly that every unit was equipped with electricity, water, and sewage lines. These houses were "evidently very simple," yet they "conformed perfectly to the needs of the occupants, who, being used to *gourbi*s, needed to adapt to an improved installation little by little." The dominant "simplicity" called for some justification and it was argued apologetically that while cost played an important role in the outcome, the Dessoliers housing still displayed the will of the authorities to do away with the "horrible plague of *bidonvilles.*"[61]

The Groupe des Cyclamens, an apartment complex in Clos Salembier, was organized as four individual but attached blocks. Louis Bérthy (whose site-abstract project for a *cité indigène* in 1939 was a horizontal scheme that quoted many aspects of local architecture) created here one hundred *type évolutif* units in six-story walk-ups, with four units per story in each block (Figs. 90 and 91). The unit sizes varied from one to

Figure 89. *(above)* Barthe, Cazalet, and Solivères, Cité Dessoliers, overall view, 1954. Figure 90. *(below)* Bérthy, Groupe des Cyclamens, perspective drawing, 1957.

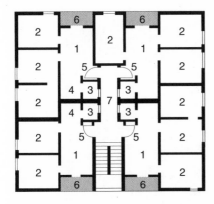

Figure 91. Bérthy, Groupe des Cyclamens, typical floor plan. (1) living room, (2) bedroom, (3) water closet, (4) kitchenette, (5) entry, (6) loggia, (7) public hallway.

four bedrooms, with three-bedroom apartments constituting the majority.[62] These were minimalist units that incorporated the few features determined to conform to the needs of "evolutionary" indigenous families: kitchenette in a corner of the living room, a loggia now reduced to a width of 1 meter (thus unusable as an extension of the living space and offering no privacy), and a water closet about 2 square meters that included a toilet, sink, and shower. The facades expressed the floor plans in a straightforward manner, the recesses of the balconies creating light and shade contrasts; a rectilinear geometry, generated by the prefabricated construction system, dominated the scheme. The architectural vocabulary and the massing aspired to Pouillon's principles in nearby Diar el-Mahçoul.[63]

Groupe des Cyclamens's east-west orientation was dictated by Gérald Hanning, the director of the Plan d'Urbanisme, to harmonize with the forthcoming Cité de Nador. Cité de Nador was built on a site cleared of squatter houses in 1955 and connected by a new road to the Route de la Femme Sauvage.[64] The architects in charge—Mauri, Pons, Gomis, and Tournier-Olliver—opted for two "bars," 100 and 72 meters long, respectively, forming between them a wide angle open to the south (Fig. 92). A predecessor of the Plan de Constantine schemes, this was perhaps the most uniform, and therefore the most economical, of all the housing projects realized under Chevallier. Each of the sixty-two units here was the same; about 35 square meters large, it consisted of a living room, a bedroom, a loggia/drying room (*loggia-séchoir*), a kitchenette, and a water closet.[65]

A review of the projects designed during the 1950s reveals a pattern shaped by adherence to a short checklist of prerequisites presumed essential. In the Cité des Eucalyptus at the border of Hussein-Dey and Maison-Carrée, architects Bize and Ducollet prioritized "maximum

Figure 92. Mauri, Pons, Gomis, and Tournier-Olliver, Cité de Nador, view, 1958.

economy, solidity, and comfort" for the 600 units they designed (Fig. 93). Of these units, 450 were accommodated in longitudinal blocks placed in rows, whereas 150 were duplexes around communal court-yards. The long blocks bordered the main road connecting Algiers to el-Harrache; the duplexes were in the back. By placing the blocks per-pendicular to each other, the architects created a hierarchy of public open spaces, interspersed with public facilities.

The 40-square-meter individual units in the higher blocks of the Cité des Eucalyptus repeated a similar configuration, the formula that had evolved from a consensus on the lifestyle of indigenous people: the combined living/cooking space opened to a terrace and a minimal bath-room space (in this case 0.75 square meter for a toilet, sink, and shower). The duplex units had a double-height living room and a kitchen-bath-room combination on the ground level and two bedrooms on the sec-ond floor (Fig. 94). A major difference from the earlier schemes was the placement of the bathroom inside the unit as opposed to its former lo-cation in the loggia, a change that stemmed in part from the diminished size of the latter. The toilet and the kitchen now became a unit (with the toilet door opening directly into the kitchen) in a most unhygienic combination. Perhaps it was again the new dimensions of the loggia that led the architects to make provisions for privacy in the Cité des Eucalyp-

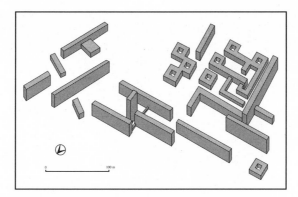

Figure 93. Bize and Ducollet, Cité des Eucalyptus, axonometric view.

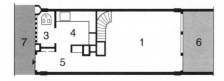

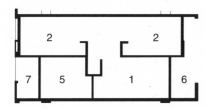

Figure 94. Bize and Ducollet, Cité des Eucalyptus, plan and section of low-rise unit. (1) living room, (2) bedroom, (3) bathroom, (4) kitchenette, (5) entry, (6) patio, (7) public hallway.

tus by including high screens that allowed for "correct ventilation" while satisfying the Muslims' "taste for apartments sealed off from the exterior." [66]

On Rue Léon-Roches at the periphery of Climat de France, Cité Taine E was built specifically for the families whose houses were expropriated in the Marine Quarter. Architects Daure, Béri, Chauveau, and Magrou again relied on the template devised for loggias, kitchens, and bathrooms. Reliance on prefabrication validated the construction of a simple rectangular scheme, a north-south oriented "bar" that was 153 meters long and 11.15 meters wide. Twelve stories high, Taine E provided 284 apartments of mostly three rooms apiece and an average of 47 square meters. Inspired by the social amenities Le Corbusier had in-

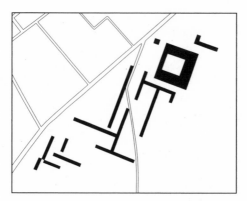

Figure 95. Nicholas Di Martino, Cité des
Asphodèles, site plan.

corporated into his Unité d'Habitation, this project designated the top
floor for a nursery school and children's playground.[67]

Thin, longitudinal blocks that could be placed with relative facility
and without constructing ample terraces on the hills of Algiers became
increasingly popular in the late 1950s. The form also catered to prefabricated construction systems efficiently and allowed for units to have
cross-ventilation, if at times through the communal corridors—the "inner streets." In the Cité des Asphodèles on the northwestern hills of
Algiers, Nicholas Di Martino attached the bars to each other, creating
T-shaped buildings and open spaces between them that were meant to
be shared by the residents (Fig. 95).[68] The facades were enlivened in a
pattern that had become customary: the depth of the loggias provided
a shadow contrast and the lattice-blocks of the water closets alluded to
local architectural forms and geometric ornaments.

As Deluz argued, Chevallier's "humanist urbanism" followed in the
footsteps of Marshal Lyautey, who had summarized his philosophy in
several memorable remarks, among them "urbanism must be implanted
first in the hearts of men."[69] Founded on the belief that urbanism could
be used as a tool to reshape people's lives and, in the colonial context,
gain the confidence of the local people by improving their living conditions, Chevallier's approach was considered the humanistic alternative
to militaristic policies. Innumerable statements about the assumed
power of good environments on people make it plain that the underlying agenda for the housing projects in Algeria was the pacification and
control of colonized people by meeting one of their basic needs. In

meeting this need, Chevallier, together with his architects and urban planners, had attempted to understand the sociocultural structures of Algerian people and address them in their projects. To do so, they turned to the discourse on the "traditional" urban forms, the Algerian house, the Algerian family, and the Algerian woman—a discourse whose history was almost as long as the French occupation. By appropriating, taming, and rationalizing the domestic settings and their urban environments, the architects attempted to enter a realm of Algerian life whose obstinate impenetrability had become a source of colonial anguish.

Realities of the Algerian War proved that housing or other kinds of social reforms would not weaken the struggle for independence. Resistance to colonial rule found shelter even in the most thoughtfully designed new housing projects. Faced with the failure of social engineering and shaped by a more technocratic mentality, the next wave of construction in Algiers focused obsessively on numbers and ignored the humanistic dimensions of Chevallier's tenure.

Plan de Constantine: 1958–61

The urban interventions done according to the provisions of the Plan de Constantine were fragmentary with clearly delineated zones, among them the ZUPs (*zones à urbaniser en priorité*), which would find their way to France. Fifty thousand housing units per year were projected, as compared to the eighteen thousand built in 1958. This quantity dictated that the form of housing be large blocks exclusively. The units designed for Muslims would "transpose the traditional houses onto vertical plans," in conformity with previous experiments.[70]

The pressing issue was the uncontrollable expansion of *bidonvilles*. The Cité Mahieddine, on a bulldozed shantytown, would consist of eighteen hundred units, in eleven blocks reserved for the fourteen hundred families that had resided in the *bidonville,* and three towers whose occupants would come from elsewhere. The huge project occupying a 7-hectare area was delegated to the architectural team of Gouyon, Bellisent, Régeste, Toillon, Dupin, and Goraguer. The two existing villas in the center, classified as "historic monuments," were preserved together with their gardens. A grid organized the site plan; the buildings were designed as simple "bars," with a single longitudinal unit occupying the entire width. Public hallways running along the entire back facades led to stairways and, in higher buildings, to elevators.[71]

Two years later, only five hundred units were completed. Yet *L'Echo d'Alger* praised, more than anything else, the "human and social" dimension of the enterprise. Residents of the *bidonville*, temporarily housed in barracks in Clos Salembier and Diar el-Keif, would now be transported to their new residences, the "hearth of [their] dreams," in army trucks.[72]

The team of Gouyon, Bellisent, and Régeste also undertook the design of Cité Faizi on Route Nationale 24, about 4 kilometers from Algiers. The four-story, 800-unit blocks repeated the bar formula, the linear blocks placed at right angles to each other. The one- and two-bedroom units were accessible once again from a back corridor (Fig. 96). The loggia had diminished considerably in size and although it was accessible from both the living room and the kitchen, because of its location off the kitchen, it served as an extension to that room. The total separation of kitchens and bathrooms—the latter much larger and better equipped than those of the earlier schemes—showed an improvement in sanitary provisions.[73]

Gouyon, Bellisent, and Régeste quickly became known as experts on low-cost housing for Algerians. They were commissioned to design the Cité des Dunes in Maison-Carrée, in collaboration with a fourth architect, Brusson. Taking advantage of the flat site, the architects exaggerated the bar scheme to its limits. The two blocks that ran parallel to each other were immense walls twelve stories high—one 200 and the other 330 meters long (Fig. 97). They sat crudely on the site, and no attempt was made to provide public spaces, parks, or gardens. The 850 apartments were lined along a back hallway intended to provide cross-ventilation to each unit. One of the last and most dreary projects to be completed by the French in Algiers, the Cité des Dunes represents best the number-oriented mentality of the Plan de Constantine technocrats.[74]

Other architects continued to build predictable schemes. For example, Challand replicated the planning principles of Cité Mahieddine in the Cité Diar es-Shems, built on the site of a large *bidonville* to the west of Clos Salembier, by placing shorter bars vertical to long ones.[75] As in the Mahieddine complex, the proximity of the blocks to each other, coupled with the heights of eight stories minimum, resulted in a very dense settlement with unpleasant leftover space between buildings.

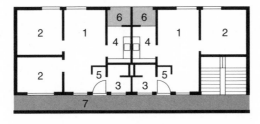

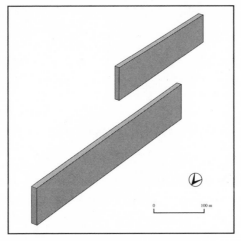

Figure 96. *(above)* Gouyon, Bellisent, and Régeste, Cité Faizi, unit plans. (1) living room, (2) bedroom, (3) bathroom, (4) kitchen, (5) entry, (6) loggia, (7) public hallway.
Figure 97. *(below)* Gouyon, Bellisent, and Régeste, Cité des Dunes, axonometric view.

The prefabricated structures had a uniform plan, by now accepted as the most efficient and economic solution for long and thin blocks (Fig. 98). A hallway in the back connected all the units to the circulation cores. A main feature that distinguished these units from the previous ones was an entry with a kitchen corner into which a relatively large bathroom opened, still a hygienically problematic arrangement. In a common pattern, the loggia accessible from the main room was later closed off by the occupants to gain extra space.

Marcel Lathuillière and Nicholas Di Martino's Cité Haouch Oulid Adda in Hussein-Dey again relied on prefabricated, four-story-high bars, in a layout described by Deluz as an example of "the misorgani-

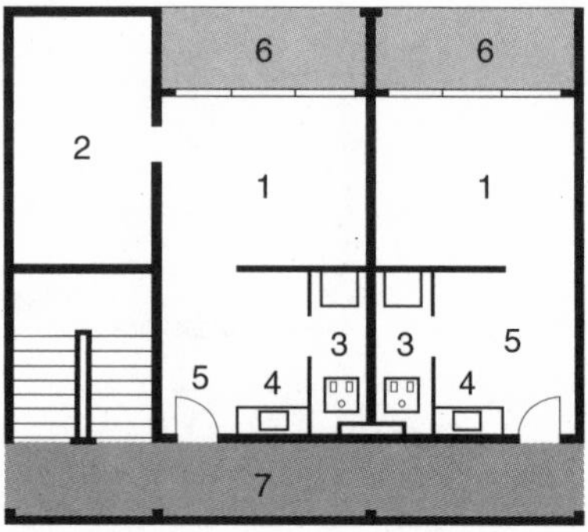

Figure 98. Challand, Diar es-Shems, plan of apartments. (1) living room, (2) bedroom, (3) bathroom, (4) kitchenette, (5) entry, (6) loggia, (7) public hallway.

zation of spaces and absence of all elements of urban life" (Figs. 99 and 100). The novelty in this scheme was the placement of a large sink off the loggia, in addition to the water closet inside the apartment. The separation of the "wet" zone in the loggia from the exterior by a latticelike panel helped to enrich the monotonous facades.[76]

In addition to their mediocre spatial planning, the housing projects of the Plan de Constantine period are characterized by poor construction. Dominated by an obsession with pace at the cost of everything else, the architects opted for building systems that allowed for the most efficient organization of the construction site. The prefabricated panels, though assembled quickly, were not insulated, and little attention was paid to their joints. Therefore, despite the persistent allusion to good environmental conditions inside the apartments (for example, cross-ventilation), the residents suffered from excessive heat and cold, as well as rainwater leaking into their units. The hasty paint job soon looked worn-out, the concrete surfaces were smeared with water leaks, the unmaintained communal spaces—the interminable corridors and stairways—became laden with dirt, and the broken glass on the windows of the communal areas were not replaced. Without exception, these buildings acquired the appearance of slums.[77]

The transformations in the approach to housing Algerians that occurred between the centennial and the end of French rule reflected a multitude of fluctuating social, cultural, political, and economic factors, but overlooked certain key changes that took place in Algerian society during the three decades of intense construction activity. Perhaps the most important among them was the impact of the Algerian War, which began to redefine the status of women and gave them an unprecedented

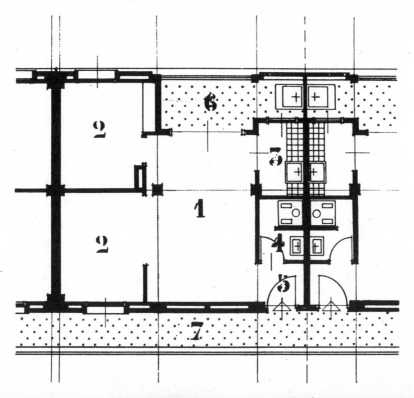

Figure 99. *(above)* Marcel Lathuillière and Nicholas Di Martino, Cité Haouch Oulid Adda, plan of unit, 1959. (1) living room, (2) bedroom, (3) water closet, (4) kitchen, (5) entry, (6) loggia, (7) public hallway. Figure 100. *(below)* Lathuillière and Di Martino, Cité Haouche Oulid Adda, view, 1959.

visibility in the public realm.[78] *El Moudjahid* argued at the time that women's roles had shifted from "knitting for soldiers and weeping for them" at home to active combat in the underground resistance, with the potential for imprisonment, torture, and death.[79] The multiple tasks women assumed during the war had broadened the sphere of their activities and the boundaries of their relations.[80] Furthermore, in the absence of men, women were obliged to carry out all the business activities outside the home. Consequently, it became common to see many women in government offices, shops, streets, and squares.[81] Even more significantly, they expressed their willing participation in the resistance by taking part in demonstrations against colonial rule and thus occupying the public spaces of the city.[82]

The war empowered the Algerian women and, within the newly enlarged framework of social interaction, the image of the encloistered woman came into question. The architects, planners, and policymakers, however, hard at work during the war years, refused to acknowledge these social changes. Reverting to the familiarity of well-established formulas, they situated the Algerian woman in a frozen past in their designs of housing units and public spaces. They continued to privilege privacy as the main need, interiorize the residential plans, and recreate "traditional" conditions for housework, and as a result they maintained the practice of restricting women's lives to the domestic realm.

In terms of the overall development of Algiers, the housing projects (not only the ones built for Algerians, but also those intended for Europeans) followed an older trend, characterized by distinct settlements that dotted the hills and were separated from each other by topographic features. The *grands ensembles* pushed the limits of the city farther as independent enclaves scattered in the landscape. Their designs pursued an internal rationale with little concern for relating to the built fabric of precolonial and colonial Algiers proper; as long as there were connecting roads, a new settlement was considered part of the greater agglomeration. One major difference from the older growth pattern was that densities of the new apartment blocks were much higher, resulting in compact patches of tall buildings, with stretches of unplanned open land between them.

The overruling intention behind the housing projects was to secure the French presence. Furthermore, construction intensified during the height of the Algerian War: between 1954 and 1962, the French built more frantically than ever and in unprecedented quantities for local populations. Military action and large-scale construction thus joined forces in the war against Algerians; their conflicting premises reinforced each other, but also displayed the dilemmas of France's colonial policies. Ultimately, the ideological agenda behind the construction projects would prove ineffective, as housing complex after housing complex turned into a center of resistance and even of military confrontation.

Epilogue

Algeria gained its independence in 1962. Since then dramatic changes have occurred in political, economic, social, and cultural spheres. The issues discussed in this book lead to inevitable questions about the developments that took place after independence and about the present-day situation. Rather than assuming the impossible task of reexamining the topics in light of the transformations of the past three decades, I chose to highlight a few themes that bridge my study to contemporary Algiers. As a conclusion to this book, I offer an open-ended inquiry that does not claim to provide comprehensive and definitive answers. My goal is modest: to begin to map in broad outlines some of the predominant tendencies in urbanism and housing since 1962 against the background of the city's colonial history and to reflect briefly and tentatively on the complicated associations that today's sociocultural scene incubates.

As the debate on the trendy term *postcolonial* suggests, the colonial period and what follows it are not separated by a great divide. In her thoughtful analysis of the term, Ella Shohat argues that *postcolonial* implies colonialism is over and thus overlooks the "economic, political, and cultural deformative traces" that are very much alive today. Masao Miyoshi makes a similar point when he states that "ours . . . is not an age of *post*colonialism, but of intensified colonialism, even though it is under an unfamiliar guise," and maintains that the present-day "global configuration of power and culture" must be understood in relation to the "historical metropolitan-colonial paradigm."[1]

The mark of thirteen decades of colonial history was not erased in the aftermath of the Algerian War. Within a different framework, the colonizer/colonized dialectic has persisted. The "overlapping experiences" of Algerians and the French, together with the "interdependence of the cultural terrains" in which they "coexisted and battled each other through projections as well as rival geographies, narratives, and histories," extend into the present day.[2] Colonial policies and cultural confrontations continue. The urban plans devised by technocrats in the colonial period were deemed universal—imbued with a scientific neutrality that could be applied to modern and independent Algeria regardless of the changes in the political structure. Yet resistance to colonial cultural hegemony and the struggle to define a distinct identity intensified and found a broad base after independence. Both trends were complex. The emphasis new Algeria placed on modernity may have played a key role in the pursuit of policies introduced during the colonial era, but now these policies carried different meanings and expressed the country's selfhood and place in the world order. Definitions of cultural identity, however, were often colored by colonial constructions of "difference."

As pointed out by Bourdieu, the war had already intensified the exchange between the colonizer and the colonized. Unlike disguised resistance, open warfare exposed everything: "Open conflict brings the two sides together just as much as it places them in opposition, because, in order to win the war, it is necessary to borrow the most efficient weapons of one's adversary, and perhaps, also, because war remains a dialogue when all is said and done." The dialogue could not be abruptly terminated once independence had been won. In effect, the themes of independent Algeria had already entered into the public realm of colonial Algeria. Again in the words of Bourdieu, "What was considered to be an imposed restraint or a gracious gift up to a few years ago is now regarded as a due right or as a prerogative won by right of conquest." During the last years of French rule, Algerians asked for their "rights" to work, to housing, to social benefits.[3]

Algiers reflected the twisted nature of the colonial and postcolonial eras in several ways. Many decisions and policies adopted by the colonial system with regard to planning and housing remained in effect, specifically in terms of formal characteristics. The focus changed, however, shifting entirely to making Algiers the capital of independent Algeria and redirecting all housing policies to provide decent shelter for Algerians. The preservation of the casbah also gained priority, due to the settlement's role in the war of decolonization and to its architectural and urbanistic character—marked by its "difference"—which responded to the search for an aesthetic expression of Algerian identity. As a curious footnote here, it is important to remember that at the time of independence, Algeria had only one Algerian architect and the government had to commission foreign architects and planners to develop and execute new projects.[4]

Algerians' claim to their city gained visibility immediately after independence by the renaming of streets and public spaces. In the context of decolonization, this act of reappropriation is related to the effort "to construct, to build, to link, to make over," because names of public places "reflect the idea that a people holds regarding its own history."[5] Street names, one of the signs of French colonialism in Algiers, were replaced by another system of signs that revealed the independence of the Algerian nation, its history, identity, and heros. The new names were written in two alphabets and two languages: Roman (French) and Arabic. If the official use of Arabic emphasized the cultural identity of independent Algeria, the pairing of two languages pointed to the connectedness of the colonial and the postcolonial eras. Bilinguality—that ambivalent condition that has continued to define and haunt Algerian culture—was inscribed into the city proper.[6]

Although one cannot talk of a methodical approach to the process of renaming, certain trends stand out. A place, not associated with a personality but making a political statement, was renamed following the same logic: perhaps the most symbolic public square in Algiers, the Place du Gouvernement (representing France), became Place des Martyres (in memory of the martyrs of the Algerian resistance); a modest street in the Agha Quarter, Rue des Colons (Street of Settlers), was translated into its opposite, Rue des Libérés (Street of the Liberated). Personality names would usually replace each other. For example, a main square or avenue bearing the name of a famed French military figure would find its equivalent among Algerians: hence Place Bugeaud, entitled in honor of Marshal Bugeaud, who later became the governor general of Algeria, became Place Abdelkadir, after the leader of the Algerian resistance to Bugeaud and his armies in the 1830s and the 1840s (Fig. 101); similarly, Colonel Salah Zamoum toppled Colonel Driant on a small street in the heights. Equal rank was not always an issue: the name of a legendary resistance fighter without any official title, such as Ali la Pointe, could take over a prominent historic military figure, such as General Randon, who fought in the Bône region in the 1840s and

Figure 101. View of Place Abdelkadir. General Bugeaud's statue was replaced by the statue of Abdelkadir.

later became the governor general of Algeria. In addition, many main avenues were renamed after Third World leaders to whom Algeria felt a political affiliation: Patrice Lumumba and Che Guevara thus entered the daily life of Algiers, together with Frantz Fanon.

In the Algerian discourse during the early years of independence, the casbah emerged as an embodiment of the essence of Algerian cultural identity—a thesis that was revisited repeatedly in the three decades that followed. The "authenticity" of its form, its mythical associations, its resilience to colonial interventions, as well as its legendary status in the war, made it an obvious symbol of national culture in a pattern that is representative of decolonization projects. As Fanon observed, "native intellectuals" searched passionately for "a national culture which existed before the colonial era," both as a precaution against being overwhelmed by Western culture and as a matter of pride and self-respect.[7]

Lesbet, for example, established a strong connection between the casbah and Algerian identity: "It is there that Algerian identity is forged and constantly reinforced. It is one of the most important basins of Algerian nationalism. The casbah expresses a triple artistic, cultural and political dimension, which gives it a national importance." Mostefa Lacheraf made a similar point by arguing that, with its "rich architectural experience" and as a site "adjusted for longevity," the casbah provided "concrete support" for "facts and acts, mental and other habits, reference points of a society, of a civilization of taste, measure." Moreover, this "civilization, stationed on the heights of the city, and notably in the courtyards, patios, [and] small streets, resisted [colonial invasion] like a last square on the battlefield."[8]

Algerians' privileging of the casbah was not entirely independent of the French discourse, however, not only because it employed a similar terminology in describing the beauties of the city, but also because it capitalized on the "difference" from French architecture and urban forms. In addition, considering the casbah as the symbol of resistance was not restricted to Algerians. The French, perhaps even reinforcing the Algerian viewpoint, also repeatedly acknowledged the adversarial position the casbah occupied during the war.

Dissociating themselves from former proposals to turn the casbah into a museum, the architects, planners, and social scientists working on the casbah after 1962 insisted that the urban fabric should be preserved in its entirety and as a living city. It was necessary to approach the casbah with a "new look" that would save it from "a certain historic marginality inherited from the colonialist vision" that regarded it as a folkloric artifact for touristic consumption.[9] A major shift in the approach after independence was the unprecedented emphasis placed on the residents of the casbah. As a first step in the rehabilitation process, a series of interviews was conducted with the inhabitants over a period of two years. Then an urbanistic analysis was carried out by COMEDOR, after which would come the preparation of intervention plans. Under the leadership of architect André Ravéreau, the "Atelier de la Casbah" documented the houses of the casbah and prepared a detailed program to be carried out in four stages, varying from urgent measures to prevent inevitable decay, to short-term operations from 1980 to 1982 that centered on three experimental construction sites, to a systematic restoration of entire blocks between 1982 and 1992, and finally to long-term projects that included the complete reconstruction of the Marine Quarter in accord with its historic structure. The latter decision, based on the rationale that the colonial interventions were not compatible with the scale of the old town, illustrates well the ultimate goals and ambitions of the project.[10]

These undertakings were much more comprehensive than any during the colonial era. Many houses on the verge of collapse were propped up; an experimental laboratory of several structures was established for analysis and to teach restoration techniques; and a pilot block of twenty-five houses was rehabilitated with financial help from UNESCO. The plans of "Atelier de la Casbah" were comprehensive, but though they produced detailed research, they remained largely unrealized in a pattern reminiscent of colonial times.[11]

Meanwhile, the problems of the colonial era continue to escalate. Densities in the casbah remain very high; houses rented out room by room are occupied in patterns they were not designed for; services are few, hygienic provisions poor, and lack of maintenance rampant—all adding to the ever-growing fragility of the built fabric. The majority of the old residents have left for "better" parts of Algiers, turning the casbah increasingly into a concentration of the subproletariat and an "antechamber of the city" for waves of rural immigrants. According to Lesbet, while in the past people lived in the casbah to "affirm" themselves, now they do so because they lack other options.[12] This situation shows a major deviation from the socioeconomic structure of the casbah in precolonial and colonial times, when a mixture of all income levels resided there.

Despite the changes and deterioration, the casbah maintains its privileged place in Algerian culture and memory and still stands as the political symbol of resistance and decolonization. Its decrepit state does not prohibit it from serving as the "universal symbol," the "inevitable sign" of Algiers that represents the city whenever it is "to be stated as an image."[13] At the same time, the political battles of contemporary Algeria refer back to the casbah to form a bridge to history. Consider, for example, the demonstration held by women demanding equality between genders, on 4 March 1985: as a reminder of Algerian women's long-term involvement in their country's destiny, they gathered in the casbah at the location where Hassiba ben Bouali was killed by French forces in 1957.[14]

Transformations in the casbah reflect developments in the entire city. The greatest issue is population growth (according to the 1987 census, over 1.5 million people lived in Algiers), around which all planning decisions revolve. It has become commonplace to blame the urban problems of Algiers on the new cross-section of its population, two-thirds of which are immigrants from the countryside. The changes brought to the capital in the last two generations have led to the emergence of the term *rurbanity* to define the dominant character of contemporary Algiers.[15] Another peculiarity of the population that complicates urban problems and calls for a radical rethinking of the housing patterns is the age factor: approximately 60 percent of Algerians are below the age of twenty.[16]

Deluz distinguishes two phases in the urbanistic activities in Algiers following independence. The first phase, which lasted until 1968, is characterized by a straightforward adoption of the plans and projects undertaken by the colonial administration, but continued under new teams. The novelty was in the emphasis given to research: a vast sociological inquiry was initiated to determine the dwelling and neighborhood types. The second phase put aside research and focused on construction. The urgency of controlling and directing the "tentacular" growth of Algiers determined the structure of the master plans drafted after 1968. Recalling the colonial schemes, they proposed to extend the city toward the heights, decrease the densities in the center, place the services on the coastal band, and concentrate industrial zones in the east. The plans from the 1970s onward devised regional solutions to "put brakes on the rural exodus" to the capital by means of decentralization. A series of settlements around the city, complete with economic and social functions, was proposed, limiting the concentration in Algiers to "capital functions" such as government, central administrations, and national scientific, social, and cultural centers.[17]

The plans were applied piecemeal, leading to the persistence of the problems inherited from the colonial period. Consequently, the coastline became heavily built, rural immigration reached a massive scale, and a serious housing crisis resurfaced and was accompanied by a rapid proliferation of shantytowns. Furthermore, land use patterns of the colonial city resulted in neighborhoods segregated according to income.[18]

Housing remained central to all planning operations. The new concept of ZHUN (*zone d'habitat urbaine nouvelle*, or new urban housing zone) worked well with the logic of regional planning and continued the former practice of ZUPs with *grands ensembles* whose urban design and architectural qualities replicated the housing schemes of the late 1950s. Due to the efficiency it brought to the building process, prefabrication became widespread, standardizing plans and facades, and compromising the quality of construction, the latter stemming from the nature of materials involved and the technical difficulties in assembling components that resulted in poor joints. Extensive areas dotted by grim uniform blocks of four to five stories high, with desolate spaces between them, now surround the city on all sides (Fig. 102). They recall the depressing environments of the Plan de Constantine projects and should be considered their descendants due to the single-minded concern for numbers as the impetus behind their spatial and aesthetic characteristics.

These projects, however, are not the only kind of new housing in Algiers. Another dominant pattern has developed since 1974, when a legislation was passed that gave each commune the right to develop the land it owned. The outcome is a curious pattern of attached or freestanding two- or three-story houses, densely packed together. While these houses are large, "luxurious," and reveal in their decorative ambitions the comfortable living standards of their owners, they do not coalesce into desirable environmental conditions, because they lack communal open spaces such as parks, playgrounds, and private gardens. The "spontaneous" *bidonvilles* on any available land around the city form the third category of new housing; "not always legal, but often legalized," their development has remained uninterrupted by political changes. Contemporary Algiers has many shantytowns scattered throughout the city: the "saturated" old *bidonvilles* that could not extend any further, former temporary housing projects that have turned into *bidonvilles* (usually in the vicinity of the HLMs), and new developments that mushroomed in the east, west, and northwest of Algiers and next to major construction sites. Their patterns reiterate the precolonial prototypes.[19]

Reacting to the grimness of new residential architecture, to the "social ruptures" attributed to collective housing blocks, and to the

Figure 102. New housing on the outskirts of Algiers.

persistent indifference among technocrats and policymakers to discussions about "typification," "normalization," and prefabrication, Algerian critics have brought back the idea of the "traditional house" and "traditional construction methods"; they argue for a nuanced synthesis of modern technology and the "cultural schema" offered by older patterns. In addition, they maintain that "modern architecture" overlooked sociocultural factors such as the family structure, the nature of social relations, the place of women, and the importance of privacy—the same issues that the architects of the colonial era attempted to address in a different framework and with a different agenda. The definitions of the "traditional Algerian house" (with specific references to the casbah of Algiers and to houses of Kabylia and Mzab) also recall the familiar colonial plans in singling out certain architectural features, such as the court, the blank facades to the street, the terrace.[20]

While the debates continue, housing presents such a serious problem in contemporary Algeria, and especially in the capital, that it is commonly considered one of the reasons for the political malaise, together with other socioeconomic issues such as employment and political freedom.[21] Scarcity of services adds to problems of space and maintenance. For example, water shortages are rampant, burdening all residents—but especially the women of the capital—with extra hardship and confining their daily lives to a tight routine of household chores. The often violent insistence of the "religiose" movement on the encloistering of Algerian women within the domestic realm, coupled with the overall housing

Figure 103. Eugène Delacroix, *Femmes d'Alger dans leur appartement* (1834).
Oil on canvas, 180 cm × 229 cm.

situation, brings the home and its association with women to the political foreground once again.[22]

   In a manifestation of the complexity of contemporary Algerian culture and its entanglements with the colonial era, much of the recent
discourse that interweaves political and cultural fields refers to colonial
formations in order to draw familiar frameworks that serve as *lieux de
mémoire*. This is especially prevalent in discussions on women's seclu-
sion and the physical environments it involves. For example, in her renowned book *Femmes d'Alger dans leur appartement,* Algerian writer
Assia Djebar writes about the central role the home can play as a prison
or as a setting of serenity by juxtaposing paintings by Eugène Delacroix
and Pablo Picasso, also titled *Femmes d'Alger.* One canvas marking the
beginning of French colonization, the other the end, the paintings
evoke strikingly different interpretations for Djebar, sparked by differences not only in the visions of the two European artists, but more important in the transformations brought by the French occupation and
the decolonization war. Djebar reads the women in Delacroix's painting
as prisoners of their houses, passive and resigned to the space around
them, dimly lighted from an ambiguous source (Fig. 103). In his second

Figure 104. Pablo Picasso, *Femmes d'Alger* (1955). Oil on canvas, 113 cm × 145.5 cm.

version of the same painting (1849), Djebar notes, Delacroix enhanced the enclosed status of these "still waiting" women by exaggerating the ambiguity of the room, enlarging the space, and diminishing the size of the female figures.[23]

Picasso obsessively reworked Delacroix's *Femmes d'Alger* during the first months of the Algerian War. From December 1954 to April 1955, he produced fifteen paintings, numerous drawings, and at least two lithographs.[24] Djebar argues that in Picasso's work, the universe of the women of Algiers was completely transformed from the precious "tragedy" into a "totally new happiness" by means of a "glorious liberation of place, [an] awakening of the body in dance, energy, free movement" (Fig. 104). Their hermetic situation has been preserved, only to be reversed into a condition of serenity, at peace with the past and the future. Djebar associates the "liberation" at home with the occupation of the city's public spaces by women resistance fighters taking part in the war.[25]

Djebar's reading of Delacroix's and Picasso's works to frame the dramatic change in women's lives during the country's *nuit coloniale* calls for continued debate and possibly disagreement, especially given Picasso's "continual struggle in the *Femmes d'Alger* series to reconcile distance with presence, possession, and watching."[26] What matters, however, is the fact that Djebar reestablishes the connection between domestic spaces and women's lives and that to do so she chooses to rely on the authority of one of the most blatant cultural symbols of French colonialism (Delacroix's painting) and the artistic tradition based on the reproductions and reinterpretations of this symbol, thereby accentuating the entanglements of her message. Her stand does not imply "giving in" to the colonizer culture, but rather deploying it to broaden her critique. Djebar is not alone in reloading colonial cultural formations with new meanings and providing complicated linkages between contemporary Algerian questions and the country's recent history. For example, in Kamal Dahane's 1992 documentary film, itself titled *Femmes d'Alger*, Delacroix's painting reemerges: the famous setting is recreated in the last scene, but now is emptied of women.

Djebar carries her association of home and prison from the colonial period to home and tomb in postcolonial times. As pointed out by Woodhull, in Djebar's novel *A Sister to Scheherazade*, the heroine is confined to a modern apartment, with a "kitchen that is like a tomb." Her struggle is to "unearth" herself from "spaces of confinement" to "spaces of liberation," which are "spaces of the town."[27] In Merzag Allouache's feature film *Bab el-Oued City* (1993), his poignant exposé of daily life in contemporary Algiers includes two female leading characters who are forced to spend their lives at home; the roof terraces continue to function as women's gathering spaces. In Dahane's documentary, too, women talk about their introverted lives and some emphasize the importance of making a statement by simply occupying the public spaces of Algiers. They assert this is an effective way of voicing their opposition to current religious-political trends aimed to keep them invisible. The interiorization of the home is juxtaposed with the publicness of urban spaces, and the sharp divide between the two deeply affects urban life.

In closing, it is proper to cast a glance, albeit a very brief one, at the cities of France. The colonial experience changed the colonizer as well, and its impact on French society and culture is there to stay. With 3.5 million North Africans living in France today, French cities display certain characteristics that recall the urban centers of Algeria. Projections point to the increase of this population to six to eight million around the turn of the twentieth century, interlocking the fates of cities and urban culture on both sides of the Mediterranean perhaps even more intimately than in the colonial era.[28] Housing is the major issue, and the edges of French cities have demonstrated developments similar to those observed in Algiers. From the *bidonvilles* of Nanterre (now demolished) that swelled with Algerians beginning in 1954 to the government-subsidized housing projects where immigrants continue to concentrate (despite various attempts at integration), the environments display similarities to their counterparts in Algiers. As urban character is a matter not only of form, but also of other signs and sensuous cues,[29] the distinctiveness of immigrant quarters is derived from the signs, the smells of goods sold in stores, the names of shops and cafés, the sounds of various languages and music, the patterns of social interaction, and the uses of public spaces.

These city fragments are filled with an urban life that reflects the "pluralities of the postcolonial heritage" and contributes to contemporary French urban culture. For the second generation of North African immigrants, identity formation is a crucial struggle within the dominant society and it is founded on biculturalism.[30] Calling themselves "Beurs" (a play on the word *arabe* pronounced backward), this group has actively carved its presence into the urban scene. The Beurs' definition of identity centers on contesting and negotiating urban spaces: they claim the urban outskirts and the housing projects as their legitimate and permanent spaces, but maintain their places of origin always in the background. Their national origins carry mythical meanings and enable the construction of a complex identity, revealed in a rich repertoire of cultural productions.[31]

Cultural intersections thus occur on both sides of the Mediterranean. If they take different forms in response to the specificity of their socioeconomic frameworks, they also enhance the deep involvement of the two places and the two eras.

Notes

Introduction

1. Two controversial terms need clarification at the outset: *colony* and *Algerians*. Administratively defined as a *département*, Algeria was not officially a colony. Nevertheless, this was a bureaucratic categorization and did not affect the power structure, which was based on the dominance of the French over Algerians. *Algerians* is an umbrella term that covers all the ethnic groups in contradistinction to colonizers. It has been used sporadically and casually in colonial discourse, with frequent counterarguments against the notion of a unified "Algerian nation" (and "Algerian people"). An intriguing argument for the long-time existence of the Algerian nation was put forward by Mostefa Lacheraf. Challenging statements by prominent Algerians (like Ferhat Abbas, who later changed his mind) and French (like Albert Camus, who did not) that denied nationhood to Algerians, Lacheraf maintained that opposition to France for 130 years could not have been pursued without national unity, if not in the form of a "nation-state" (*état nation*) in the form of a "community state" (*état communauté*). See Mostefa Lacheraf, *L'Algérie: nation et société* (Paris, 1965), 9. Lacheraf's association of the Algerian nation with resistance to colonialism is echoed by Christopher Miller, who broadens it to African nationalism: "The original African nationalism is one of resistance to colonialism from within." For Miller, however, the origin of African nationalism is in the struggle, not the presence of a nation. See Christopher L. Miller, "Nationalism as Resistance and Resistance to Nationalism in the Literature of Francophone Africa," *Yale French Studies* 82 (1993): 74–75.

2. French colonial policies regarding urbanism and architecture have constituted a major field of interest in recent scholarship. Janet Abu-Lughod's pioneering book, *Rabat: Urban Apartheid in Morocco* (Princeton, N.J., 1980), provided English-speaking readers with an acute critical study. About a decade later, Paul Rabinow published *French Modern: Norms and Forms of the Social Environ-*

ment (Cambridge, Mass., 1989) and devoted a large section to the urban policies of Marshal Hubert Lyautey in Morocco. Gwendolyn Wright's *The Politics of Design in French Colonial Urbanism* (Chicago, 1991) looked at the cities of Morocco, Vietnam, and Madagascar. On Algeria, there is only one book in English: David Prochaska's masterful *Making Algeria French* (Cambridge, England, 1990), which focuses on Bône (present-day Annaba). So far, Algiers has entered the discourse sporadically and solely in terms of Le Corbusier's unrealized projects for the city.

3. Eric J. Hobsbawm, *The Age of Empire, 1875 –1914* (New York, 1987), 76.

4. Edward Said, *Culture and Imperialism* (New York, 1993), 11 – 12 (italics in original).

5. Spiro Kostof, *The City Shaped* (London, 1992), 25, 9, 11.

6. Kevin Lynch, *The Image of the City* (Cambridge, Mass., 1960), 9, 4.

7. Henri Lefebvre, *The Production of Space,* trans. Donald Nicholson-Smith (Oxford, 1991), 17.

8. Frantz Fanon, *The Wretched of the Earth,* trans. Constance Farrington (New York, 1968), 38 – 39.

9. Le Corbusier, "Le Folklore est l'expression fleurie des traditions," *Voici la France de ce mois* 16 (June 1941): 31; idem, *La Ville radieuse* (Paris, 1933), 230 – 231.

10. Lefebvre, *The Production of Space,* 17.

11. Janet Abu-Lughod, "On the Remaking of History: How to Reinvent the Past," in Barbara Kruger and Phil Mariani, eds., *Remaking History* (Seattle, 1989), 112.

12. Kostof, *The City Shaped,* 11, 13.

13. Lefebvre, *The Production of Space,* 90, 116.

14. Eric J. Hobsbawm, "From Social History to the History of the Society," in Felix Gilbert and Stephen R. Graubard, eds., *Historical Studies Today* (New York, 1972), 14 – 16.

15. Homi K. Bhabha, "The Other Question: Difference, Discrimination and the Discourse of Colonialism," in Russell Ferguson, Martha Gever, Trinh T. Minh-ha, Cornel West, eds., *Out There: Marginalization and Contemporary Culture* (Cambridge, Mass., 1990), 72, 85 – 86.

16. Ibid., 71 – 87; H. Bhabha, "Of Mimicry and Man: The Ambivalence of Colonial Discourse," *October* 28 (October 1984): 125 – 133. See also Benita Parry, "Problems in Current Theories of Colonial Discourse," *Oxford Literary Review* 9, nos. 1 – 2 (1987): 27 – 58, especially 28 – 29 and 41 – 42.

17. Peter Hulme, *Colonial Encounters: Europe and the Native Caribbean, 1492 –1797* (London, 1986), 2.

18. Michel Leiris, "L'Ethnographe devant le colonialisme," *Les Temps modernes* 6, no. 58 (August 1950): 358, translated as "The Ethnographer Faced with Colonialism," in Michel Leiris, *Brisées: Broken Branches,* trans. Lydia Davis (San Francisco, 1989), 112.

19. I thus extend Christopher Miller's argument that "a fair reading of African literature demands engagement within, and even dependence on, anthropology" to a fair reading of architecture and cities. See Christopher L. Miller, *Theories of Africans* (Chicago, 1990), 4.

20. The material discussed in this book revolves around certain key events

and dates, but it is beyond the scope of my project to provide the historic background. I offer the following list not as a comprehensive bibliography on the history of Algeria, but as a selection that expands on the critical moments of my analysis. C.-R. Agéron, *Modern Algeria: A History from 1830 to the Present,* tr. and ed. M. Brett (London, 1991); idem, *Politiques coloniales au Maghreb* (Paris, 1973); idem, *L'Histoire de l'Algérie contemporaine: de l'insurrection de 1871 au déclenchement de la guerre de libération (1954)* (Paris, 1979); J. Berque, *French North Africa: The Maghrib between the Two World Wars,* tr. J. Stewart (New York, 1967); Frantz Fanon, *A Dying Colonialism* (New York, 1967); D. C. Gordon, *The Passing of French Algeria* (London, 1966); A. Hourani, *A History of the Arab Peoples* (Cambridge, Mass., 1991); C.-A. Julien, *History of North Africa: Tunisia, Algeria, Morocco, from the Arab Conquest to 1830* (New York, 1970); Lacheraf, *L'Algérie;* A. Laroui, *The History of the Maghrib* (Princeton, N.J., 1977); John Ruedy, *Modern Algeria: The Origins and Development of a Nation* (Bloomington, Ind., 1994); L. Valensi, *On the Eve of Colonialism: North Africa before the French Conquest 1790 –1830* (New York, 1977). For comprehensive bibliographies, see Michael Brett's Bibliography, in Agéron, *Modern Algeria: A History from 1830 to the Present,* and Ruedy's Bibliographical Essay, in *Modern Algeria: The Origins and Development of a Nation.*

21.   Consider Marshal Lyautey's famous statement on colonies as laboratories of modernism.

22.   Albert Sarrault, *Grandeur et servitude coloniales* (Paris, 1931), 220–221.

23.   Raoul Girardet, *L'Idée coloniale en France* (Paris, 1972), 176, 186.

24.   Gustave Mercier, speech made in 1930 and quoted in Winifred Woodhull, *Transfigurations of the Maghreb* (Minneapolis, 1993), 41.

25.   The Colonial Exposition held in Paris a year later nurtured the climate of "the greatest France." Literature on the 1931 Colonial Exposition is extensive; see, in particular, C.-R. Agéron, "L'Exposition coloniale de 1931: mythe républicaine ou mythe impériale?" in P. Nora, ed., *La République* (Paris, 1984), 561–591; Eugene Lebovics, *True France* (Ithaca, N.Y., 1992); Patricia Morgan, "The Civilizing Mission of Architecture: L'Exposition Coloniale Internationale de 1931 à Paris" (Ph.D. diss., Princeton University, 1994).

Chapter 1.   The Casbah and the Marine Quarter

1.   The term *casbah* was derived from the citadel located at the highest point of the fortifications surrounding the town.

2.   In the words of colonial architectural historian A. Maitrot de la Motte-Capron, Algerian architecture expressed a very clear "*amour du cube.*" See A. Maitrot de la Motte-Capron, "L'Architecture indigène nord-africaine," *Bulletin de la Société de Géographie d'Alger et de l'Afrique du Nord* 37, no. 131 (1932): 293.

3.   Roger Le Tourneau, "Al Djaza'ir," in *Encyclopedia of Islam* (Leiden, 1960), 519–520.

4.   Ibid., 520; Djaffar Lesbet, *La Casbah d'Alger. Gestion urbaine et vide sociale* (Algiers, [c. 1985]), 194–195. In 1816, the citadel became the residence of the dey of Algiers.

5.   André Raymond, *The Great Arab Cities in the 16th–18th Centuries* (New York, 1984), 10.

6. The Janina Palace burned in 1844; it was then demolished. Today the al-Jadid Mosque is on the present-day Place des Martyres (formerly Place du Gouvernement).

7. Le Tourneau, "Al Djaza'ir," 520; André Ravéreau, *La Casbah d'Alger. Et le site créa la ville* (Paris, 1989), 35–36; Jean Michel de Venture, *Alger au XVIIIe siècle,* second ed. (Tunis, [c. 1980]), 9–10.

8. Raymond, *Great Arab Cities,* 9. Le Tourneau, "Al Djaza'ir," 520–521; Ravéreau, *La Casbah d'Alger,* 35–36. While the records are clear about the cosmopolitan nature of the population of Algiers, the available population figures are vague, making it difficult to quantify the city's population for any period before 1830. They vary dramatically, from 60,000 at the end of the sixteenth century to 100,000 in 1634; from 50,000 at the end of the eighteenth century to 30,000 in 1830. For Algiers of this period, see also William Spenser, *Algiers in the Age of Corsairs* (Norman, Okla., 1965).

9. Jean-Michel de Venture, for example, describes the streets of eighteenth-century Algiers as "extremely narrow," not even wide enough for three persons to walk side by side. He also elaborates on the darkness of the streets caused by houses bridging the two sides and by projecting second stories. Venture, *Alger au XVIIIe siècle,* 3, 10.

10. Lamberto Deho and Daniele Pini, "Tipologia edilizia e morfologia urbana della Casbah di Algeri," *Parametro* 17 (June 1973): 30.

11. Ravéreau, *La Casbah d'Alger,* 40–42. Venture's observations in the eighteenth century contradict this statement; he characterizes the streets of Algiers as dirty and foul-smelling. See Venture, *Alger au XVIIIe siècle,* 10.

12. Janet L. Abu-Lughod, "The Islamic City—Historic Myth, Islamic Essence, and Contemporary Relevance," *International Journal of Middle Eastern Studies* 19, no. 2 (May 1987): 162–164.

13. Georges Marçais, "Maisons et villas musulmanes d'Alger," *Documents algériens* 26 (1 January 1948–31 December 1948): 347.

14. Ravéreau, *La Casbah D'Alger,* 40.

15. On the houses of Algiers, see Lucien Golvin, *Palais et demeures d'Alger à la période ottomane* (Aix-en-Provence, 1988). Although Golvin focuses on several case studies from upper-class houses, he includes some more modest examples and discusses the general principles.

16. Ravéreau, *La Casbah d'Alger,* 38–39. For the distribution of mosques, religious schools, public fountains, and baths, see Marcello Balbo and Guido Moretti, "La Casbah nello sviluppo di Algeri," *Parametro* 17 (June 1973): 7–8, and Lesbet, *La Casbah d'Alger,* 197–198.

17. Le Tourneau, "Al Djaza'ir," 520; André Raymond, "Le Centre d'Alger en 1830," *Revue de l'occident musulman et de la Meditérranée* 31, no. 1 (1981): 73–74. Relying on a number of sources, Raymond reconstructed a map of the central zone of the lower city in 1830 (see 84).

18. A *waqf* (known in the Maghreb as *habous*) is a permanent endowment of land or real estate made by an individual and secured by a deed of restraint. Through this act, the owner stipulated that the property be used for good purposes. The principles to be followed were regulated in detail: the purpose had to be compatible with Islam and pleasing to God; the object of the endowment had to be of a permanent nature and made in perpetuity. *Waqfs* varied

from religious buildings to educational ones, to all kinds of public works (roads, aqueducts, bridges), to charitable institutions (hospitals, hostels, laundries, kitchens, baths). Every *waqf* had a manager, in addition to several technically skilled people on salary, responsible for its repair; a local judge supervised the maintenance. For *waqf*s, see H. A. R. Gibb and H. Bowen, *Islamic Society and the West*, vol. 1 (New York, 1957), 2, 164; *Encyclopedia of Islam* (Leiden, 1960), 1096–97.

19. Roland Barthes, "Myth Today," in Susan Sontag, ed., *A Barthes Reader* (New York, 1982), 93–94, 104.

20. Woodhull, *Transfigurations of the Maghreb*, 19; J. Lorraine, *Heures d'Afrique* (1899), quoted in Yvonne Knibiehler and Régine Goutalier, *La Femme aux temps des colonies* (Paris, 1985), 40.

21. M. Bernard, *D'Alger à Tanger* (n.d.), 1, quoted in Judy Mabro, ed., *Veiled Half-Truths: Western Travellers' Perceptions of Middle Eastern Women* (London, 1991), 35.

22. Lucienne Favre, *Tout l'inconnu de la casbah d'Alger* (Algiers, 1933), 10 ("sex appeal" is in English in the original).

23. Le Corbusier, *La Ville radieuse*, 260.

24. Le Corbusier, *Poésie sur Alger* (1950; facsimile reprint, Paris, 1989), 16.

25. Le Corbusier, "Le Folklore est l'expression fleurie des traditions," 31.

26. *L'Algérie de nos jours* (1893), quoted in Mabro, *Veiled Half-Truths*, 31–32.

27. Favre, *Tout l'inconnu de la casbah d'Alger*, 249. The contrast between the French town and the casbah was conveyed to broad audiences in Julien Duvivier's popular film *Pépé le Moko* (1937), even though the movie was shot entirely in the studio.

28. Eugène Fromentin, *Une Année dans le Sahel*, seventh ed. (Paris, 1888), 24, 27–28. *Ville blanche* is italicized in the original text.

29. Fanon, *The Wretched of the Earth*, 51.

30. "Il Seminario al Comedor. Conclusioni," *Parametro* 17 (June 1973): 39.

31. Théophile Gautier, *Voyage pittoresque en Algérie*, ed. M. Cottin (1845; reprint, Geneva, 1973), 190.

32. See, for example, "Projets pour 1834," Service Historique de l'Armée de Terre, Château de Vincennes, Paris (hereafter SHAT), Génie. Alger. Art. 8, section 1, carton 3, which specifies, among other less important conversions, the resettlement of the Third Battalion of the African Army in a house on the Rue de la Casbah. "Projets pour 1834," ibid., mentions the continuation of the appropriation of houses near the casbah and their transformation into workshops. "Mémoire sur l'état actuel de la place. Projets pour 1837," ibid., carton 4, also notes the conversion of several houses near the casbah into workshops.

33. Quoted in Alf Andrew Heggoy, *The French Conquest of Algiers, 1830: An Algerian Oral Tradition* (Athens, Ohio, 1986), 22–23.

34. "Rapport au Comité du Génie. Séance du 1 octobre 1831," SHAT, Génie. Alger. Art. 8, section 6.

35. Le Baron Louis André Pichon, *Alger sous la domination française, son état présent et son avenir* (Paris, 1833), 118–119.

36. René Lespès, *Alger, étude de géographie et d'histoire urbaines* (Paris, 1930), 205–206.

37. "Rapport au Comité du Génie. Séance du 11 octobre 1831," SHAT, Génie. Alger. Art. 8, section 6.

38. Raymond, "Le Centre d'Alger en 1830," 75–76.

39. Lespès, *Alger,* 206–208; Pichon, *Alger sous la domination française,* 266–267; Ministère de la Guerre, "Extrait du Comité des fortifications, séance du 31 décembre 1833," Archives Nationales, Dépôt d'Outre-Mer, Aix-en-Provence (hereafter AOM). As this last document indicates, the desire to regularize the fourth side of the Place du Gouvernement to create *"une place parfaitement rectangulaire"* persisted. Another attempt to bring order to this side of the square by means of an obelisk or fountain dates from 1840. See correspondence between Directeur de l'Intérieur and Ministre de l'Intérieur, Algiers, 27 June 1840 and 19 July 1840, AOM.

40. "Rapport fait au Ministre de l'Intérieur," 8 January 1834, AOM.

41. Lespès, *Alger,* 213–221.

42. "Projet pour Alger" and "Projets pour 1834," SHAT, Génie. Alger. Art. 8, section 1, carton 3.

43. M. Pasquier-Bronde, "Alger. Son développement depuis l'occupation française," in J. Royer, ed., *L'Urbanisme aux colonies et dans les pays tropicaux,* vol. 1 (La-Charité-sur-Loire, 1932), 33–35; P.-L. Nougier, "La Transformation de l'ancien quartier de la Marine," *Chantiers* 14 (January–March 1954): n.p.

44. "Rapport au Conseil d'Administration, Direction de l'Intérieur," 27 August 1845, AOM; Lespès, *Alger,* 315–324; "Projet d'accordement de la Place du Gouvernement avec Boulevard de l'Impératrice," SHAT, Secrétariat du Comité des Fortifications, séance du 21 janvier 1865; Federico Cresti, "The Boulevard de l'Impératrice in Colonial Algiers (1860–1866)," *Environmental Design* 1 (1984): 54–59.

45. "Projet général d'agrandissement de la Casbah," SHAT, Génie. Alger. Art. 8, section 1, carton 5.

46. For discussions of the early phase of French planning in Algiers, also see Federico Cresti, "Algeri dalla conquista francese alla fine del secondo impero," and Luc Vilan, "Algeri o il lettro di procuste: la nascita della citta coloniali in Algeria nell'800," *Storia urbana* 10, nos. 35–36 (April–September 1986): 41–76, 77–106.

47. "Transformation du quartier Bab-Azoun," Procès verbal, 29 September 1917, AOM.

48. "Rapport du Comité des Fortifications. Séance du 14 mars 1884," SHAT, Génie. Alger. Art. 8, section 6.

49. Lespès, *Alger,* 398–400. Reminding the French authorities that already four of the largest and most beautiful mosques of Algiers had been demolished, Algerian advisors voiced a protest in 1885 against the demolition of the al-Kabir and al-Jadid. See ibid., 400, n. 2.

50. Pasquier-Bronde, "Alger," 38–39.

51. "Rapport au Conseil d'Administration, Directeur de l'Intérieur," 27 August 1845, AOM; "Extrait des registres des déliberations du Conseil Municipal de la ville d'Alger. Session extraordinaire. Séance du 26 novembre 1859," AOM.

52. Jean-Jacques Deluz, *L'Urbanisme et l'architecture d'Alger* (Algiers, 1988), 13.

53. Lespès, *Alger,* 278–279.

54. "Rapport," addressed to M. le Maréchal Compte Randon, gouverneur général d'Algérie, 5 May 1858, AOM.

55. Quoted in Lespès, *Alger*, 305.

56. Fromentin, *Une Année dans le Sahel*, 17–18.

57. Lesbet, *La Casbah d'Alger*, 39–48.

58. Fanon, *The Wretched of the Earth*, 38–39.

59. R. Randau, "Un Coin du vieil Alger qu'il faut préserver," *L'Afrique du nord illustrée* (1 April 1938).

60. Lespès, *Alger*, 170–171.

61. On Lyautey in Morocco, see Abu-Lughod, *Rabat*, 131–173; Rabinow, *French Modern*, 277–319; and Wright, *Politics of Design in French Colonial Urbanism*, 85–160.

62. Quoted in Abu-Lughod, *Rabat*, 141.

63. Quoted in Norman Daniel, *Islam, Europe, and Empire* (Edinburgh, 1966), 489.

64. Quoted in Abu-Lughod, *Rabat*, 143.

65. Quoted in ibid., 142.

66. Henri Prost, "Le Développement de l'urbanisme dans le protectorat du Maroc, de 1914 à 1923," in Royer, *L'Urbanisme aux colonies*, vol. 1, 60, 68.

67. Henri Prost, "Rapport général," in Royer, *L'Urbanisme aux colonies*, vol. 1, 21–22; see also Abu-Lughod, *Rabat*, 145.

68. Charles Montaland, "L'Urbanisme en Algérie, ses directives pour l'avenir," in Royer, *L'Urbanisme aux colonies*, vol. 1, 51; Pasquier-Bronde, "Alger," 39.

69. Jean Bévia, "Alger et ses agrandissements," *L'Architecture* 43, no. 5 (15 May 1930): 183.

70. Ella Shohat and Robert Stam, *Unthinking Eurocentrism* (London, 1994), 23.

71. "Vers un meilleur aménagement: les projets et les mesures préventives," *Chantiers* (March 1935): 180, 184. For Prost, Danger, and Rotival's master plan, see the next section in this chapter and Chapter 2.

72. René Lespès, "Les Villes," in *Les Arts et la technique moderne en Algérie 1937* (Algiers, 1937), 25–26.

73. Ibid., 26.

74. Gouvernement Général de l'Algérie, Direction Générale des Affaires Indigènes et des Territoires du Sud, Service de l'Economie Sociale Indigène, *Pour les paysans et les artisans indigènes* (Algiers, 1939), 140–141. To hasten and increase production and to provide more "precision" to the work, these schools and workshops promoted the use of modern machinery.

75. Le Corbusier, *La Ville radieuse*, 229, 244; idem, letter to the Prefect of Algiers, 18 May 1942, Fondation Le Corbusier (hereafter FLC); idem, Questionnaire C, 1931–35, FLC; idem, note for M. Sabatier, 6 May 1941, FLC; and idem, "Proposition d'un plan directeur d'Alger et de sa région pour aider aux travaux de la Commission du Plan de la Région d'Alger et comme suite à la séance du 16 juillet 1941," FLC. I have analyzed Le Corbusier's projects in Algiers in terms of their colonial implications in "Le Corbusier, Orientalism, Colonialism," *Assemblage* 17 (April 1992): 58–77.

76. Le Corbusier, "Proposition d'un plan directeur."

77. Ibid.

78. R. P. Letellier (des Pères Blancs), *Les Indigènes de la Casbah* (Algiers: 19ème Corps de l'Armée, Etat Major, Cours de formation islamique, 3 December 1941), 2–5. In 1952 a study reiterated the common pattern of one family per room, the room being 5 to 10 square meters, with very poor ventilation and daylight. See Paul Debauffre, "Habitat en Algérie," *Documents nord-africains* 42 (February 1952): 3.

79. E. Pasquali, "La Casbah en 1949," *Bulletin municipal officiel de la ville d'Alger* 10 (August 1949): 6. The density in the upper casbah was recorded as 2,600 to 3,800 people per hectare as compared to the average density of 1,060 people per hectare for the entire commune of Algiers. According to some interpretations, this amounted to an overpopulation of 25,000 people. See Georges Boni, "Le Cas d'Alger," *Bulletin économique et juridique* 172 (April 1954): 138; "Bilan général de l'aide à la construction de 1946 à 1953," *Documents algériens* 42 (1 January 1953–31 December 1953): 95.

80. E. Pasquali, "Aperçus sur la 'Casbah' d'Alger de l'époque phénicienne à nos jours—Démographie de la Casbah," *Bulletin municipal officiel de la ville d'Alger* 3 (March 1951): n.p., and ibid., 4 (April 1951): n.p.

81. M. Kaddache, "La Casbah de nos jours," *Documents algériens* (1 January 1951–31 December 1951): 237, 240–241.

82. Ibid., 231–237.

83. Ibid., 229–230; *Bulletin municipal officiel de la ville d'Alger* 4, 5–6, (April, May–June 1950): n.p.

84. *L'Echo d'Alger,* 11 June 1959.

85. General de Gaulle quoted in République Française, Délégation Générale du Gouvernement en Algérie, Direction du Plan et des Etudes Economiques, *Plan de Constantine 1959–1963. Rapport général* (June 1960), 33, 336.

86. M. Baglietto, "Un Vaste projet municipal: l'aménagement de la Casbah," *L'Echo d'Alger,* 13 February 1960; idem, "Le Conseil municipal du Grand-Alger devant un problème humain: l'aménagement de la Casbah," *L'Echo d'Alger,* 17 February 1960.

87. Lesbet, *La Casbah d'Alger,* 61–62.

88. Albert-Paul Lentin, *L'Algérie entre deux mondes. Le Dernier quart d'heure* (Paris, 1963), 111. The entire city was divided into three zones: central Algiers and two-thirds of the casbah; the remaining one-third of the casbah and the west of Algiers; and east of Algiers. See ibid., 124.

89. Ibid., 126–134.

90. *L'Echo d'Alger,* 29 March 1956, 27–28 May 1956, 9 January 1957 (the newspaper reported that about five hundred men were registered as construction workers), and 23 September 1956. See also Henri Alleg, Jacques de Bonis, Henri J. Douzon, Jean Freire, and Pierre Haudiquet, *La Guerre d'Algérie,* vol. 2 (Paris, 1981), 183.

91. Lentin, *L'Algérie entre deux mondes,* 131–135.

92. *El Moudjahid* 74 (15 December 1960). The tract was signed by Union Générale des Travailleurs Algériens, Union Générale des Etudiants Musulmans Algériens, Jeunesse Algérien, and Union des Femmes Algériennes.

93. *El Moudjahid* 75 (19 December 1960): 352, 356, 358. One eventful day reveals the fervor and scale of collective action in the casbah. On 11 December 1960, at 9:45 A.M., 10,000 people crowded its streets, shouting "[Ferhat] Abbas

to power" and "Muslim Algeria." At 2:30 P.M. hundreds of young people carrying FLN flags still marched the narrow streets to the chants of women crowded at windows. By 5:30 P.M. large crowds—FLN processions—again filled the streets of the casbah.

94. "Le Plan d'aménagement de la région algéroise," in *Travaux nord-africains,* 17 December 1932.

95. Deluz, *L'Urbanisme et l'architecture d'Alger,* 16. Although refined and detailed further by Tony Socard, the project became known as the Prost project.

96. Lespès, "Les Villes," 9; Joseph Sintes, "Le Quartier de la Marine et la Casbah" in *Travaux nord-africains,* 31 December 1932. According to Sintes, prostitution was so rampant that Muslim residents felt compelled to write "honnête maison" on their doors.

97. F. Gauthier, "Le Quartier de la Marine," *Feuillets d'El-Djezair* (July 1941): 33. Comité du Vieil Alger was established to preserve precolonial Algiers. Its activities included designating buildings that should be classified historic monuments, organizing lectures and walking tours in the casbah, and publishing a journal, *Feuillets d'El-Djezair.* Among its members were Georges Marçais and Muhammad Racim. See M. Orif, "De l'Art indigène à l'art algérien," *Actes de la recherche en sciences sociales* 75 (November 1988): 38.

98. "Vers un meilleur aménagement," *Chantiers* (March 1935): 186.

99. Ibid., 185.

100. Lespès, "Les Villes," 12; "Vers un meilleur aménagement," 186; Jean Alazard, "L'Urbanisme et l'architecture à Alger de 1918 à 1936," *L'Architecture* 50, no. 1 (15 January 1937): 25. The new housing projects were to be constructed in the Bab el-Oued Quarter and in the southern suburbs.

101. J.-P. Fauve, *Alger capitale* (Paris, 1936), 30, 36.

102. Ibid., 67, 69; J.-P. Fauve, "Confirmation mathématique des vues qui précèdent," 7 June 1934, FLC.

103. The idea of placing a skyscraper at the location was criticized even by those who were typically Le Corbusier's defenders. Fauve, for example, argued that the proposed building "profiled in a disastrous manner on the casbah, the pure gem of Algiers," despite the same vision of the project to develop a civic center near the Place du Gouvernement. See Fauve, "Confirmation mathématique."

104. Le Corbusier, "Note financière annexe au Projet C de l'urbanisation du Quartier de la Marine à Alger," 1934, FLC; idem, Questionnaire B, 1931–35, FLC; idem, "Proposition d'un Plan Directeur d'Alger et de sa région pour aider aux travaux de la Commission du Plan de la Région d'Alger et comme suite à la séance du 16 juillet 1941," FLC.

105. See Mary McLeod, "Le Corbusier and Algiers," *Oppositions* 16–17 (1980): 55–85.

106. Omar Racim's letter was published in *Tribune d'Alger républicain,* 16 August 1947. The editors qualified their position by stating that while they thought the letter was "interesting," the opinion expressed belonged solely to the author.

107. P. Loviconi, "La Transformation du Quartier de l'Ancienne Préfecture," *Bulletin municipal officiel de la ville d'Alger* 11 (September 1949): 11.

108. P. L. Nougier, "La Transformation de l'ancien quartier de la Marine," *Chantiers* 14 (1954): n.p.

109. *Travaux nord-africains,* 6 December 1956.

110. Ibid., 12 March 1959; Deluz, *L'Urbanisme et l'architecture d'Alger,* 74–76; *Travaux nord-africains,* 6 December 1956. By late 1956, 328 of the 1,250 projected units had been built in Bab el-Oued. Obviously, 1,250 units for 15,000 people displaced from the Marine Quarter meant very high densities for the new housing projects.

111. *Travaux nord-africains,* 19 March 1959.

112. Deluz, *L'Urbanisme et l'architecture d'Alger,* 74.

113. "Urbanisation du quartier de la Marine," *Alger-revue municipale* (spring 1959): 48.

114. *Travaux nord-africains,* 6 December 1956; Deluz, *L'Urbanisme et l'architecture d'Alger,* 74.

Chapter 2.   An Outline of Urban Structure

1. This chapter does not claim to be a comprehensive survey, but an outline that explains the essence of city-building activities under the French. For a thorough and meticulous survey of urban history on Algiers that covers the years 1830 to 1930, see Lespès, *Alger.* For a well-illustrated but brief summary of architecture and urbanism in Algiers under French rule (until the 1960s), see X. Malverti, "Alger: Meditérranée, soleil et modernité," in Institut Français d'Architecture, *Architectures françaises outre-mer* (Paris, 1992), 29–64. I have not dealt with the history of the harbor of Algiers. On this topic, see Yves Layes, *Le Port d'Alger* (Algiers, 1951).

2. Quoted in Pasquier-Bronde, "Alger," 33.

3. The term *à la Vauban* is used in 1951 by M. Molbert, chief engineer of the city of Algiers, who criticized the short vision of the first French planners in Algiers and who mocked the fact that the fortifications had to be demolished a century later "without having received a single gunshot." See M. Molbert, "L'Urbanisme et son application à Alger," *Bulletin municipal officiel de la ville d'Alger* 5 (May 1951): n.p. On fortifications, see Lespès, *Alger,* 235–237.

4. "Extraits du Journal des Débats du 18 juin 1842," SHAT, Génie. Alger. Art. 8, section 1, carton 7.

5. Lespès, *Alger,* 223, 336–337.

6. Molbert, "L'Urbanisme et son application à Alger"; Lespès, *Alger,* 251–257.

7. François Béguin, *Arabisances* (Paris, 1983), 106; Lespès, *Alger,* 255.

8. Lespès, *Alger,* 263–265.

9. Pasquier-Bronde, "Alger," 36–37; Deluz, *L'Urbanisme et l'architecture d'Alger,* 13; Lespès, *Alger,* 357–364.

10. Lespès, *Alger,* 265–266.

11. Ibid., 325–329, 355; Louis Presse, *Algérie et Tunisie* (Paris, 1888), 12, 14–15. The location of a new casino was a much debated affair. Eugène de Redon proposed to place it in Bab el-Oued, with a commanding view of the sea; among

other locations considered were the Boulevard Gambetta, Boulevard de la République, and Square Bresson. See Lespès, *Alger,* 425. The British interest in Algiers as a place of *hivernage* was short-lived.

12. Lespès, *Alger,* 340–42.

13. Ibid., 349–352.

14. Ibid., 376–383.

15. Ibid., 398–399.

16. Ibid., 400–401.

17. Ibid., 405–406.

18. Ibid., 411–413, 417.

19. Ibid., 413–414.

20. Ibid., 430–435; J. Alazard, "L'Urbanisme à Alger," *Le Monde colonial illustré* 80 (April 1930): 92.

21. Lespès, *Alger,* 408–409. The increase by 22,000 in the indigenous population of the *intra-muros* between 1896 and 1926 is especially noteworthy. The overall population increase in the same area during these three decades was 34,000.

22. Molbert, "L'Urbanisme et son application à Alger."

23. Alazard, "L'Urbanisme à Alger," 93; Lespès, *Alger,* 438–439.

24. "Vers un meilleur aménagement," *Chantiers* (March 1935): 180; Molbert, "L'Urbanisme et son application à Alger"; Lespès, *Alger,* 8–9.

25. "Vers un meilleur aménagement," 180–183; Lespès, *Alger,* 16–18. Deluz, *L'Urbanisme et l'architecture d'Alger,* 19–20.

26. Lespès, *Alger,* 13.

27. Deluz, *L'Urbanisme et l'architecture d'Alger,* 20.

28. Literature on Le Corbusier's projects in Algiers is extensive. For an indepth discussion, see McLeod, "Le Corbusier and Algiers," 55–85. For the projects, see Le Corbusier, *Ouevre complète, 1938–1946* (Zurich, 1964). Curiously enough, Le Corbusier was challenging Prost and Danger's proposals in another Mediterranean city at the time. With the support of Turkish modernist architects, he had taken on the design of an alternative master plan for Izmir. See Izmir Files, FLC.

29. Le Corbusier, *Poésie sur Alger,* 17, 11–13.

30. Le Corbusier, *La Ville radieuse,* 233.

31. Le Corbusier, *Quand les cathédrales étaient blanches* (Paris, 1937), 46–47.

32. Le Corbusier, *Poésie sur Alger,* 38, 44.

33. Cotéreau quoted in Deluz, *L'Urbanisme et l'architecture d'Alger,* 12.

34. Reynaud quoted in Girardet, *L'Idée coloniale en France,* 176–99.

35. Resituating Le Corbusier within the historic context of colonial urban design, R. Cozzolini and A. Petruccioli argue that Le Corbusier's viaduct scheme is derived from Chassériau's arcades. See R. Cozzolini and A. Petruccioli, "Algeri—Le Corbusier—Algeri," *Spazio e Società* 15–16 (September–December 1981): 110. Le Corbusier himself expressed his fascination with the arcades in numerous sketches and acknowledged their influence on his own designs.

36. Deluz, *L'Urbanisme et l'architecture d'Alger,* 18.

37. McLeod, "Le Corbusier and Algiers," 73.

38. An outstanding example that makes reference to the viaduct of Obus A

is the Immeuble-Pont Burdeau from 1952. The long and narrow building is situated in a valley and is designed to connect the two hills on two sides. Its asphalt roof acts as a portion of a major traffic artery. For Le Corbusier's influence on architects practicing in Algiers, see Deluz, *L'Urbanisme et l'architecture d'Alger,* 41–52.

39. M. Sgroi-Dufresne, *Alger 1830 –1984: Stratégies et enjeux urbains* (Paris, 1986), 18.

40. René Maunier, *Sociologie coloniale* (1932), quoted in Robert Descloitres, Jean-Claude Réverdy, and Claudine Descloitres, in *L'Algérie des bidonvilles* (Paris, 1961), 21.

41. Sgroi-Dufresne, *Alger 1830 –1984,* 24–25.

42. Ibid., 29; Deluz, *L'Urbanisme et l'architecture d'Alger,* 55.

43. Sgroi-Dufresne, *Alger 1830 –1984,* 29.

44. Ibid., 29–30; Deluz, *L'Urbanisme et l'architecture d'Alger,* 55, 57.

45. "Plan d'urbanisme de la région algéroise," *Chantiers* 2 (1951).

46. "Les Grandes lignes du Plan d'Urbanisme de la région algéroise," *Chantiers* 7 (1952).

47. The population of Algiers had increased from 308,321 in 1948 to 355,000 in 1954, pushing the overall density from 224 to 258 people per hectare. The change in the European population was from 179,546 to 192,890, whereas the Muslim population had grown from 128,775 to 162,150. It was noted alarmingly that within nine years, the number of Muslims living in Algiers would equal the number of Europeans and the total number would reach 460,000. See "Alger, ville dont la population s'accroit [chaque année] de 10,000 habitants," *Alger-revue municipale* (May 1955). According to computations by Sgroi-Dufresne, 99.2 percent of Hussein-Dey's population was Muslim, followed by 76.5 percent of Bouzarea, 70–71 percent of Algiers and Maison-Carrée, and 61.6 percent of Kouba. In contrast, the communes of St.-Eugène, Birmandreis, and el-Biar were heavily European. See Sgroi-Dufresne, *Alger 1830 –1984,* 36.

48. Descloitres, Réverdy, and Descloitres, *L'Algérie des bidonvilles,* 30–31, 39–43, 52–53; "Alger, lutte pour resoudre le douloureux problème de la casbah et des bidonvilles," *Alger-revue municipale* (May 1955); Sgroi-Dufresne, *Alger 1830 –1984,* 36. The segregation was especially striking in certain quarters. For example, in 1954, in Bab el-Oued 92 percent of a total population of 45,905 consisted of Europeans, and in the Rue Michelet area, where 52,674 people lived, this percentage was 94. In contrast, 97 percent of the 41,467 residents of the upper casbah were Muslims, and Mahieddine was 100 percent Muslim. See Descloitres, Réverdy, and Descloitres, *L'Algérie des bidonvilles,* 41.

49. Deluz, *L'Urbanisme et l'architecture d'Alger,* 63.

50. Jacques Chevallier, *Nous, algériens* (Paris, 1958), 141.

51. For the organization and personnel of the agency, see "Le Bureau du plan de la ville d'Alger," *Alger revue* (May 1955). Among the members of the team was Robert Descloitres, who studied the *bidonvilles* and later published the results of his studies.

52. Chevallier quoted in Sgroi-Dufresne, *Alger 1830 –1984,* 48.

53. Association pour l'Etude du Développement de l'Agglomération Algéroise, *Alger, méthode de travail, étude du site* (Algiers, 1958), 4–5, 13.

54. Deluz, *L'Urbanisme et l'architecture d'Alger,* 64–65; Sgroi-Dufresne, *Alger 1830–1984,* 48–49.

55. Deluz, *L'Urbanisme et l'architecture d'Alger,* 66–67; Sgroi-Dufresne, *Alger 1830–1984,* 48–49.

56. *L'Echo d'Alger,* 7 May 1958. The first is in the ravine of the Femme Sauvage and reaching to Diar el-Mahçoul; the second is the Boulevard Aquilina between Climat de France and Boulevard Lettre-de-Tassigny. For the construction of the 500-meter-long Boulevard Aquilina, named after a military commandant whose widow had provided the funds, a shantytown was bulldozed. A stela, placed at the entrance of the avenue, paid homage to Commandant Aquilina, to the "'apostle of *bidonvilles,*' . . . who knew how to use the treasures of his endless goodness on these lands formerly occupied by *bidonvilles,* and deserves the respect and the affection of the disinherited."

57. Deluz, *L'Urbanisme et l'architecture d'Alger,* 101–102.

58. République Française, Délégation Générale, *Plan de Constantine,* 348.

59. Deluz, *L'Urbanisme et l'architecture d'Alger,* 105–106.

60. Ibid., 102; République Française, Délégation Générale, *Plan de Constantine,* 352. The concept of ZUP has survived in French urbanism to the present day and become identified with working-class neighborhoods with large-scale housing projects. Today, immigrants from North Africa are concentrated in ZUPs of French cities.

61. *L'Echo d'Alger,* 26 February 1959.

62. For tram and trolley lines, see *L'Echo d'Alger,* 3 March 1959; for the subway project, see ibid., 19 November 1959.

63. Sgroi-Dufresne, *Alger 1830–1984,* 100.

64. See *L'Echo d'Alger,* 28 February 1959, 4 March 1959, 6 March 1959, and 11 March 1959.

65. Deluz, *L'Urbanisme et l'architecture d'Alger,* 106.

Chapter 3.   The Indigenous House

1. Djamila Amrane, *Les Femmes algériennes dans la guerre* (Paris, 1991), 45.

2. Marnia Lazreg, *The Eloquence of Silence: Algerian Women in Question* (New York, 1994), 99. Lazreg argues that the family served as a buffer against colonialism for women because it was central to their lives. I stretched the concept to the spatial realm.

3. Pierre Bourdieu, *The Algerians,* tr. Alan Ross (Boston, 1962), 157. Cultural resistance to colonialism is an important theme that has recently enjoyed scholarly attention. For example, Djilali Sari argues that the reappropriation and reaffirmation of Algerian cultural patrimony (as resistance to colonialism) began in the later part of the nineteenth century amid the "ruin and the rabble of the vestiges of the medinas" in literature, music, and visual arts. See Djilali Sari, "Role des médinas algériennes dans la dynamisation culturelle et identitaire," paper presented at the American Institute for Maghribi Studies Annual Conference, "The Living Medina: The Walled Arab City in Literature, Architecture, History," Tangier, 29 May–3 June 1996. In her masterful study, Julia Clancy-

Smith analyzed religious resistance to colonialism; see Julia Clancy-Smith, *Rebel and Saint: Muslim Notables, Popular Protest, and Colonial Encounters* (Berkeley, 1994).

4. "Rapport du chef du Génie sur la place d'Alger, 1831," SHAT, Génie. Alger. Art. 8, section 1, carton 1, quoted in Aleth Picard, "Architecture et urbanisme en Algérie: d'une rive à l'autre (1830–1962)," *Revue du monde musulman et de la Méditerranée* 73/74 (1996): 122.

5. The term *ethnography* as I use it adheres to James Clifford's definition, which distinguishes it from ethnology, social anthropology, and cultural anthropology. Ethnography is "a more general cultural predisposition that cuts through modern anthropology and that this science shares with twentieth-century art and writing. The ethnographic label suggests a characteristic attitude of participant observation among the artifacts of defamiliarized cultural reality." James Clifford, *The Predicament of Culture* (Cambridge, Mass., 1988), 121.

6. Philippe Lucas and Jean-Claude Vatin, *L'Algérie des anthropologues* (Paris, 1975), 26–27. From the 1880s on, racial differences between Berbers and Arabs were emphasized to serve a divide-and-conquer strategy. See Fanny Colonna and Claude Haim Brahimi, "Du Bon usage de la science coloniale," in *Le Mal de voir* (Paris, 1976), 231–234.

7. As Colonna and Brahimi point out, Masqueray himself did not argue that the racial characteristics of Berbers allowed them to be assimilated more easily than the Arabs, but simply maintained that they were *assimilables*. See Colonna and Brahimi, *Le Mal de voir*, 238.

8. Bourdieu, *The Algerians*, 4, 59–65.

9. Lucas and Vatin, *L'Algérie des anthropologues*, 31.

10. Augustin Bernard, *Enquête sur l'habitation rurale des indigènes de l'Algérie* (Algiers, 1921), 123–124; Augustin Berque, "L'Habitation de l'indigène algérien," *Revue africaine* 78 (1936): 47–50.

11. Bernard, *Enquête sur l'habitation rurale*, 117–121.

12. Clifford, *Predicament of Culture*, 61, 122.

13. William Marçais, preface to Amélie-Marie Goichon, *La Vie féminine au Mzab* (Paris, 1927), vii–viii. Between these lines, it is possible to read an implicit agenda to delimit the boundaries of women's participation in the profession to the domestic sphere.

14. These books also strive, in varying degrees, to influence the colonial policies regarding Algerian women, family, and society. They thus present themselves as agents of the French order and civilization even when they dissent from colonial policies. Auclert's main areas of inquiry—marriage, polygamy, divorce, and prostitution—were studied by Goichon and Gaudry, too. If Auclert did not have the academic background to investigate the material culture and daily life patterns of Algerian women with a rigorous ethnographic methodology, she knew where to look. For example, her sporadic references to physical settings and to residential forms ("where life flowed inside the courtyards and in houses without windows") reemerged in Goichon's and Gaudry's work as areas that deserved to be explored with scientific scrutiny in order to shed light on daily life and social relationships. See Hubertine Auclert, *Les Femmes arabes en Algérie* (Paris, 1900), 4, 24.

15. Goichon, *La Vie féminine au Mzab*, 1. Seeing Algerian women as "guard-

ians of tradition" is an enduring theme in ethnographic discourse. Three decades after Goichon, Bourdieu repeated a similar observation: "[Kabylian] women play an essential role in ensuring the permanence of tradition." See Bourdieu, *The Algerians,* 95.

16. Goichon, *La Vie féminine au Mzab,* 41, 24 – 25, 100 – 104. Goichon refers the readers to M. Mercier's *Civilisation urbaine,* a "technical study," for further information on houses of Mzab.

17. The educational role of photographic documentation in ethnography reached a threshold in Paris between 1937 and 1950, under the curatorship of Thérèse Rivière, herself a prominent ethnographer and photographer. Among the various exhibitions organized during Rivière's tenure, the 1943 display on Aurès occupies a special place. The 123 photographs Rivière selected among the 6,000 she had taken in 1935 – 36 were in the spirit of the ethnographic photography of Goichon and Gaudry. Rivière did not treat photography as subsidiary to text, however, but gave it a primary narrative function. For example, she recorded the work process by a chronological series of images that focused on detail. With the majority of her subjects as women at work, she expanded on Goichon's and Gaudry's work. As pointed out by David Prochaska, the women in Rivière's photographs were never depicted as sex objects; they therefore offered a corrective to the other colonial photographic genre, the commercial postcard. See David Prochaska, "L'Algérie imaginaire," *Ghardiva* (winter 1989 – 90): 33 – 35. A selection of Thérèse Rivière's photographs has been published by Fanny Colonna, who also wrote an introduction to the collection. See Fanny Colonna, *Aurès/Algérie 1935 – 36. Photographies de Thérèse Rivière* (Algiers, 1987).

18. Mathéa Gaudry, *La Femme chaouia de l'Aurès* (Paris, 1928), 280 – 286.

19. Ibid., 17 – 32, 25 – 26, 31, 287.

20. Thérèse Rivière, "L'Habitation chez les Ouled Abderrahman Chaouia de l'Aurès," *Africa* 11, no. 3 (1938): 294 – 304.

21. Laure Bosquet-Lefevre, *La Femme Kabyle* (Paris, 1939), 30, 182 – 183.

22. Germaine Laoust-Chantreaux, *Kabylie, côté femmes. La Vie féminine à Aït Hichem, 1937 –1939* (Aix-en-Provence, 1990), 30 – 44. Note that the study was not published at the time it was written.

23. Montaland, "L'urbanisme en Algérie," 51 – 52.

24. For example, Gaudry's book enjoyed immense success at the time. See Denise Brahimi, *Femmes arabes et soeurs musulmanes* (Paris, 1984), 168.

25. "L'Habitat musulman," *Informations algériennes* 19 (February 1942): 71.

26. René Lespès, "Projet d'enquête sur l'habitat des indigènes musulmans dans les centres urbains d'Algérie," *Revue africaine* 76, nos. 362 – 363 (1935): 433 – 434; idem, "Les Villes," 4.

27. *L'Architecture d'aujourd'hui* 3 (1936): 26; H. Marchand, *La Musulmane algérienne* (Paris, 1960), 47 – 50.

28. For the architectural representation of Islam in the world's fairs, see Zeynep Çelik, *Displaying the Orient: Architecture of Islam at Nineteenth-Century World's Fairs* (Berkeley, 1992).

29. Berque, "L'Habitation de l'indigène algérien," 63, 87, 94. For a discussion of these projects, see Chapter 5.

30. Augustin Berque, *L'Algérie, terre d'art et d'histoire* (Algiers, 1937), 323 – 327. To adapt the indigenous house to European needs and habits, Berque pro-

posed certain alterations that would enable the architects to design "dream villas" in Algeria.

31. Le Corbusier, *La Ville radieuse,* 230, 233; idem, "Le Folklore est l'expression fleurie des traditions," 31.

32. Ibid., 230.

33. Jean de Maisonseul, "Pour une architecture et un urbanisme Nord-Africains," *Revue d'Alger* 8 (1945): 353–358.

34. Ibid., 353–354.

35. Ibid., 355–356.

36. Ibid., 356–357.

37. Ibid., 357.

38. J. Scelles-Millie, "L'urbanisme en Algérie," *Entr'Aide française* 9 (November 1946): 7.

39. See Linda Nochlin, "The Imaginary Orient," *Art in America* 71, no. 5 (May 1983): 120–129, 186–191. For comprehensive surveys of Orientalist painters, see Linda Thornton, *Women as Portrayed in Orientalist Painting* (Paris, 1985) and idem, *The Orientalists, Painter-Travellers 1828–1908* (Paris, 1983).

40. See Malek Alloula, *The Colonial Harem,* tr. Myrna Godzich and Wlad Godzich (Minneapolis, 1986).

41. Abdelghani Megherbi, *Les Algériens au miroir du cinéma colonial* (Algiers, 1982), 192.

42. R. P. Letellier (des Pères Blancs), *La Famille indigène devant les problèmes sociaux modernes* (Algiers, n.d.), 5–6.

43. Congrès Internationaux d'Architecture Moderne (CIAM) 9, Aix-en-Provence, Groupe CIAM Alger, "Bidonville Mahieddine," 1953, FLC.

44. Alleg et al., *La Guerre d'Algérie,* vol. 1, 144.

45. Descloitres, Réverdy, and Descloitres, *L'Algérie des bidonvilles,* 84–85. Berque indeed mentioned the *bidonvilles* in his article "L'Habitation de l'indigène algérien." A report from 1949 qualifies the *bidonvilles* as "ancient, sometimes fifty years old." See Jean-Claude Isnard, *Les Problèmes du logement dans l'agglomération algéroise* (Ecole Financière Nationale d'Administration, Section Economique et Financière, December 1949), mim. report, AOM.

46. Descloitres, Réverdy, and Descloitres, *L'Algérie des bidonvilles,* 91–103; Bourdieu, *The Algerians,* 64.

47. Descloitres, Réverdy, and Descloitres, *L'Algérie des bidonvilles,* 78–79, 27, 30–31.

48. Ibid., 35; Bourdieu, *The Algerians,* 64–65; Isnard, *Les Problèmes du logement,* 6; Alleg et al., *La Guerre d'Algérie,* vol. 1, 146. Unemployment figures were alarming. According to Bourdieu, in 1954, 30 percent of adult urban males were unemployed or worked only part-time; Alleg argues that about one out of every two (male) Algerians had neither a profession nor regular work.

49. Descloitres, Réverdy, and Descloitres, *L'Algérie des bidonvilles,* 56–59, 67–71; "Les Bidonvilles: Genèse et résorption. L'Experience du Clos-Salembier," *Alger revue* (spring 1961): 26.

50. Descloitres, Réverdy, and Descloitres, *L'Algérie des bidonvilles,* 13–18, 70–71. Although the poor conditions of squatter settlements in Algiers had alarmed the city officials quite early, no action was taken to improve them. For

example, the municipality declared the settlements of el-Kattar and Mahieddine unsanitary in 1941, and decided to demolish the shacks and build rehousing projects for the residents. No part of the program was executed, but in 1943, the municipality built fountains, latrines, a main sewage line, and a main street in these settlements. See Isnard, *Les Problèmes du logement*, 7, 16.

51. Jean de Maisonseul, "Djenan el-Hasan," in *Roland Simounet. Pour une invention de l'espace* (Paris, 1986), 17. For Simounet's work in Algiers, see Chapter 5.

52. CIAM 9, Aix-en-Provence, Groupe CIAM Alger, "Bidonville Mahieddine," FLC.

53. Ibid. The largest CIAM congress to date, the Ninth Congress (1953) focused on a charter of habitation that aimed to bring a radical critique to the functionalist mechanism of the Athens Charter by emphasizing the notion of "man" and relations between "men." Under the leadership of architects such as Alison and Peter Smithson and Aldo Van Eyck, discussions shifted to "patterns of inhabitation." Simounet thus found a sympathetic environment for his study of the merits of squatter housing.

54. "Pour un habitat humaine," *L'Architecture d'aujourd'hui* 60 (1955): 4.

55. See, for example, Descloitres, Réverdy, and Descloitres, *L'Algérie des bidonvilles*, 12.

56. Furthermore, villagers seeking refuge in the *bidonvilles* from the bombarded countryside enabled the older squatter settlers to acquire a comprehensive vision of the war. For example, in the summer of 1956, refugees from the burned and bombarded villages of Mitija (at the foot of the Atlas mountains) and Kabylia flocked to the Mahieddine settlement, the most extensive *bidonville* of Algiers. Their stories mixed with those of the urban resistance, complementing each other and unifying the struggle. See Alleg et al., *La Guerre d'Algérie*, vol. 1, 168–169.

57. Ibid., 144. The daily papers of Algiers frequently reported demolition and rehousing operations carried out by the army. For example, *L'Echo d'Alger* reported on 3 September 1957 that the 248 shacks in the *bidonville* known as Descuns in Maison-Carrée were bulldozed by army forces and the families were scattered into four areas. According to the same newspaper of 25 November 1957, similar operations had marked the end of another squatter settlement, the Glacière in Hussein-Dey. On 18 December 1959, *L'Echo d'Alger* printed a photograph showing the demolition of 225 squatter houses whose residents were relocated.

Chapter 4.   Housing the Algerians: Policies

1. René Lespès, *Pour comprendre l'Algérie* (Algiers, 1937), 36.

2. Sarrault, *Grandeur et servitude coloniales*, 108, 102–103, 108, 116, 119.

3. Lespès, "Projet d'enquête," 434, 436.

4. Louis Morard, "L'Algérie: ce qu'elle est, ce qu'elle doit devenir," *Le Monde colonial illustré* 87 (November 1930): 272. The growing importance given to low-cost housing was fueled by the creation of the Office des Habitations à Bon Marché (HBM) de la Ville d'Alger (Office of Low-Cost Housing of the

City of Algiers) in 1921. This office assumed the construction and management of low-cost housing projects. The first three groups of HBM housing, Rochambeau (1923), Bobillot (1925), and Picardie (1927), were for Europeans. See *Chantiers* (March 1935): 177–178.

5. A. Seiller and M. Lathuillière, "Le Problème de l'habitat indigène en Algérie," *L'Architecture d'aujourd'hui* 3 (1936): 22.

6. Lespès, "Projet d'enquête," 435–436; idem, *Pour comprendre l'Algérie*, 38.

7. Alazard, "L'Urbanisme et l'architecture à Alger de 1918 à 1936," 26.

8. Direction de l'Intérieur et Beaux-Arts, 3ème Bureau, "Proposition de la Commission des Réformes musulmanes," 4 March 1944, "Projet de décision soumis au gouvernement," 4 April 1944, and "Note sur l'habitat urbain musulman," 16 January 1946, AOM.

9. Tony Socard, "L'Urbanisme en Algérie," *Rafales* 135 (12–19 October 1946). For a discussion of these projects, see Chapter 5.

10. Scelles-Millie, "L'Urbanisme en Algérie," 6.

11. Deluz, *L'Urbanisme et l'architecture d'Alger*, 53–54.

12. Le Docteur Montaldo, "L'Habitat économique et social en Algérie," *Technique et architecture* 12, nos. 1–2 (1953): 46.

13. Jacques Stamboul, "L'Urbanisme," *Encyclopédie mensuelle d'outre-mer* (Paris, 1954), 208.

14. Paul Messerschmitt, "Problèmes actuels," *Bulletin économique et juridique* 172 (April 1954): 128. Messerschmitt cites a total of 40,000 residents in *bidonvilles*. According to a government report, the number is 53,000, with 17,200 people in Algiers proper, 22,000 in Hussein-Dey, and 14,000 in Maison-Carrée. See République Française, Présidence du Conseil, Commissariat Général au Plan de Modernisation et d'Equipement, *Rapport général de la commission d'étude et de coordination des plans de modernisation et d'équipement de l'Algérie, de la Tunisie et du Maroc*, June 1954, 131.

15. Messerschmitt, "Problèmes actuels," 128–129. For the Boucle-Perez housing project, see Chapter 5.

16. Cabinet du Ministre d'Algérie, *Algérie* (1957), 165.

17. Ibid., 128. HLMs (*habitations à loyer modéré*) were considered the main solution to housing problems in Algiers in the 1950s. Financing could be done in several ways, mostly by the offices of HLM with loans from the Caisse des Dépôts et Consignations; it was common to hold competitions for designs. Another means was by *location-attribution* with Sociétés Coopératives, Crédit Immobiliers, or Sociétés Mutuelles. For financing of HLMs, see Yves Duconge, "Problèmes du financement de la construction en Algérie," *Bulletin économique et juridique* 170 (April 1954): 133–135; for their organizational structure, see René Montaldo, "Le Rôle des organismes d'H.L.M. en Algérie," *Bulletin économique et juridique* 170 (April 1954): 130–132, 135. For the financing of low-cost housing in general, see Cabinet du Ministre d'Algérie, *Algérie*, 158–161.

18. "Rapport de M. André Bakouche, rapporteur général de la Commission d'Habitat, adopté par l'Assemblée Algérienne le 29 mars 1956," *Travaux nord-africains*, 29 March 1956.

19. Commissariat à la Reconstruction, "Arrête relatif à l'amélioration des populations rurales en Algérie," Algiers, 25 September 1956, AOM (this decree

also applied to rural populations); Cabinet du Ministre d'Algérie, *Algérie,* 169, 164.

20. Sgroi-Dufresne, *Alger 1830–1984,* 47–48.

21. René Pottier, "Alger, ville pilote," *Encyclopédie mensuelle d'outre-mer* 68 (April 1956): 177.

22. *L'Echo d'Alger,* 14 August 1958.

23. Ibid., 13 July 1959.

24. *The Constantine Plan for Algeria* (New York, May 1961), 9.

25. République Française, Délégation Générale, *Plan de Constantine, 1959–1963,* 337. The other numbers were 32,000 for 1960, 42,000 for 1961, and 53,000 for 1962.

26. Ibid., 339, 341. For financial aspects of the housing programs of Plan de Constantine, see ibid., 342–347.

27. *Europe France Outre-mer* 388 (June 1962): n.p.

28. "Les Bidonvilles: Genèse et resorption," 28.

29. *L'Echo d'Alger,* 15 May 1959.

30. "Les Bidonvilles: Genèse et resorption," 28.

31. Ibid., 28–29.

32. Louis Bertrand, *Alger* (Paris, 1938), 139–140, 143.

33. Scelles-Millie, "L'urbanisme en Algérie," 7. See also Chapter 3.

34. Pottier, "Alger, ville pilote," 175.

35. Gouvernement Général de l'Algérie, Direction Générale des Affaires Indigènes et des Territoires du Sud, Service de l'Economie Sociale Indigène, *Pour les paysans et les artisans indigènes* (Algiers, 1939), 135–137. The report pointed to one such project under construction: Ain-Bouchekif, 15 kilometers outside Tiaret.

36. Berque, "L'Habitation de l'indigène algérien," 75–76. For various rural housing experiments, see ibid., 76–85.

37. Michel Cornaton, *Les Regroupements de la décolonisation en Algérie* (Paris, 1967), 60–61.

38. *El Moudjahid,* 10 May 1959.

39. Cornaton, *Regroupements de la décolonisation,* 57, 60–65.

40. Gouvernement Général de l'Algérie, Commissariat à la Reconstruction, "Arrêt relatif à l'amélioration de l'habitat traditionnel des populations rurales en Algérie," 25 September 1956, AOM.

41. Cabinet du Ministre de l'Algérie, *Algérie,* 165–166.

42. Cornaton, *Regroupements de la décolonisation,* 68–71; Bourdieu, *The Algerians,* 164. For Sarrault's use of the term, see Sarrault, *Grandeur et servitude coloniales,* 79.

43. Bourdieu, *The Algerians,* 163.

44. *L'Echo d'Alger,* 2 July 1959; Cornaton, *Regroupements de la décolonisation,* 74; *El Moudjahid,* 10 May 1959.

45. *L'Echo d'Alger,* 20 October 1959 and 29 July 1960.

46. Bourdieu, *The Algerians,* 169. Bourdieu maintains that even if the army officers had sought to consult the users, most likely they would have gotten no cooperation.

47. Cornaton, *Regroupements de la décolonisation,* 83–84. For an extremely

effective visual presentation of the *regroupement* practices, see Marc Garanger, *La Guerre d'Algérie* (Paris, 1984), 42–57.

48. Bourdieu, *The Algerians,* 171. For Bourdieu's analysis of the Kabyle house, see ibid., 6–7.

49. Secrétariat Social d'Alger, *De l'Algérie originelle à l'Algérie moderne* (Algiers, 1961), 37.

50. Cornaton, *Regroupements de la décolonisation,* 84–89.

51. Rita Vindes, "Est-il permis que des enfants meurtent de faim dans les 'camps de regroupement' en Algérie," *El Moudjahid,* 5 January 1960.

52. Cornaton, *Regroupements de la décolonisation,* 99–102.

53. Quoted in ibid., 102.

54. *El Moudjahid,* 10 May 1959.

55. Descloitres, Réverdy, and Descloitres, *L'Algérie des bidonvilles,* 12.

56. Cornaton, *Regroupements de la décolonisation,* 94–95.

Chapter 5. Housing the Algerians: *Grands Ensembles*

1. Deluz, *L'Urbanisme et l'architecture d'Alger,* 190.

2. I borrow the term *arabisance* from François Béguin, who defines it as "arabization of architectural forms imported from Europe." See Béguin, *Arabisances,* 1. These early projects have a strong link to the new medinas built in Morocco in the 1910s and the 1920s.

3. A. Loeckx and P. Vermeulen, *L'Habitat moderne à Alger (1925–1975),* part 2 (Leuven, 1988), 5–6, 45; Deluz, *L'Urbanisme et l'architecture d'Alger,* 40.

4. Jean-Jacques Deluz and Joëlle Deluz-La Bruyère, "L'Alloggio sociale a Algeri durante il periodo coloniale (1920–1962)," *Storia urbana* 10, nos. 35–36 (April–September 1986): 120.

5. "Les Réalisations," *Chantiers* (March 1935): 196.

6. *Plan d'aménagement de Maison-Carrée. Dossier urbain,* May 1933, AOM.

7. Deluz, *L'Urbanisme et l'architecture d'Alger,* 40; Deluz and Deluz-La Bruyère, "L'Alloggio sociale," 120. Of the intended 816 units covering 8 hectares, only 210 were constructed.

8. *Chantiers* 2 (1951).

9. *Bulletin municipal officiel de la ville d'Alger* 11 (September 1949); *Chantiers* 7 (1952); Loeckx and Vermeulen, *L'Habitat moderne à Alger,* part 2, 7–8.

10. Chevallier, *Nous, algériens,* 140.

11. *Bulletin municipal officiel de la ville d'Alger* 10 (October 1953): n.p.

12. F. Pouillon, *Mémoires d'un architecte* (Paris, 1968), 168, 171.

13. "Programme municipal de construction de 2000 logements," *Chantiers* 14 (1954); *Travaux nord-africains,* 6 October 1955; Deluz, *L'Urbanisme et l'architecture d'Alger,* 62.

14. Pouillon, *Mémoires,* 220. Pouillon's reference to designs for "the airplane captain" is a critique of Le Corbusier's urbanism.

15. Loeckx and Vermeulen, *L'Habitat moderne à Alger,* part 2, 20.

16. Pouillon, *Mémoires,* 205.

17. Pouillon proudly recorded that in fifteen days over five hundred palm trees were planted in Diar el-Mahçoul. See ibid., 196.

18. Loeckx and Vermeulen, *L'Habitat moderne à Alger,* part 2, 23.

19. *Travaux nord-africains,* 6 October 1955. Concrete was used for foundations, floor slabs, and for paving the terraces.

20. *Type évolutif* is a curious term that merits some discussion. The word *évolutif* does not refer to the housing type per se, but to the occupant—an immigrant coming from a *bidonville,* the casbah, or the countryside. Considered semi-urban, this person would be in the process of evolution (toward being urban, civilized, and ultimately Westernized), but not "evolved" yet. For further discussion of the term, see Deluz and Deluz-La Bruyère, "L'Alloggio sociale," 130.

21. *Travaux nord-africains,* 6 October 1955.

22. Pouillon, *Mémoires,* 308.

23. *Travaux nord-africains,* 6 October 1955.

24. Lentin, *L'Algérie entre deux mondes,* 146.

25. *L'Echo d'Alger,* 22 March 1957. The reporter continued (tongue in cheek) that teachers who go through enormous difficulties to educate both Muslim and European children of Algiers were thus rewarded.

26. Mohamed Terki, "Bezouich," in Musée National du Moudjahid, *Nora: Témoignages-Nouvelles* (Algiers, 1984), 75.

27. For the construction of the new artery between the two projects, see *L'Echo d'Alger,* 6 July 1957 and 11 July 1957.

28. For further documentation on Diar es-Saada, see Bernard Félix Dubor, *Fernand Pouillon* (Paris, 1986), 48–55.

29. "Les Bidonvilles: Genèse et resorption," 24–25, 27.

30. For discussions of site plans, see Dubor, *Pouillon,* 67; Loeckx and Vermeulen, *L'Habitation moderne à Alger,* part 2, 27; and G. Geenen, A. Loeckx, and N. Naert, *Climat de France* (Leuven, 1991), 10–28.

31. Jacques Berque, "Médinas, ville neuves et bidonvilles," *Cahiers de Tunisie,* 21–22 (1958): 37; Geenen, Loeckx, and Naert, *Climat de France,* 15.

32. Geenen, Loeckx, and Naert, *Climat de France,* 34.

33. Ibid., 35.

34. *Travaux nord-africains,* 7 March 1957.

35. Ibid.

36. Pouillon, *Mémoires,* 206–208.

37. Dubor, *Pouillon,* 66.

38. Pouillon, *Mémoires,* 207.

39. Lentin, *L'Algérie entre deux mondes,* 146–147.

40. Pouillon, *Mémoires,* 205, 208.

41. Lentin, *L'Algérie entre deux mondes,* 147, 151.

42. Simounet's studies of squatter settlements are discussed in Chapter 4.

43. P.-A. Emery, "L'Architecture moderne en Algérie: 1930–1962," *Techniques et architecture* 329 (March 1980): 57; Maisonseul, "Djenan el-Hasan," in *Roland Simounet,* 20 (the words *naturellement* and *simplement* are underlined in the text). Simounet himself elaborated on the major difference between Pouillon and himself during an interview with the author: "Je respecte le site; Pouillon agresse le site" (I respect the site; Pouillon attacks the site). Furthermore, he criticized Pouillon for designing "sans penser aux hommes" (without thinking of men). For Simounet, Pouillon's insensitivity to the site, context, and culture

stemmed from his coming directly from France—unlike Simounet, who was "from Algeria." Simounet, interview with the author, Paris, 26 April 1993.

44. For this project, see "Cité 'La Montagne' à Hussein-Dey (Alger)," *Cahiers scientifiques et techniques du bâtiment* 32 (1958): n.p.; Deluz, *L'Urbanisme et l'architecture d'Alger*, 91–92; and Deluz and Deluz-La Bruyère, "L'Alloggio sociale," 133.

45. Simounet recalls that Béri contacted him fifteen days before the deadline to help them with the project. Intrigued by the problem and appalled at the inefficiency of Daure and Béri ("They had not designed a single unit. They only had naive sketches"; in addition, they were total outsiders to the culture: "They had never seen an Algerian woman make coffee before"), 26-year-old Simounet assumed the design of units. Simounet, interview with the author.

46. "Cité 'La Montagne.'"

47. Lentin, *L'Algérie entre deux mondes*, 26. The vaults did not act as strong barriers to vertical additions and the residents of these units, compelled by growing families, topped their vaulted spaces by concrete-frame-brick infill structures in a totally different architectural vocabulary.

48. La Montagne's other "horizontal" settlement, designed by architects Régeste and Bellisent, was to the west. Here the units had nonusable flat roofs; once again, the residents added extra stories to accommodate their families' needs. Although growth control was the admitted concern for the architects of both schemes, their design solutions could not prohibit additions. With the later random interventions, the Montagne Quarter acquired the image of a spontaneous development, resembling more the *bidonvilles* than the aesthetically self-conscious schemes of the same period. See Deluz, *L'Urbanisme et l'architecture d'Alger*, 92.

49. Ibid., 78. In some publications, this project is referred to as "de Solliers."

50. Simounet's contribution to the Carrière Jaubert remained restricted to the design stage; the project was completed by Daure and Béri in 1959. See Loeckx and Vermeulen, *L'Habitat moderne à Alger*, part 2, 53.

51. Deluz, *L'Urbanisme et l'architecture d'Alger*, 80.

52. *Roland Simounet*, 44.

53. *Travaux nord-africains*, 8 November 1956 and 28 March 1957; *Roland Simounet*, 44; Deluz, *L'Urbanisme et l'architecture d'Alger*, 80. Simounet argued that by grouping the bathrooms into a *hammam*, he could afford to give the residents more "luxurious" facilities. Simounet, interview with the author. Inevitably, temporary housing turned into permanent housing, making sanitary conditions even more intolerable. The residents had to wait until independence, when the city administration connected water to each unit.

54. Simounet claimed that he worked on the design of Djenan el-Hasan "in tranquility, with my heart [*tranquillement, avec mon coeur*]" and reached a solution that was "evident" and "very simple." Simounet, interview with the author.

55. The slope varied between 30° and 50°.

56. *Travaux nord-africains*, 8 November 1956 and 28 March 1957; *Alger-revue* (February 1957); *Chantiers* 32 (1959); Deluz, *L'Urbanisme et l'architecture d'Alger*, 78; Simounet, interview with the author.

57. Simounet described, for example, the food preparation process in the *bi-*

donvilles. Women worked sitting down and used large utensils; therefore European-style counters and sinks would not accommodate their needs and separate kitchens did not make sense. Simounet, interview with the author.

58. *Chantiers* 32 (1959).

59. For a critique of Djenan el-Hasan, see Loeckx and Vermeulen, *L'Habitat moderne à Alger,* part 2, 57–58.

60. *Travaux nord-africains,* 24 November 1955.

61. Ibid., 19 April 1956.

62. There were six units with four bedrooms, sixty-four with three, twenty-four with two, and a single one with only one bedroom. In addition, six shops were located on the ground floor.

63. *Travaux nord-africains,* 27 September 1956; *Chantiers* 32 (1959).

64. *Travaux nord-africains,* 6 October 1955.

65. *Chantiers* 32 (1959).

66. *Travaux nord-africains,* 3 November 1955, 2 February 1956, and 27 June 1957; Loeckx and Vermeulen, *L'Habitat moderne à Alger,* part 2, 43–44.

67. *Travaux nord-africains,* 8 November 1956 and 23 October 1958; *L'Echo d'Alger,* 22 October 1958. The complete project had twelve other buildings three to seven stories high, and again with terraces for communal use; the total number of units reached 464.

68. Deluz, *L'Urbanisme et l'architecture d'Alger,* 85–86.

69. Ibid., 101.

70. Ibid., 101–102. Two ZUPs were designated for Algiers: Les Annassers, with some housing for indigenous people, and Rouiba-Reghaia.

71. *Travaux nord-africains,* 4 December 1958 and 6 March 1958.

72. *L'Echo d'Alger,* 29 September 1960. Meanwhile, the city continued to clear the *bidonvilles,* which still mushroomed in the Climat de France area. In 1960, the 120 newly built shacks were torn down to be replaced by twelve housing blocks. The four-story, "logéco" (*logement économique*) buildings would shelter a total of 188 families which were now temporarily settled in Diar el-Keif. See *L'Echo d'Alger,* 15 November 1960.

73. *Travaux nord-africains,* 24 July 1958.

74. *L'Echo d'Alger,* 4–5 September 1960; Loeckx and Vermeulen, *L'Habitat moderne à Alger,* part 2, 50.

75. Deluz and Deluz-La Bruyère, "L'Alloggio sociale," 139.

76. Deluz, *L'Urbanisme et l'architecture d'Alger,* 105; *Chantiers* 32 (1959).

77. For a critique of the Plan de Constantine, see Deluz, *L'Urbanisme et l'architecture d'Alger,* 105.

78. Women "terrorists," for example, entered the public realm not only through their activities, but also through the media. It became common to see their photographs printed in the colonial, metropolitan, and even international news. To cite one memorable instance, on 24 July 1958 *L'Echo d'Alger* printed a photograph of four legendary FLN figures: Zohra Drif, pointing a gun at the camera, Samia Lakdari (who had placed a bomb in the Milk Bar), Djamila Bouhired (condemned to death for her activities, though her sentence was converted to life imprisonment), and Hassiba ben Bouali (killed later during an attack in the casbah). The caption mocked their struggle: "Emancipation for them consists of holding a gun or a pistol to be equal with murderers."

79. *El Moudjahid,* 31 May 1960.

80. Ibid., 3 August 1959 and 31 May 1960. While a significant number of women were active militants, others provided refuge for the members of resistance groups, acted as contact agents and guides, and collected funds; those with professional skills, mainly nurses and secretaries, also offered their services. In addition, women were instrumental in initiating literacy campaigns and providing education in hygiene in the countryside. For a comprehensive discussion on the multiple tasks of women during the war, see Amrane, *Les Femmes algériennes dans la guerre,* 115–147, and Lazreg, *Eloquence of Silence,* 138.

81. *L'Echo d'Alger,* 13 September 1958.

82. For women's participation in political demonstrations, see Amrane, *Les Femmes algériennes dans la guerre,* especially 202–215. Algerian women's participation in political rallies had begun much earlier. For example, veiled women took part in a political rights demonstration in Algiers in 1936. See Lazreg, *Eloquence of Silence,* 96.

Epilogue

1. Ella Shohat, "Notes on the 'Post-Colonial,'" *Social Text* 31–32 (1992): 105; Masao Miyoshi, "A Borderless World? From Colonialism to Transnationalism and the Decline of the Nation-State," *Critical Inquiry* 19, no. 4 (summer 1993): 750, 728.

2. Said, *Culture and Imperialism,* xx.

3. Bourdieu, *The Algerians,* 187, 160.

4. Deluz, *L'Urbanisme et l'architecture d'Alger,* 123. Abderrahman Bouchema was the unique Algerian architect in the country. As an active opponent to the colonial regime, his career under the French remained limited to designing houses for Algerians. After 1963, his office became one of the most important in Algiers.

5. Leonard Kodjo quoted in Christopher Miller, *Theories of Africans* (Chicago, 1990), 102, note 71. Miller provides a short summary of Kodjo's unpublished paper titled "Noms de rues, noms des maîtres" (1987), which focuses on street names in Abidjan, Ivory Coast. For an excellent analysis of street names in Annaba (formerly Bône) with reference to French colonization and Algerian decolonization, see Prochaska, *Making Algeria French,* 209–215.

6. A great deal has been written on bilinguality in Algeria. Consider, for example, Assia Djebar's thoughts on the topic:

French is my "stepmother" tongue. Which is my long-lost mother-tongue, that left me standing and disappeared? . . . Mother-tongue, either idealized or unloved, neglected and left to fairground barkers and jailers. . . . Burdened by my inherited taboos, I discover I have no memory of Arab love-songs. Is it because I was cut off from the impassioned speech that I find the French I use so flat and unprofitable? . . .

This language was formerly used to entomb my people; when I write it today I feel like the messenger of old, who bore a sealed missive which might sentence him to death or to dungeon. By laying myself bare in this language I start a fire which may consume me. For attempting an autobiography in the former enemy's language. (Assia Djebar, *Fantasia: An Algerian Cavalcade,* tr. Dorothy S. Blair [London, 1985], 214–215)

On the languages of Algeria today (written Arabic, Maghribi Arabic, dialects of Berber, and French), see Kenneth Brown, "Lost in Algiers: Ramadan 1993," *Mediterraneans* 4 (summer 1993): 15–16.

7. Fanon, *The Wretched of the Earth*, 209–210.

8. Lesbet, *La Casbah d'Alger*, 1; Lacheraf, preface to Ravéreau, *La Casbah d'Alger*, 28–29.

9. Lacheraf, preface, 10.

10. "Sauvegarde de la Casbah d'Alger," *Techniques et architecture* 329 (March 1980): 82–85. For accounts of postindependence projects for the casbah, see also Deluz, *L'Urbanisme et l'architecture d'Alger*, 118–119, and Lesbet, *La Casbah d'Alger*.

11. Bernard Pagand, "Constantine et les grandes médinas nord-algériennes entre ruines et projets," in *Maghreb: Architecture et urbanisme. Patrimonie, tradition et modernité* (Paris, 1990), 95–96.

12. Lesbet, *La Casbah d'Alger*, 64. Similar conditions dominate other Algerian cities as well. In Tlemcen, for example, the medina is now only a "place of transit" for newcomers, a situation that makes the already vulnerable fabric of the old city even more fragile. See Daoud Brikci, "Mutations des médinas d'Algérie: le cas de Tlemcen," paper presented at the American Institute for Maghribi Studies Annual Conference, 1996.

13. I borrow this terminology from Barthes's analysis of the Eiffel Tower. See Barthes, "The Eiffel Tower," in Sontag, *Barthes Reader*, 237.

14. The incident is cited in Lazreg, *Eloquence of Silence*, 197.

15. Brown, "Lost in Algiers," 13–14.

16. Nadir Abdullah Benmatti, *L'Habitat du tiers-monde (cas d'Algérie)* (Algiers, 1982), 168. According to the 1987 census, 44 percent of the country's population is younger than fifteen, and 72 percent younger than thirty. See *Recensement général de la population et de l'habitat du 20 mars 1987* (Algiers, 1989), 110.

17. Deluz, *L'Urbanisme et l'architecture d'Alger*, 111–113; Sgroi-Dufresne, *Alger 1830–1984*, 118.

18. Sgroi-Dufresne, *Alger 1830–1984*, 233.

19. Deluz, *L'Urbanisme et l'architecture d'Alger*, 114–115; Sgroi-Dufresne, *Alger 1830–1984*, 213; Benmatti, *L'Habitat du tiers-monde*, 178.

20. Benmatti, *L'Habitat du tiers-monde*, 179–182; Sidi Boubekeur, *L'Habitat en Algérie* (Lyon, 1986), 22–24, 177.

21. See, for example, *New York Times*, 6 June 1995.

22. Lazreg offers to replace the term *fundamentalism* by *religiosity*. She uses the term *religiose movement* to "identify the groups involved in order to emphasize the manipulation of religion as a tool of justification and acquisition of political power." See Lazreg, *Eloquence of Silence*, 209.

23. Assia Djebar, *Femmes d'Alger dans leur appartement* (Paris, 1979), 170–178. It is not Delacroix's "superficial Orient"—a popular subject in recent art historical discourse—that Djebar cares to dissect. She focuses instead on the subtler implications of the painting, especially the fact that the scene makes the observer conscious of his unwarranted presence in the intimacy of this room, which is enclosed on the women frozen in an act of waiting.

24. For a comparative discussion of various versions of Picasso's *Femmes d'Alger*, see L. Steinberg, "The Algerian Women and Picasso at Large," in Stein-

berg, *Other Criteria: Confrontations with Twentieth-Century Art* (New York, 1972), 125–234.

25. Djebar, *Femmes d'Alger*, 186–189. Djebar establishes a metaphorical relationship between fragments of women's bodies and the explosives they carried under their clothes. She also provides a critique of women's condition in Algeria in the aftermath of the independence by arguing that the grenades women hid under their clothes "as if they were their own breasts" exploded against them.

26. Steinberg, *Other Criteria*, 130. Picasso's sympathy for the Algerian War is expressed most blatantly in his drawing of Djamila Boupasha, whose accounts of torture had made her a cause célèbre in France and throughout the world. The portrait was published in 1962 on the cover of *Djamila Boupasha*, written by Gisèle Halimi, with an introduction by Simone de Beauvoir.

27. Woodhull, *Transfigurations of the Maghreb*, 84–85.

28. These figures are taken from John A. McKesson, "Concepts and Realities in a Multiethnic France," *French Politics and Society* 12, no. 1 (winter 1994): 20.

29. Abu-Lughod, "The Islamic City," 160–161.

30. H. Adlai Murdoch, "Rewriting Writing: Identity, Exile, and Renewal in Assia Djebar's *L'Amour, la fantasia*," *Yale French Studies* 83 (1993): 87–89.

31. Samia Mehrez, "Azouz Begag: Un di Zafas di Bidoufile (Azouz Begag: Un des enfants du bidonville) or the *Beur* Writer: A Question of Territory," *Yale French Studies* 82 (1993): 25–42.

Selected Bibliography

Archives

Archives Nationales, Dépôt d'Outre-Mer, Aix-en-Provence (AOM)

Fondation Le Corbusier, Paris (FLC)

Service Historique de l'Armée de Terre, Château de Vincennes, Paris (SHAT)

Journals and Newspapers

Alger revue

Algéria

L'Architecture

L'Architecture d'aujourd'hui

Bulletin économique et juridique

Bulletin municipal officiel de la ville d'Alger

Cahiers scientifiques et techniques du bâtiment (CSTB)

Chantiers

Documents algériens

Documents nord-africains

L'Echo d'Alger

El Moudjahid

Encyclopédie mensuelle d'outre-mer

Entr'Aide française

Informations algériennes

Le Monde colonial illustré

Revue africaine

Techniques et architecture

Travaux nord-africains

Books and Articles

Abu-Lughod, Janet. "The Islamic City—Historic Myth, Islamic Essence, and Contemporary Relevance." *International Journal of Middle Eastern Studies* 19, no. 2 (May 1987): 155–176.

———. "On the Remaking of History: How to Reinvent the Past." In *Remaking History*, edited by Barbara Kruger and Phil Mariani, 111–129. Seattle, 1989.

———. *Rabat: Urban Apartheid in Morocco*. Princeton, N.J., 1980.

Algérie contemporaine. Algiers, 1954.

Alleg, Henri, Jacques de Bonis, Henri J. Douzon, Jean Freire, and Pierre Haudiquet. *La Guerre d'Algérie*. 3 vols. Paris, 1981.

Alloula, Malek. *The Colonial Harem*. Translated by Myrna Godzich and Wlad Godzich. Minneapolis, 1986.

Amrane, Djamila. *Les Femmes algériennes dans la guerre*. Paris, 1991.

Les Arts et la technique moderne en Algérie 1937. Algiers, 1937.

Association pour l'Etude du Développement et de l'Agglomération Algéroise. *Alger, méthode de travail, étude du site*. Algiers, 1958.

Auclert, Hubertine. *Les Femmes arabes en Algérie*. Paris, 1900.

Béguin, François. *Arabisances*. Paris, 1983.

Benmatti, Nadir Abdullah. *L'Habitat du tiers-monde (cas d'Algérie)*. Algiers, 1982.

Bernard, Augustin. *Enquête sur l'habitation rurale des indigènes de l'Algérie*. Algiers, 1921.

Berque, Augustin. *L'Algérie, terre d'art et d'histoire*. Algiers, 1937.

———. "L'Habitation de l'indigène algérien." *Revue africaine* 78 (1936): 43–100.

Berque, Jacques. "Médinas, ville neuves et bidonvilles." *Cahiers de Tunisie* 21–22 (1958): 5–41.

Bertrand, Louis. *Alger*. Paris, 1938.

Bhabha, Homi. "Of Mimicry and Man: The Ambivalence of Colonial Discourse." *October* 28 (October 1984): 125–133.

———. "The Other Question: Difference, Discrimination and the Discourse of Colonialism." In *Out There: Marginalization and Contemporary Culture*, edited by Russell Ferguson, Martha Gever, Trinh T. Minh-ha, and Cornel West, 71–87. Cambridge, Mass., 1990.

Boubekeur, Sidi. *L'Habitat en Algérie*. Lyon, 1986.

Boulanger, Pierre. *Le Cinéma colonial*. Paris, 1975.

Bourdieu, Pierre. *The Algerians*. Translated by Alan C. M. Ross. Boston, 1962. First published in French in 1958.

Bousquet-Lefevre, Laure. *La Femme Kabyle*. Paris, 1939.

Brahimi, Denise. *Femmes arabes et soeurs musulmanes*. Paris, 1984.

Cabinet du Ministre d'Algérie. *Algérie*. 1957.

Çelik, Zeynep. "Le Corbusier, Orientalism, Colonialism." *Assemblage* 17 (April 1992): 58–77.

Chevallier, Jacques. *Nous, algériens*. Paris, 1958.

Clifford, James. *The Predicament of Culture*. Cambridge, Mass., 1988.

Colonna, Fanny. *Aurès/Algérie 1935–36. Photographies de Thérèse Rivière*. Algiers, 1987.

Colonna, Fanny, and Claude Haim Brahimi. *Le Mal de voir*. Paris, 1976.

The Constantine Plan for Algeria. New York, May 1961.

Le Corbusier. "Le Folklore est l'expression fleurie des traditions." *Voici la France de ce mois* 16 (June 1941): 27–32.

———. *Poésie sur Alger*. 1950. Facsimile reprint, Paris, 1989.

———. *Quand les cathédrales étaient blanches*. Paris, 1937.

———. *La Ville radieuse*. Paris, 1933.

Cornaton, Michel. *Les Regroupements de la décolonisation en Algérie*. Paris, 1967.

Cresti, Federico. "The Boulevard de l'Impératrice in Colonial Algiers (1860–1866)." *Environmental Design* 1 (1984): 54–59.

Deluz, Jean-Jacques. *L'Urbanisme et l'architecture d'Alger*. Algiers, 1988.

Deluz, Jean-Jacques, and Joëlle Deluz-La Bruyère. "L'Alloggio sociale a Algeri durante il periodo coloniale (1920–1962)." *Storia urbana* 10, nos. 35–36 (April–September 1986): 107–152.

Descloitres, Robert, Jean-Claude Réverdy, and Claudine Descloitres. *L'Algérie des bidonvilles*. Paris, 1961.

Djebar, Assia. *Fantasia: An Algerian Cavalcade*. Translated by Dorothy S. Blair. London, 1985.

———. *Femmes d'Alger dans leur appartement*. Paris, 1979.

Dubor, Bernard Félix. *Fernand Pouillon*. Paris, 1986.

Fanon, Frantz. *A Dying Colonialism*. Translated by Haakon Chevalier. New York, 1967.

———. *The Wretched of the Earth*. Translated by Constance Farrington. New York, 1968.

Fauve, J.-P. *Alger capitale*. Paris, 1936.

Favre, Lucienne. *Tout l'inconnu de la casbah d'Alger*. Algiers, 1933.

Fromentin, Eugène. *Une Année dans le Sahel*. Seventh ed. Paris, 1888.

Garanger, Marc. *La Guerre d'Algérie*. Paris, 1984.

Gaudry, Mathéa. *La Femme chaouia de l'Aurès*. Paris, 1928.

Gautier, Théophile. *Voyage pittoresque en Algérie*. 1845. Reprint edited by M. Cottin, Geneva, 1973.

Geenen, G., A. Loeckx, and N. Naert. *Climat de France*. Leuven, 1991.

Girardet, Raoul. *L'Idée coloniale en France*. Paris, 1972.

Goichon, Amélie-Marie. *La Vie féminine au Mzab*. Paris, 1927.

Golvin, Lucien. *Palais et demeures d'Alger à la période ottomane*. Aix-en-Provence, 1988.

Gordon, David. *Women of Algeria: An Essay on Change.* Cambridge, Mass., 1968.

Gouvernement Général de l'Algérie, Direction Générale des Affaires Indigènes et des Territoires du Sud, Service de l'Economie Sociale Indigène. *Pour les paysans et les artisans indigènes.* Algiers, 1939.

Heggoy, Alf Andrew. *The French Conquest of Algiers, 1830: An Algerian Oral Tradition.* Athens, Ohio, 1986.

Hobsbawm, Eric J. *The Age of Empire, 1875–1914.* New York, 1987.

Isnard, Jean-Claude. *Les Problèmes du logement dans l'agglomération algéroise* (Ecole Financière Nationale d'Administration, Section Economique et Financière, December 1949). Mim. report, AOM.

Knibiehler, Yvonne, and Régine Goutalier. *La Femme aux temps des colonies.* Paris, 1985.

Kostof, Spiro. *The City Shaped.* London, 1992.

Lacheraf, Mostefa. *L'Algérie: nation et société.* Paris, 1965.

Laoust-Chantreaux, Germaine. *Kabylie, côté femmes. La Vie féminine à Aït Hichem, 1937–1939.* Aix-en-Provence, 1990.

Lazreg, Marnia. *The Eloquence of Silence: Algerian Women in Question.* New York, 1994.

Lefebvre, Henri. *The Production of Space.* Translated by Donald Nicholson-Smith. Oxford, 1991.

Leiris, Michel. "L'Ethnographe devant le colonialisme." *Les Temps modernes* 6, no. 58 (August 1950): 357–374. English translation in M. Leiris, *Brisées: Broken Branches,* translated by Lydia Davis. San Francisco, 1989.

Lentin, Albert-Paul. *L'Algérie entre deux mondes. Le Dernier quart d'heure.* Paris, 1963.

Lesbet, Djaffar. *La Casbah d'Alger. Gestion urbaine et vide sociale.* Algiers, [c. 1985].

Lespès, René. *Alger, étude de géographie et d'histoire urbaines.* Paris, 1930.

———. *Pour comprendre l'Algérie.* Algiers, 1937.

———. "Projet d'enquête sur l'habitat des indigènes musulmans dans les centres urbains d'Algérie." *Revue africaine* 76, nos. 362–363 (1935): 431–436.

———. "Les Villes." In *Les Arts et la technique moderne en Algérie 1937.* Algiers, 1937.

Letellier, R. P. (des Pères Blancs). *La Famille indigène devant les problèmes sociaux modernes.* Algiers, n.d.

———. *Les Indigènes de la Casbah.* Algiers, 19ème Corps de l'Armée, Etat Major, Cours de formation islamique, 3 December 1941.

Le Tourneau, Roger. "Al Djaza'ir." *Encyclopedia of Islam.* Leiden, 1960.

Loeckx, A., and P. Vermeulen. *L'Habitat moderne à Alger (1925–1975).* Leuven, 1988.

Lucas, Philippe, and Jean-Claude Vatin. *L'Algérie des anthropologues.* Paris, 1975.

Lynch, Kevin. *The Image of the City.* Cambridge, Mass., 1960.

Mabro, Judy, ed. *Veiled Half-Truths: Western Travellers' Perceptions of Middle Eastern Women.* London, 1991.

Maisonseul, Jean de. "Pour une architecture et un urbanisme Nord-Africains." *Revue d'Alger* 8 (1945).

Malverti, Xavier. "Alger: Méditerranée, soleil et modernité." In Institut Français d'Architecture, *Architectures françaises outre-mer.* Paris, 1992.

Marchand, Henri. *La Musulmane algérienne.* Paris, 1960.

McLeod, Mary. "Le Corbusier and Algiers." *Oppositions* 16–17 (1980): 55–85.

Megherbi, Abdelghani. *Les Algériens au miroir du cinéma colonial.* Algiers, 1982.

Mehrez, Samia. "Azouz Begag: Un di Zafas di Bidoufile (Azouz Begag: Un des enfants du bidonville) or the *Beur* Writer: A Question of Territory." *Yale French Studies* 82 (1993): 25–42.

Miller, Christopher. *Theories of Africans.* Chicago, 1990.

Miyoshi, Masao. "A Borderless World? From Colonialism to Transnationalism and the Decline of the Nation State." *Critical Inquiry* 19, no. 4 (summer 1993): 726–751.

La Municipalité d'Alger vous présente quelques images, Alger d'hier et aujourd' hui. Algiers, 1957.

Murdoch, H. Adlai. "Rewriting Writing: Identity, Exile, and Renewal in Assia Djebar's *L'Amour, la fantasia.*" *Yale French Studies* 83 (1993): 71–92.

Musée National du Moudjahid. *Nora: Témoignages-Nouvelles.* Algiers, 1984.

Nochlin, Linda. "The Imaginary Orient." *Art in America* 71, no. 5 (May 1983): 120–129, 186–191.

Nora, P., ed. *La République.* Paris, 1984.

Parametro 17 (June 1973) (entire issue).

Parry, Benita. "Problems in Current Theories of Colonial Discourse." *Oxford Literary Review* 9, nos. 1–2 (1987): 27–58.

Pichon, Le Baron Louis André. *Alger sous la domination française, son état présent et son avenir.* Paris, 1833.

Pouillon, Fernand. *Mémoires d'un architecte.* Paris, 1968.

Presse, Louis. *Algérie et Tunisie.* Paris, 1888.

Prochaska, David. "L'Algérie imaginaire." *Ghardiva* (winter 1989–90): 29–38.

———. *Making Algeria French.* Cambridge, England, 1990.

Rabinow, Paul. *French Modern: Norms and Forms of the Social Environment.* Cambridge, Mass., 1989.

Ravéreau, André. *La Casbah d'Alger. Et le site créa la ville.* Paris, 1989.

Raymond, André. "Le Centre d'Alger en 1830." *Revue de l'occident musulman et de la Mediterr'née* 31, no. 1 (1981): 73–81.

———. *The Great Arab Cities in the 16th–18th Centuries.* New York, 1984.

République Française, Délégation Générale du Gouvernement en Algérie, Direction du Plan et des Etudes Economiques. *Plan de Constantine, 1959–1963. Rapport général.* June 1960.

République Française, Présidence du Conseil, Commissariat Général au Plan de Modernisation et d'Equipement. *Rapport général de la commission d'étude et de coordination des plans de modernisation et d'équipement de l'Algérie, de la Tunisie et du Maroc.* June 1954.

Rivière, Thérèse. "L'Habitation chez les Ouled Abderrahman Chaouia de l'Aurès." *Africa* 11, no. 3 (1938): 294–311.

Roland Simounet. Pour une invention de l'espace. Paris, 1986.

Royer, J., ed. *L'Urbanisme aux colonies et dans les pays tropicaux.* 2 vols. La-Charité-sur-Loire, 1932.

Said, Edward. *Culture and Imperialism*. New York, 1993.

Sarrault, Albert. *Grandeur et servitude coloniales*. Paris, 1931.

Secrétariat Social d'Alger. *De l'Algérie originelle à l'Algérie moderne*. Algiers, 1961.

Sgroi-Dufresne, M. *Alger 1830–1984: Stratégies et enjeux urbains*. Paris, 1986.

Shohat, Ella. "Notes on the 'Post-Colonial.'" *Social Text* 31–32 (1992): 99–113.

Shohat, Ella, and Robert Stam. *Unthinking Eurocentrism*. London, 1994.

Socard, Tony. "L'Urbanisme en Algérie." *Rafales* 135 (12–19 October 1946).

Sontag, Susan, ed. *A Barthes Reader*. New York, 1982.

Steinberg, L. *Other Criteria: Confrontations with Twentieth-Century Art*. New York, 1972.

Thornton, L. *The Orientalists, Painter-Travellers 1828–1908*. Paris, 1983.

———. *Women as Portrayed in Orientalist Painting*. Paris, 1985.

Venture, Jean Michel de. *Alger au XVIIIe siècle*. Second ed. Tunis, [c. 1980].

Woodhull, Winifred. *Transfigurations of the Maghreb*. Minneapolis, 1993.

Illustration Sources and Credits

FIG. 1, *Chantiers,* March 1935; FIG. 2, John McKenna; FIG. 3, Bibliothèque Nationale, Département des Estampes et de la Photographie; FIG. 4, photograph by the author; FIG. 5, Golvin, *Palais et demeures d'Alger;* FIG. 6, photograph by the author; FIG. 7, Le Corbusier, *La Ville radieuse;* FIG. 8, *Algéria* 1, no. 6, August 1933; FIG. 9, Golvin, *Palais et demeures d'Alger;* FIGS. 10 and 11, Le Corbusier, *Poésie sur Alger,* © 1997 Fondation Le Corbusier, Paris/Artists Rights Society, New York/ADAGP, Paris; FIG. 12, SHAT; FIG. 13, Bibliothèque Nationale, Département des Estampes et de la Photographie; FIG. 14, Pichon, *Alger sous la domination française;* FIG. 15, *Algéria* 2, no. 12, February 1934; FIG. 16, Bibliothèque Nationale, Département des Estampes et de la Photographie; FIG. 17, John McKenna; FIG. 18, Deluz, *L'Urbanisme et l'architecture d'Alger;* FIG. 19, *Algéria* 1, no. 3, May 1933; FIG. 20, *Chantiers* 4, 1954; FIG. 21, Le Corbusier, *La Ville radieuse;* FIG. 22, Alleg et al., *La Guerre d'Algérie,* vol. 3; FIG. 23, *Chantiers,* March 1935; FIG. 24, *Chantiers* 2, 1951; FIG. 25, Deluz, *L'Urbanisme et l'architecture d'Alger;* FIG. 26, *Chantiers* 4, 1954; FIG. 27, *Alger revue,* spring 1959; FIG. 28, John McKenna; FIG. 29, AOM; FIG. 30, Deluz, *L'Urbanisme et l'architecture d'Alger;* FIG. 31, *Documents algériens* 1 January 1951–31 December 1951; FIG. 32, Bibliothèque Nationale, Département des Estampes et de la Photographie; FIG. 33, John McKenna; FIG. 34, line drawing by Bill Nelson; FIG. 35, photograph by the author; FIG. 36, *Chantiers* 7, 1952; FIG. 37, *Les Arts et la technique moderne en Algérie 1937;* FIG. 38, Le Corbusier, *Poésie sur Alger,* © 1997 Fondation Le Corbusier, Paris/Artists Rights Society, New York/ADAGP, Paris; FIG. 39, Le Corbusier, *La Ville radieuse;* FIG. 40, Deluz, *L'Urbanisme et l'architecture d'Alger;* FIG. 41, *Chantiers* 2, 1951; FIGS. 47 and 48, *L'Architecture d'aujourd'hui,* 1935; FIG. 49, Le Corbusier, *La Ville radieuse;* FIGS. 50–52, Thornton, *Women as Portrayed in Orientalist Painting;* FIG. 53, Boulanger, *Le Cinéma colonial;* FIG. 54, courtesy Marc Garanger; FIG. 55, Descloitres, Réverdy, and Descloitres, *L'Algérie des bidonvilles;* FIGS. 56 and 57, courtesy Marc Garanger; FIG. 58, line drawing by Bill Nelson; FIG. 59, *Algéria,* March 1933; FIG. 60, *Chantiers,* April

Index

Compositor: G & S Typesetters, Inc.
Text: 10/13 Galliard
Display: Galliard
Printer and binder: Thomson-Shore, Inc.